Miraculous Interventions III
2012 - The Miraculous Year

by Deborah Aubrey-Peyron

A diary following the year 2012's miraculous occurrences in healing, blessings, and even through sorrows.

"For thou shalt go to all that I send thee, and whatsoever I command thee thou shalt speak. Be not afraid of their faces: for I am with thee to deliver thee, saith the Lord."
Jeremiah 1: 7-8 KJV

Home Crafted Artistry & Printing
New Albany, Indiana
2013

Books by Deborah Aubrey-Peyron

Miraculous Interventions
True life stories of miraculous
events that have shaped the author's
life and those she has known.

Christmas Chaos.
A family with three unruly boys have a
less-than-fortunate run-in with St. Nicholas.
An illustrated children's Christmas story
told with humor, verse
and Christ, of course.

Miraculous Interventions II
Modern Day Priests, Prophets, Pastors
& Everyday Visionaries
Amazing stories from various ministers
who walk in the office of the miraculous.
These are their experiences with the Lord
and the divine interventions they have witnessed.

Miraculous Interventions III
2012 – The Miraculous Year
A diary following the year 2012's
miraculous occurrences in healing,
blessings, and even through sorrows.

Best of the Miraculous Interventions Stories
Sample stories from the series
plus a bonus preview of
Christmas Chaos.

Miraculous Interventions III
2012 - *The Miraculous Year*

by Deborah Aubrey-Peyron

A diary following the year 2012's miraculous occurrences in healing, blessings, and even through sorrows.

"For thou shalt go to all that I send thee, and whatsoever I command thee thou shalt speak. Be not afraid of their faces: for I am with thee to deliver thee, saith the Lord."
Jeremiah 1: 7-8 KJV

To Lisa,
God Bless you
Long Lost Sister!
So glad to see you
again!
Much Love,
Deb

1/21/17

#_48_ of first 200

Deborah Aubrey-Peyron, author

ISBN-13: 978-0-9893714-1-4
ISBN-10: 0989371417

Home Crafted Artistry & Printing
Mary Dow Smith, Chief Editor
1252 Beechwood Avenue
New Albany, IN 47150
Contact information:
e-mail HomeCraftedArtistry@yahoo.com
e-mail peyronsinjesus@yahoo.com

Special Order
Special discounts are available on quantity purchases of 25 or more copies. Speaking or signing engagements may be arranged upon request. Please e-mail or write to the above address.
"Miraculous Interventions" **is a trademark of Deborah Aubrey-Peyron and is reserved exclusively for this series of books.**

Cover design by Mary Dow Bibb Smith
Photographs are author's photographs.
Scripture on cover quoted from
Matthew 10:27 NIV
Jeremiah 1:7-8 KJV

DEDICATION

To the teachers who inhabited this book and blessed my life.

Fr. Mike and Patti Olsen
Parson Zeb and Rabbona* Joy Son
Pastor Chris Powell
Pastor Keith Taylor
Pastors Tom and Bridgette McCullum

To my new little sister Crystal, a bright star on my horizon and her husband, David. Thank you for coming into my life, teaching me, growing me as an example of Jesus on this Earth and most especially, for loving me.

Always, for my husband Mark, my sons and their wives, Ben and Amanda, Andy and Samantha, David, and our grandchildren, Lily and Matthew.

And for you, dear readers, this book is dedicated for you.

"Beloved, I wish above all things
that thou mayest prosper
and be in health,
even as thy soul prospereth."
3 John 2

Love and blessings,
Deb

*Rabbona is an endearing term "for a female rabbi, or my female teacher."Joy Son has a Masters in Jewish-Christian studies and is an ordained Messianic Minister. She is my Rabbona or Rabbi.

11

ACKNOWLEDGMENTS

As always, I thank the God of all flesh, (especially this flesh) for sending Jesus to save us. And for sending the Great Comforter to guide me through this life, reminding me over and over again whose I really am. I want to thank on paper the whole new batch of friends God sent into my life the spring of 2012:

Crystal and David Murray, who I now call family. David, who prayed down the power of Heaven in my time of need. Crystal, helper in all things electronic. How could so much brains be inside such a little person? Finally, after 53 years, I got to meet you. I missed you before I knew there was a you.

Pastors Zeb, Joy, and Chris and all the gang at Christian Cowboy Church. You are my secret smiles when my life needs a hand up. You have all taken up residence in my heart.

My dear sweet family, Mark, my husband, and our sons Ben, David and Andy and their families. You all encourage and help me daily.

To Lisa Bonneck, who once again has come on board as our editor to produce a product that is worthy to praise the Lord with. You make me look good on paper. One day I may actually have to pay you.

Mary, my publisher, co-worker, cover designer, and all around good gal. What have we started here? A series on miracles for our Lord's glory.

Who would have thought, two momma's from southern Indiana, writing and publishing books, could have caught the attention of the Vatican in Rome?

We received a beautiful letter with an Apostolic Blessing, a Christmas card and an autographed picture of Pope Benedict XVI.

Where do we go from here?

Last but not least,
Annie Frances Peyron
March 18, 2012 – November 30, 2012
Our one and only baby girl
Ra and Da love you
We will see our little sugar bug in Paradise.

"And I will meet you in the garden,
where life all begins anew.
Roses, flowers, jasmine,
there I will wait for you"

INTRODUCTION

"Be not afraid
I go before you always
Come follow me
and I will give you rest."

The term "be not afraid" is used 365 times in the Bible -- one for every day of the year. That came in very handy during the year of 2012.

When the Lord of Hosts showed me that this book was to be called "The Miraculous Year," I was sure it would be filled with amazing, wonderful happy times and miracles. And it was.

The funny thing, though, about miracles, they usually come when they are most needed - when circumstance are much less than perfect and you are hanging on by the shear thread of your faith.

Sigh.

So be it.

And so it was more times than I cared to recount.

As the year of 2012 unfolded, it seemed to go through "seasons" —

—Seasons of healings and miracles

—Seasons of blessings, wonders and prophesy-

—Signs, wonders, and events that took place far away from the natural

—Even seasons of sorrows and mysteries—great illnesses and death, and in December, a possible miracle for us, even we were remembered - for a season. Enjoy your walk. Let's get started.

MAMA
MOMMA
MOMMAH

There is a spirit
that comes upon some,
full of compassion and love
and even a lot of fun.

Though the days flew by
as all life winds down,
for that I did try
to earn a gold crown.

For this reason, I was sent here,
to be there for each and one another.
In joy, laughter, sorrow or tear,
I am simply made,
a mother.

**For the ones who counted first —
you taught me to count.**

* With three little boys, they each decided they would
spell my name differently so I would know which one
had given me a card or note of love.

Season I
Healings and Words of Knowledge

*Jeremiah 1: 5 "**Before** I formed you in the womb, I knew you; before you were born, I separated you for myself.*

I have appointed you....."

*Psalm 41: 3 "**The Lord** sustains them on their sick bed and restores them from their bed of illness."*

To me, *life is like a soccer game. From the moment the game begins, you push your hardest and don't slow down, for if you do, you get behind. You're on a team with your teammates, faith, strength, belief, hope, love, courage and honor. Against you are failure, greed, tragedy, hardships, depression and pain. They are all in your way of reaching your goal, which is becoming the person you are meant to be. And you play your heart out, making all the moves you feel right and take down your opponents one by one, until you reach that moment when your goal is right in front of you. All you have to do is find the faith to take the shot.*

And when the final buzzer sounds, and judgment day comes, you shall not fear it. For you hear the crowd chanting your name in the greatness of what you have accomplished. You have reached your goal of becoming everything you were meant to be.

You have won.

You are victorious.

John David Higginbotham (17 yrs. old)

THE ANOINTING
(Jan. 1st)

The year 2011 had ended well, and we looked forward to January 1st. Mark and I had already set our plans in motion. Our new good friends, Larry and Marilynn Crosier, had agreed to go with us to see a church in Louisville, Kentucky, where the priest and his congregation were seeing angelic orbs and smelling frankincense and myrrh.

In the car, I was slightly upset at the prospect of being late for mass. Not to worry, Larry driving at the helm felt no matter what my watch said, we would be right on time. And we were. It seemed the good Anglican priest, Father Mike Olsen, his wife Patti, and their congregation were also ten minutes late in starting. I am in continuous amazement of how God orchestrates the smallest details in our lives for the benefit of our faith and trust in Him.

As Marilynn, Larry, Mark and I entered the church, we were greeted with warm smiles and hellos from Father Mike and members of his church.

Father Mike greeted us, "You're just on time. We're about to start. Have a seat." Patti, his wife, was already at the piano ready to sing to the Lord. Their small congregation stood in attendance as Father Mike entered from the back of the church with the Holy Bible and a large cross carried behind him by altar boys (or whatever they call them now). Father Mike led praise and worship before the mass officially started. He prophesied for the New Year as the Holy Spirit led him. "This is the year of angels and miracles. The war between good and evil is raging now." (Just as I had seen in my dream years ago. That was what the angel beside me had said.)

Father Mike quoted Jeremiah 33:3, "Call unto me, and I will answer thee, and show thee great and mighty things, which thou knowest not." He went on, "From this rock I will build my church and the gates of hell shall not prevail against it. Dance like a child before the Lord." What a beginning.

In my heart, I asked to smell the Lord when He was nearby. Instantly, both Mark and I smelled incense. Father Mike was still before the Lord and gave more utterance. "The joy of the Lord is your strength. Release the joy! Don't be discouraged anymore! The angels are pouring out new wine. There is freedom in this place. Let me bind and heal your wounds. The enemy has no more place here in you. The work is complete. All is forgiven! Now is the time to be blessed. I am calling you to a higher place."

Marilynn felt he was talking directly to her. God was bringing her from having a wounded spirit to new life. New friends. To a new position where she could rejoice. Marilynn felt she was back in the army of God and there was work to do. As we sang praises, I felt compelled to take pictures in the church. In almost every picture you could see many "angelic orbs." During the last part of Father Mike's prophesy before starting mass, Marilynn and I felt these words were for us. "This is the year that you break off the power that caused you harm and discouragement. No more. Let go of the words that said you were not worthy or no good."

Then Father Mike started the mass. From the opening of the mass until after communion, the charismatic liturgy went on as expected. Larry and Marilynn enjoyed the solemnity of the service and felt the closeness of the Holy Spirit in the church.

The homily was about man. It was about man being made a little lower than the angels. All things are under his feet. We are no longer slaves but children of God. We are heirs. Have the mind of Christ. Empty ourselves. Be obedient. Father Mike started with the gospel of Luke and moved on to the book of Psalms, "How majestic is the name of God! See God as big as He is. His name is above all names! Call upon Jesus. Remember to plead the blood of Jesus over all your circumstances. His name is above doubt or fear. Jesus comes for His own, and you are seated with Him in glory."

"There is a whole other realm that the church does not address much; the supernatural realm of angels and miracles. God is here. He is above our circumstances. He is in the glory realm. Call on angels to bring you help. Plant seeds in others. With praise on our lips, we will see the manifestation of God. Praise silences your foes and enemies. Praise the Lord, and watch all your enemies leave. Have a Biblical imagination! See miracles all around you. Be like Jesus. Go do the work of the Gospel. Consider what God can do. God wants us to believe from small to large. Remind God of what He has said to us in His scriptures. When we make our God big, anything is possible. All our problems become small."

After communion, Father Mike came forward to the front of the altar. He called out, "Someone here has back pain. Come forward to be healed."

I knew this was Marilynn's time for a full healing.

I whispered, "Go! He is talking to you!"

As she walked up to the altar, Father told this story: "The oil vial I have in my hands was miraculously translated into the home of another pastor who gave it to me. The vial has a little slip of paper stating where it is from taped to it. It is miraculous oil sent to us from God."

He anointed each person with oil from this vial. Father started to pray over Marilynn. Mark stood in back of her in case she needed to be caught. I stood beside her. Mike told Marilynn he saw angels all around her and in her home. He had no way of knowing there were angel statues all over their house. As he prayed, her back healed instantly and she was slain in the spirit. Father Mike cried out, "God calls you daughter with a purpose for intercessory prayer."

The next one up was Larry. He called Larry a rock, and said, "You should keep paper beside the bed because you are going to see angels and have angelic visitations. Write down what you see." Larry was slain in the spirit.

Father Mike then went to the other side of the church for more healing prayers. Mark got in line over there. After a few minutes, it was his turn to be ministered to. It was as if Mike could read Mark's mind. Father Mike stated, "God has heard you. He is answering the prayers you have had in your heart right now. I see good, very good things for you. I see a new path."

With Father Mike's eyes closed, standing in front of Mark, he stretched out his right arm and pointed directly at me and said, "I see radio and television interviews for you. It is all good."

He anointed several other people and then walked back to our side of the church and prayed over more people. I stood ready to catch anyone that would need it. When he finished with everyone else in line, Father turned and looked at me. He said, "I might as well tell you too." I stood before him, both hands raised, to receive what he had to say.

Father Mike looked up to somewhere the natural eye couldn't see. He spoke, "I see angels on Jacob's ladder. You have God's ear this year, 2012. God has heard your cry. I see you with a wreath on your head as a crown. You are running the race. Keep running the race! You are just getting started. You have arrived at your destiny, your purpose in life. You will smell the angels; the very aroma of God. The Throne room. You will smell the rose of Sharon; roses and flowers. I see your boys walking closer with the Lord. God is opening doors for you both that no man can close. He will show your path clearly. Be filled with joy!"

Then Father Mike prepared and gave the final blessing to close the mass. The women all went to the kitchen to prepare the meal. The men helped take down the New Year's decorations. Father blessed the meal, and we all went into fellowship.

It was then that other parishioners came forward and said they had been watching us during mass. They knew we had Catholic backgrounds because we knew all the right responses to the prayers. Our backgrounds had told on us!

All four of us helped clean up at the end of the evening. We walked out with the other parishioners, taking items out to their cars for them. We were just closing Larry's trunk when I heard Father Mike calling my name and running out of St. Columba to catch us.

"Deborah! Deborah!"

"Yes Father Mike? I'm here. What is it?"

"God has spoken to me."

"Oh my! What did our Lord have to say?"

I stood breathless, waiting for his answer.

He said to me, "God said to give this miraculous oil vial to you."

I heard immediately in my spirit, "**Now it begins.**"

My knees swayed beneath me. My voice would not come out of my mouth.

I ran back to the car finally crying out, "Thank you! Thank you!" We all jumped up and down as we got in the car to head back to Mom's. All I could think of in my head was "Don't drop it, don't break it, and don't blow it. REALLY don't blow it!"

We hadn't gotten four miles down the road when I noticed the little vial that wasn't two-thirds full had miraculously filled up and was overflowing out onto my hands. God, through this vial, was anointing my hands for His work.

I shouted out to the rest of my friends in the car and told them what was happening. They could see the oil coming out of a tightly closed vial, now full to overflowing.

Immediately I knew what to do. I anointed Marilynn with oil and prayed for her ministry of intercessory prayer. Then I anointed my husband for a healing ministry. I did not anoint the driver, Larry, in case he might be slain in the Spirit again!

Our spirits were as high as kites by the time we arrived back at Mom's. We knew when we dropped off our car earlier that she was sick with the flu. We all knew what we had to do as we went into the living room. I asked if we could pray over her.

She said, "Yes, of course."

With hands still covered in oil, we laid hands on her and prayed for her to be healed.

At the end of the prayer, I did not realize that I was still under the anointing. I said to her, "Awe Mom, when we leave, you are going to cough up all this goop and be just fine." Everyone laughed. Even I thought I was speaking in the flesh.

As it turned out, I spoke prophesy. When we left, Mom coughed up all the infection. She was immediately hungry and had to eat before going to bed.

The next day, she called Sandy, her daughter, and told her, "I've had a miracle! I've had a miracle!"

Over the next several days, utilizing the anointing oil, we saw physical manifestations of miracles over and over: healings from surgeries, averting of disasters, words of knowledge, prophesies, etc...

By the third day of the New Year, I was told in the Spirit I would be writing a third book right alongside book two. It would be called "2012: The Miraculous Year."

So be it.

SIGNS AND WONDERS
(Jan. 2nd)

Mark woke up worse than ever with the rash that had been troubling him for a month. Red and angry welts were all over his skin. I was told in the spirit to take his picture. I anointed him all over with miraculous oil and told him to lie down in bed until he felt okay to get up.

I made breakfast and called Mark to come to the kitchen. To my surprise, he looked much better. His hands had new pink skin where there had been welts. Mark was smiling. I prayed in my heart for someone to show this to, and to tell them what happened. I wanted Andy, our son, the Advanced Care EMT, to see this. Fifteen minutes later, he called. Andy was in Corydon and wanted to come over and have breakfast with us.

When Andy arrived, we told him the whole story.

"Wow! Amazing," said Andy.

Andy looked at the picture taken just one hour ago and at the evidence before him on Mark's skin. Thomas Andrew was our witness to the latest goodness of God.

"This is miraculous, Momma." Andy stated.

We thanked Andy for having stopped by on his busy schedule.

Later that day, we went to Mt. St. Frances for a charismatic mass. For the first time in 15 years, I was asked to give a praise report at the end of mass, ."..and oh, by the way, could you please anoint people and pray over them for their needs?"

"Why sure." I cried.

At the end of mass, I got up and gave my witness of what had gone on the last two days. Mary, my friend, also spoke of how God placed it on her heart to ask me to pray over people. In the 15 years I have gone to mass there, no one had ever asked me to lead prayer over people. One of those we prayed over was Billie. She had undergone surgery for an abscess that was as big as her fist. The doctor said it would take six weeks to heal. She wanted to go back to work the next week. Could we pray for her? I said yes immediately. Then I went into prayer in my heart and asked the Lord to guide me. I felt in the spirit to pray for her quick recovery. I looked forward to her praise report.

**I found out a few days later that she did indeed heal in four days.

THREE
(Jan. 3rd)

A CALL FROM A FRIEND

I received a call from Clare. There was trouble afoot. She had strong premonitions about her daughter. We prayed in agreeing prayer to avert disaster. We cried out to send it back to hell where it belonged.

Afterwards, I brought her up to date on all that had gone over the last week. She said, "Be careful. What you say under anointing will come true. Ask God to guide you."

I had also been asked to print notes from a sermon that had been given the week before. It was on overcoming doubt. It went like this:

"Don't be afraid! Let it all come. We serve an on-time God. He will be right on time. On this Earth, we say *about time,* but God says *on time.* Go with what God is telling you."

That evening I felt told in my spirit It was confirmed to me, I would be writing two books at the same time. I even got the names...

Miraculous Interventions II Modern Day Priests, Prophets, Pastors & Everyday Visionaries and

Miraculous Interventions III: 2012, The Miraculous Year

And I was also given the name for the next book, *Miraculous Interventions IV: The Gathering*

I could see 2012 would be off to a busy start.

A HEALED HEART

Miss Vicki Sampson did not feel well. I received a word to pray over her heart. God would provide for her health. After I prayed, she felt better.

PROPHESY FOR IVIE

Pastor Ivie had been fighting cancer off and on for almost 25 years. We were tired of it. When she called me that day, before I could stop it, I said, "Ivie, the cancer is gone. You are cancer free. It won't even be in your cells."

When Ivie got home, back to South Carolina, she had a message from her doctor's office that said just that. What a belated Christmas present.

What a day!

What a God!

MINISTERING ANGELS
(Jan. 5th)

What an amazing year, and it was only the fifth day! I was not sure on how to proceed, so I asked the Lord to send me ministering angels to help guide me. He did. I took calls from two of my favorite apostles of the Lord. Once again, Pastor Ivie Dennis showed up over the phone as well as Pastor Lee Schwarz.

Pastor Ivie started out, "The cancer cells are dead and I am cancer free. I have asked God to wrap it up. Also, the Lord told me to tell you that your house is already paid for with the money from your books."
"So be it."

That afternoon, I was able to give my witness report on what had happened over the last five days to Pastor Lee. He weighted his reply with these words, "Go with the direction of the Holy Spirit. Obey Him only. What God tells us to do is right. Everything else is sin. This is not our own decision to make. You have been given this vial for a reason. Remember it is holy oil. It is the widow's cruise. Remember the very poor woman who ministered to Elijah? The last of her oil and meal lasted them 18 months. She never ran out of her provision for the rest of her life. Now this is important. Remember to thank God for His provision every day!"

I promised Lee I would. He went on with words of wisdom.

"God takes care of us in little and big ways. God wanted you to know and see what you did with your gift of the vial. The very first thing you did in the car was share it. You have gone from helper to healer. It may make you weary, but God will provide your strength."

Then words of knowledge came to him for me.

"Keep anointing Mark. He is under attack."

Lee felt God was working for us in a new way. He laughed and said, "It will be a trip. This whole year. This is an exciting beginning to your year. This is the start of your next book. If this is the beginning, where will it go from here?"

Lee went on to say, "Let the Spirit speak. Don't you worry about what's coming out of your mouth. Commit these gifts for His glory. Do what you are given to do. Remember, you have no power. It's all God's power! You have a gift. It's been years in the making. Be careful of intrusion of yourself in the process. Don't try to outthink God. Watch your ego because we're all human."

I took all Lee's advice to heart.

"The more power you see God display in you, the more potential ego problems could exist. Guard yourself, or you could be lost as an instrument. Your usefulness could be lost for the Kingdom. Even illness and death could come on you if you lose your way. Be careful of New Age."

I could see all this could come with a price.

Lee spoke plainly, "Don't lose your effectiveness for the Kingdom. Stay well grounded. Pray every day! You will work miracles under God's care and anointing."

Suddenly, I felt very heavy with the weight of all that would be accomplished.

There were no prospects of Lee and Anne coming back to Indiana soon. Their finances weren't good, and they were headed for bankruptcy court. It would allow them to breathe a little easier. They needed to get rid of debt that they had been carrying for 20 years. I was assured that they would love to make the trip by car or train as soon as they could arrange it.

Right before we got off the phone, Lee said this came to him about my husband. "Wipe away Mark's tears and his rash. He has emotional and spiritual tears."

That evening, we had church at Believer's Fellowship. After the service, I asked Pastor Schuppert if he had a moment. I told him the whole story of the last five days. He said, "Wow!" Then Fred told me of the pain he had been experiencing in his body. I asked if he would like me to pray over him with the anointing oil. He said, "Yes." His wife, Jeanne, Mark and myself anointed and prayed over Fred for his total healing.

I told him I would look for his good report.

When Mark and I arrived home, I anointed Mark's body all over and asked for a total healing for him; mind, body and spirit.

After all, I am his wife. It was the least I could do.

BATTLES
(Jan. 6th)

Mark came home sick from work with the flu and sinus infection. I got up out of my chair and retrieved the anointing oil. As was becoming our custom, I prayed and anointed my husband. In a little while, his temperature went back to normal and he felt much better.

By 1 a.m. he was still better. By 4 a.m. he was not so good. And by 5:30 a.m. he came down sick again. It seemed to be everywhere I looked.

Mary, my publisher was also home sick with the flu. She had slept all day.

And Karen, my editor, was in a bad state. Her faithful dog had died while she was at work. She was having a hard time with it.

I stayed home and ministered to my husband. I felt overflowing love for him. In just a few days, I had seen so many healings take place that I wanted the same for my dear one.

"Where was Mark's healing, Lord?"

11:58 P.M.
(Jan. 7th)

Mark stayed home, still sick with the flu virus and sinusitis. I took care of him all day. I anointed my husband several times for a healing. I even resorted to giving him medicine so he would feel better until his healing came. I sang uplifting songs to comfort both of us. While Mark took a nap, I talked to God about this matter.

"Lord, it's the seventh day of the year. These are miraculous times upon us. But today I am at home with a sick husband who is not healed. Am I not to see or experience anything miraculous today?"

I waited for my answer.

Evening came, and after a nice dinner, we watched a couple of Christian movies together. It was a very nice evening despite Mark's illness.

At 11:00 p.m., I thought there would be no miracle that day, and I have to admit to having been a little bit let down. But the day was not over.

Mark felt in his heart to turn on the television and look for a Christian station. We found Perry Stone and Sid Roth and the Hunter Group. All had wonderful messages. By the end of the last show, they prayed over the audience there and at home. She asked us to put our hand over our hearts for a healing. We did. Immediately, I felt hot heat through my hand and into my chest. I started crying out, "Free! Free!" No more emotional chains in my heart to hurt or lack. I was healed. God did not forget me!

The time when it was over?

11:58 p.m., the last few minutes of the day.

Mark also felt peace overflow his body. Warmth came to his heart too. Yet his physical healing did not come.

I pondered all these things in my heart.

EPIPHANY OF YESHUA
(Jan. 8th)

Mark slept well through the night. The next morning, he was better but not completely healed. His mucous had cleared, and his itching was down to just a few areas. I had diligently taken care of my husband over that weekend and canceled all plans to go out.

What I had not told Mark was that I felt illness come on too. I was under attack with a raw throat, runny sinuses and fatigue. What I had not understood that morning was that my heart had been prepared for my instant healing the night before.

I got up and fixed breakfast for us. I prepared a batch of lemon muffins sent to us from South Carolina by Pastor Ivie and her husband, Ray. While I waited in the kitchen for the muffins to bake, Mark sat in the living room in his easy chair. It was then that I went to the bathroom and called out for help.

"Lord. I cannot do all you have set on my plate to do this week with our books, meeting Mary, taking care of my husband and being sick myself. Please send your holy angels with healing."

I went back in the kitchen and prepared our plates and drinks. I took them into the living room for a lite meal. Our Christmas lights were gently glowing, the Angels CD that Andy had given us was softly playing in the background, and Mark was on the floor before the Lord in Adoration.

When I came around the living room corner I bumped right into an angelic presence with my healing. Fire flowed from the top of my head to the soles of my feet. Instantly my head cleared, fatigue left me, my throat was well and clear. Glory to God.

I joined my husband on the floor in grateful tears and smiles. After prayers of thanksgiving, we got up and ate our breakfast. It was only 8:30 in the morning. Oh, my Lord. My soul cried out. What else have You for us on this holy Epiphany of Yeshua? Now we were ready to go to our friend's house for lunch.

On the way to John and Cathy's, our son Ben called us wanting our opinion on Jeremiah 10: 2-5.

"When did you start this study, Son?" I asked.

"January 1st."

That was the day Fr. Mike prophesied Ben would come back to the Lord in a strong manner.

At John and Cathy's, Cathy told this story. Her sister Billie came to prayer group three days after we had prayed for her at mass. Billie told everyone after we had prayed for her on Monday night, she got rapidly better every day. The word I had been given while praying for her, which I spoke out loud, had been "rapidly better." Instead of six weeks, her healing came in four days.

We praised God for such a wonderful message.

A CHRISTIAN ATMOSPHERE
(Jan. 9th)

Once again the same fight came overnight. Mark got up with thick yellow mucous. We prayed to God before taking anything. Then we went into praise and thanksgiving. Mark had a standing appointment to see a dermatologist later that afternoon.

Good news. We arrived and walked into the office and I knew within seconds it was a Christian office. I heard praise music in the background. On the office walls, there were scripture verses. How wonderful. We knew we were in the right place.

I told them up front we only had so much money, but we would be happy to make payments. When the time came to check out, Mark's bill was less than half of what we expected. And when we went to pick up his medications the cost was reduced on two of the highest medicines. We still had money left over. As if that wasn't enough, while we were waiting we saw that there was a 75% off Christmas special going on. We picked up a 12 place setting of Christmas dishes for $10.00. I had always wanted Christmas dishes and never had the money to get any.

During the evening, we put away our few Christmas decorations that we had gotten out. We also decided to watch a movie. While it was playing, we received a call from a friend who was very upset about hearing of her friend with a terminal illness. Mark started immediately with prayer over the phone.

At the end of the day, right before bed, I started

with diarrhea. I called out to Mark for prayer. He put on praise music and led me to bed. I heard in my spirit, *"all means all."* I knew it meant my healing. My bowels were restored and we rejoiced of winning another battle. Praise God.

I was up until midnight writing praise reports.

JUST ENOUGH.
(Jan. 11th)

With Mark down sick, having the rash and needing a specialist, it took almost all the available funds we had. Our main account had $12.00 and $8.00 of that was due out in fees. And my little account had $12.00 in it with $5.00 in fees coming out. I prayed before I left the house.

"Lord, we have little money and no ibuprofen for Mark while he is recovering. Please, we need some miracle money."

I left to go to the bank, determined to close my account to buy the medicine Mark needed. I arrived at the bank and requested my balance.

Well, the balance I had written down was all wrong. My account had $20.00 more in it. I took out $10.00 for Mark's medicine and kept my account open.

"Thank you Lord for caring that my account stay open and still be able to get what we needed."

When Mark came home that night, he came in with several bags of groceries. Immediately, I cried out, "Where did you get the money for that?"

Mark met my cry with exuberance.

"I got a $25.00 tip!"

"Oh boy! Groceries in the house!"

On our time God made sure we had just enough to meet our present needs. Like our friend Pastor Lee said, "He's a giver of the big and the small blessings." We need to learn to accept them all. At the end of the day, we each had $5.00 in our checking accounts and savings. We called it good.

MARY
(Jan. 12th)

Of course, with all the praise and worship and thanksgiving we were sending up, we had no idea another illness was at our door. It arrived at 3:30 the next morning. From 3:30 that morning until 4:30's victory, Mark and I were, for a second time, in a battle for my health. Diarrhea once again beset me with no cause. We went directly into praise with scriptures. We read Psalm 59 and Proverbs 31. I anointed myself and requested Heavenly help. For a second time in less than one week, illness was sent flying back to the abyss. I thanked God for His graciousness. Glory to the Almighty. His peace had entered my situation.

Mary had spent the night. She woke up sick. I put oil on her sinuses and they opened right up.

We worked on the business of *Miraculous Interventions* and *Christmas Chaos*! While we were working, it started to snow. Snow! Didn't we have somewhere we needed to go? Mary and I drove in it and had a blast. What a gift. We felt like two young-ens enjoying the season. After all, it was snowflakes that had gotten us into all of this. We drove to Mary's house to work on her computer, but the screen quit working soon after we sat down to work. This meant trouble. We prayed, but to no avail. We went to Office Depot to finish what we had started. The assistant manager met us at the counter. Mary told her what happened. She replied, "Mary, I'm moving and putting my things in storage. You can borrow my screen until September if you like." Problem solved. No coincidence. All God!

REMINDER
(Jan. 13th)

Mark came into the kitchen that morning for breakfast with a text message from Fr. Mike. It said simply, "Angel pics?"

I called and left him a message that I would get the pictures to him quick.

He called me at 11 a.m. that same morning with a story to tell me.

Mike said, "Last night, I was in bed and felt a Heavenly visitation. I took a quick picture of myself. There was a swoosh of color over my head. I had been visited. "

He told the one that would understand everything he had said.

You bet I believed him.

MAN VISIONS
(Jan. 16th)

Father Mike and his wife Patti came over for a visit. We thought it was time we took them out to see our homeland. From the first step, they loved it.

"Breath taking."

Father Mike saw something he had never seen before. He saw an angel on our property doing cart wheels. Then he asked if we ever thought of putting a chapel on it. In the original design four years ago, that was our exact plan.

We all went back to our home and had a wonderful dinner. They stayed until midnight and told us story after story of how good God had been to them during their life together.

That night Mark had a dream that he saw the robe of God — from his elbow to his hand. There was a smoky blue and white all around this vision. Then he saw a beautiful sunrise with gold in it.

FIRE FALL!

(Jan. 17th)

Last night Mary's monitor blew.
That morning my monitor blew.
I had to wait and see what good the Lord had in store for us.

My best friend of 38+ years, Vicki Sampson, called to warn me of impending bad weather. I showered and got dressed quickly as sirens started. I went to my friend Gail's home with her daughter and grandchild.

Once it was over, I came back to the house and laid down to take a nap. I was feeling a little sorry for myself. I asked God once again, "Lord, aren't you ever going to bless me just a little bit more?"

As I was falling asleep, I felt fire consume my whole head all the way to my neck. The same way it did when Pastor Fred prayed over me, and the Holy Spirit fell with virtue and power. As it embedded itself in me, I sang, "I love you Lord. And I lift my voice. To worship you, oh my soul rejoice. Take joy my King, in what you hear. Let it be a sweet, sweet sound in your ear." Then I fell asleep.

I remember hearing words come out of a fog, "wisdom, discernment, miracles."

That evening, our son Andy called.
And did he have a story to tell me.
Of course I wrote it down.

TWINS FOUR YEARS APART!
(Jan. 17th)

"Momma! I have something awesome to tell you." Thomas Andrew, our youngest son had started the conversation. I was all ears.

"Do tell!"

Andy started, "I was working out at the gym today and hurt my intercostal (ribs) muscles right lateral. I had a bulge in the area. Later in the day, I called Ben to ask what to do about it. During the conversation, I mentioned I was hurting. Ben asked me if it was on my right side intercostal muscles, describing exactly what I was feeling. I was amazed and said, 'Yes.' He said he had been hurting there all day and wondered what he had done to himself. Then he asked me if my right shoulder was giving me any trouble. I said, 'Yeah,' to that. It was popping and I didn't know what I had done to it. He said it wasn't me, it was him. He had hurt his shoulder. We were feeling each other's pain. Then he asked me if I ever felt like I was his twin. (Ben had a twin that had passed away at 12 weeks gestational age.) I said, 'Yeah,' and he said, 'Me too!'"

Andy asked me, "Do you think this is possible?"

My reply? "With God, all things are possible. Absolutely! Remember when Ben was having his cardiac event in the army? You came home and knew there was something wrong with him."

Andy replied, "Yeah, just like a twin four years apart."

This does not surprise me one bit. God answers the prayers of a child.

46

When Ben was very young, he missed his twin and used to pray for God to send him back.

Wait! You haven't read the verification.
Read on.

VERIFICATION ONE YEAR LATER
(Jan. 6th 2013 for this story's purpose)

It was the first Charismatic Mass of the year at Mount St. Frances for the year 2013. I had spent the day being a good helper to my Momma and Mom Peyron. By 6 p.m. that evening, I had dinner on the table for Mark and myself. During the course of the meal, my husband remarked of his fatigue and asked if I minded if he stayed home from mass that evening.

"Of course not."

While the meal was coming to a close, we opened the mail. There was a letter from Washington D.C. for me and Mary, my publisher. I didn't know anyone there, but evidently they knew us. I had sent my books to the Vatican for Pope Benedict XVI's year of faith and sharing. We had received a response!

There were two pictures signed by Pope Benedict, two Christmas cards from the Vatican and a letter. I couldn't wait to tell Mary that night at church! My sister was about to be on cloud nine. Mark agreed to do dishes, so I could get to church a little early.

Singing and praising had already begun when I entered Mt. St. Frances. I sat a few pews away from Mary. After a quick service (Father wasn't feeling well), Mary walked over to me and sat down in front of me. I was all smiles as I showed our now "prize possession" and read her the generous letter. Mary cried as she told me of her prayer that very morning about our work together. Prayers were answered in 12 hours.

As we talked further about answered prayer, we discussed several other books. One book had a passage about a child in Heaven seeing a miscarried sibling who had no name because their momma had not named it. I told Mary that when I was young, before I had my three miscarriages including Ben's original twin, I had named all my babies from their conceptions. They weren't very inventive names, but they were better than none. Mary asked what they were.

"Baby Face" "Bright Star" "Baby Twin"

Mary thought for a moment and said, "What if their names were in Latin or Hebrew?"

"What would that make them?" I asked.

Baby Face: Fidas, Bright Star: Stella, Baby Twin: Thomas. Mary added, "Don't forget Annie Frances: Full of Grace." (See page 237)

There it was. Thomas the twin. Ben's twin. What he had prayed as a little boy had come back to us. Thomas "the twin" Andrew had come back just for us.

Fast forward to the fall of 2013 and the typing of all these stories: I was at Mary's home since I had no computer or home of my own yet. As I was typing this very story up at her house, dinner was almost ready, and we were called to the kitchen.

Over the meal, Mary asked what I was typing, and I told her and her family the story of "Twins four years apart." As eerie as it sounded, Mitch had an ending to the story that set it apart.

He said, "Today is a special commemorative day on the secular calendar."

"Really? What?"

"National Pregnancy and Infant Loss Remembrance Day."

"Oh, my gosh!"

"I can't believe it!" We cried out together.

Time has no meaning to God. All things come together for good for those that love the Lord and trust ....

Even when it's weird.

MARCHING ORDERS
(Jan. 18th)

What an amazing day! As I look back on it, I had no idea that morning how mighty and fast the Holy Spirit would move through that day.

I had already planned a very busy day. A luncheon with a local group of business women met at noon. Then I was going to see friends with my husband in the evening. But God is a wonderful re-arranger, and how He managed to fit it all in, (in one day) is one of the miracles documented here.

Shortly after Mark arrived at work, he called me. Buster had called and was worried about Fred's health. He thought we should all go over and pray for Fred and Jeanne that evening.

"Send the word out, Wife."

I made calls as instructed and then made a quick call to Karen who had agreed to come on board as one of my editors for the book published in 2012. An hour flew by quickly as we brought each other up to date on our daily life events. Karen has always been a wonderful help to me.

I did a fifteen minute workout and was ready to clean up to go to the luncheon when my phone rang. It was Pastor Ivie from South Carolina. All we had to do was greet each other and it felt like we were in the same room.

"Hello beautiful woman of God!" I heard Ivie's cheery voice across the miles.

"Hello beautiful woman of God. How are you?" I responded.

"All is well with my soul and God has done great

and mighty things in my life. He has also shown me a vision for your direction. Are you ready to receive it?"

"Are you kidding me? Paper! I need paper! Don't talk until I have something to write on." My enthusiasm spilled over, and I heard appreciative laughter from my sister in Christ Jesus.

I found the two journals I had laid aside, one for her and one for the year 2012. I sat myself at the kitchen table and prepared to write.

"Okay, go."

Praise reports and a word from God began.

Ivie started, "Well my sister, let's begin with a thanksgiving prayer." Ivie went down the line of recent victories in her life and mine to be thankful for. Then she spoke a request to God for wisdom, knowledge, revelation and confirmation. As she spoke, she confirmed another word exactly given to me on January 1st of that year from Fr. Mike Olsen.

Ivie saw a laurel, a wreath about my head, me walking in stride. It was the same thing Fr. Mike saw about me running a race. It was my destiny.

Then the Lord showed her big exponential growth steps in every area of my life.

"Get ready quick! You may be overwhelmed temporarily. Things are going to move for you now." She saw the word "promoted."

Pastor Ivie saw me go from being shackled with the Mary Syndrome (feeling unworthy), to being freed. She saw the deep-rooted fear of messing up and it breaking off of me. God Himself cut off the root. The very hand of God unshackled me. God told her to tell me this, "F.E.A.R. stands for *False Evidence Appearing Real*. Don't believe it. The *what if* faith syndrome. Walk by faith."

Ivie saw the hand of God unshackle me. I twirled around free, smiling. Then I started running the race with a good stride. Ivie told me what I had been told by others and I had long suspected. I have the heart of an evangelist walking in the office of a prophet as God gives the gift.

Then Pastor Ivie spoke to me of her miracle. As she was preparing for a new job making $9.00 an hour on an as needed basis, she had to go by the hospital to pick up a doctor's clearance to go back to work. It was then she saw a sign for a company that some of her friends owned. They needed help. Ivie faxed them her resume' and went right over to see them. As she walked through the door, they were reading her resume'. Immediately, she received a $4.00 an hour raise and started six days later.

Her report? "God always gives us better than what we ask for."

As we were ending the conversation, I asked her to pray for Brother Fred's health. Of course, she said she would.

I proceeded to get ready for the afternoon. At 11:00 a.m., Clare showed up right on time, and off we went to the ladies luncheon. All during the meeting, I felt in my spirit to pray for Fred right then! I grabbed Clare, and we both prayed for him in the middle of the meeting. During the luncheon, I told Trudy and Clare about the meeting set for later that day. Clare said she had to go to a funeral home that evening. Trudy piped right up and said, "Clare! There is nothing you can do for that man in the funeral home, but you can come and help pray for Fred and Jeanne tonight." The order was given!

We ran some errands and did some light shopping while we waited for Mark to get off work. At 5:30, Trudy and I were sitting on my couch talking when a word of knowledge dropped into my head. I knew Brother Bill hadn't been called.

"Oh my! No one has called Brother Bill." I ran to the phone and dialed his number. Bill's usual cheery voice answered.

"Hello, Sister Debbie."

"Brother Bill. Has anyone contacted you about tonight?" I already knew the answer.

"No. What's tonight?"

"The church is going over to pray for Fred and Jeanne. We're evicting the demon that's attacking their health and wealth."

"What time are we meeting?"

"6 p.m."

"Okay. See you in half an hour."

"Whew. Thank you God for that word to call our brother and tell him to come to the Schuppert's. I am sure we are going to need him."

All hands were due on deck.

Mark arrived home at 5:45 p.m. In two minutes, we were all back out the door. The mission field awaited us.

The first one to arrive was Clare, then Trudy, then us. A few minutes more and the Wards, Brother Bill and finally, Brother Buster came in. He was the one who had listened to the Lord's prompting and started it all.

Jeanne had just finished teaching music class and had put all the chairs in a circle for our group. Fred came in the room wearing a coat. He was cold, and his legs and hips ached. Enough of that; it had to go.

We all held hands, heads bowed in reverence, and Brother Bill as an elder of the church, started the prayers.

The battle over this territory began in earnest.

"In the name of Jesus." Bill prayed healing and health back to Fred's body. He bound satan the liar and cast him down and out! Each of us prayed as the Holy Spirit gave us utterance. Demands were made to give back all the devil had stolen from them. Pain and suffering had to go. It had no place there. Financial burdens had to leave as well.

Shouts, tears, words of knowledge and laying on of hands were administered as we cried for victory to come marching in. As the prayers died down, we were led to pray for blessings to shower down on the Schuppert household and, in fact, on all in our little church.

How many were there, you ask?

Why, I thought you would know.

Twelve: Youngest to oldest, we numbered twelve. Of course we did.

If twelve was good enough for our Lord, it was good enough for Fred.

By 7 p.m., a feeling of peace settled over the Schuppert residence.

We still had one more errand to run before our evening was finished. We left our little home church, picked up a meal on the road and took off for the Horne's. We did not know our prayer work was not yet done for the day.

Mark and I arrived shortly after dark to see the

new renovations Rick and Lisa were doing at their home. With a big flashlight, Rick showed us around the outside. What marvelous changes were in store for this family of six.

When we went inside Lisa showed us the remodeled living room, kitchen and bathroom.

"How exciting." I cried.

We sat at their kitchen table and caught up with each other's lives. When I told the story of the miraculous oil and how it had come to me, Rick had a question.

"Did you bring it with you?"

"Yes, I did."

"Can you please pray for my elbow. It hurts."

"Sure we can."

I thanked God and asked for His provision for healing. I anointed Rick and we all took turns and prayed over him. We told Rick when we left that we would look for a good report.

It was the end of another busy day in the Lord's service.

DISSIPATE
(Jan. 22nd)

Mark and I started out the day making a lunch and dinner meal for our pastor and his wife - our pleasure.

The rest of the day was spent cooking a dish for a seven person birthday party in the family. It was an expensive weekend.

It was during the cooking phase that I received a strong word from the Lord, *"Peace, be still."* I knew bad weather was coming.

"Pray all day, dissipate; dissipate!"

We made our rounds with the food we had prepared and headed to the birthday party. When we arrived, I asked if we could spend the night at the Royal house due to the dark clouds that marched behind us as we drove over. As the night wore on, the local weathermen took over the broadcasting to warn their listening viewers. Tornado activity was bearing down on our region.

True to the word I was given earlier in the day, I prayed over and over again for it to dissipate. In the late night hours, curled up on a blow up mattress in their basement, we watched, time after time, on the radar, front after front dissipate as it hit the Clark County border. Right before our eyes, evidence of all that was unseen, fell apart. There was no tornado activity at all.

"Thank You, Lord. Your words are true over man's. *Peace, be still* 2000 years ago, still meant *Peace, be still* now.

PRAYER AND FASTING
(Jan. 23rd)

It was the last day of my 21 day prayer fast. That morning, I said my last prayer of thanksgiving to God for sparing our region from tornadoes. I had hoped for it to usher in good for our family, for God's presence to be felt more deeply in our lives, and for God's spirit to move even more in my life with dreams. I was not disappointed.

Lisa called to remind me about being their babysitter that afternoon and evening. As we talked, a word of knowledge and great love for her came over me, and I cried. I told her what happened. I told her the message given to me for her.

"It is okay to be all God has gifted you to be. Your children will be fine."

I felt in my heart a small bit of God's love for her. It was almost overwhelming.

I watched their children that afternoon, and then Mark came home. We had dinner, played games, painted together, and watched movies.

"Do you know that you are awesome?" the two youngest of the four, Adam and Kate said.

Two sweet little faces looked up to us with smiles. We smiled back.

"No, but if you hum a few bars, I am sure we can fake it..."

My attempt at a joke went right over their dear little heads.

Later that evening, Mom and Dad picked up their children and all their gear with thanks for our help.

While we got ready for bed, I pondered the word of knowledge I had been given earlier in the day for Lisa and the love I felt come through. Surely, it had touched my heart as much as hers. Then, having that same love come back to me through their children was truly heart-warming.

Their children spoke from their hearts.

"I want to stay here and play for a long time." Six-year-old Adam spoke.

"Wow. The picture you drew was awesome. But I bet you already knew that." said Alex, the oldest child.

"Yes, but not as clearly as you did." I responded with a smile.

NOW I LAY ME DOWN TO SLEEP...
(Jan. 23rd)

As my husband and I laid down to sleep, Mark prayed a lovely prayer for beautiful dreams of our Lord to fill our heads. And they did.

In my first dream, I heard, "The wealth of the sinner is laid up for the just." I felt someone out of my past was going to come and help me in a big way.

Near the morning, another dream came with clarity.

I thought I saw the outside of our promised home on Nicholas Drive. It was already built, and we were living there. I saw Mark and myself walk out the front door as if off to work. Mark turned to lock the door as I was walking down the steps. It was a beautiful, clear spring day.

In my head, I was planning the day's events. I was busy going about the Lord's work on a higher level than before.

In that dream, all my dreams had come true.

BLESSINGS FROM ABOVE
(Jan. 26th)

Every day there had been a miraculous event, healing, gift or mending of a heart. And it was not even the end of January.

Early that morning, as I was singing praise to God, I felt the power of the Holy Spirit, Jesus and God visit. I fell to my knees and welcomed them all.

The day started out wonderful. My first client had lost 24 pounds since the beginning of the year. What a marvelous start to his "new you."

After he left, I had some errands to do. A Christmas store in our town was going out of business. She was retiring and moving to Florida. Nice for her; maybe nice for me. I walked into her store and looked at all the pretty things that I normally couldn't afford but now had a chance to buy. I looked at the music boxes on display. I had always wanted to find the one I had so long ago; it had been a gift for my first baby. My husband at the time took the beautiful music box and crushed it to dust in front of me. I needed to replace it as a reminder of Baby Face who had died in my womb. What were the odds that I could find such a present for myself? Why, with God all things are possible!

As I looked around through their boxes, in the back, almost hidden, there it was. There was even a special price on it.

"Could you please open the case and get that one out for me?"

Excitement grew in my chest.

"Oh dear, the cashier replied, "You don't want that one. It's damaged. It can't sing."

"That's okay," I replied. "I'll hear my baby sing in Heaven."

She looked at me, perplexed at my response, but I'm sure she figured it took all kinds and rang me up. She boxed up my treasure and off I went with tears in my eyes, rocking a box for a baby I never got to hold.

I stopped by Mark's work to show him my new-found treasure. I figured since he was a bench jeweler, maybe he could fix it.

I said, "Honey, it can't sing but it reminded me of the music box I had for Baby Face, so I had to get it. Can you fix it?"

Mark searched his memory of the story that I had told him in our first years of marriage, nodded his head, and said he would see what he could do.

By the end of the afternoon, I received a call from one of my favorite stores in Louisville, Kentucky, Tonini's Church Supply. They had carried all my books to date, and Mr. Tonini himself had called me "the Miracle Lady." Chris, Mr. Tonini's son, did all the purchasing for the store. They needed more books. And could I please put them on the list of stores for the next in the series?

"Absolutely."

It was a day filled with gifts, verifications that God never forgot my wounds, and He sent healing balms for my heart 27 years later.

As nice as that day was, the next day was filled with attacks on me and my family.

ATTACKED!
(Jan. 27th)

We moved Ben and Amanda the next morning. Mark took the day off, and we started early. We had enough people help that we were all done by 3:30 that afternoon. Several of the helpers left, but we stayed behind to wait for Amanda to come home from work.

Ben's back was hurting after all the exertion which he said with his mouth and his movements.

"Ohhhh..." Ben stretched his lower back muscles.

Mark and I looked at each other. I told him the story of the anointing oil and how I just happened to have it on me.

"Would you like me to pray over you?" I asked.

He responded by turning around, his back to me, and lifted his shirt. Mark and I both prayed over him as I anointed him.

By that time, Amanda came bouncing into their house.

"You're all done? Wow."

We all went out to eat dinner at a little, local family-owned restaurant. Mark bought dinner. Our last errand was to take them to the grocery store and shop together, then back home.

On the way home, Andy called to tell us he was okay.

"What do you mean, you're okay? What are you talking about?" I looked at my husband with concern rising in my voice.

"I was exposed to bad fumes in the ambulance that I was driving today. They checked me out in the hospital, but I am going to be okay. I gave thanks to the Lord." I could hear the relief in his voice and then in mine.

"Yes sweetheart. We are so glad that you are fine. Please stay safe."

As we fell asleep later that evening, we asked God for pleasant dreams. I fell asleep saying the *Our Father*.

I dreamed I was working for a king in a big castle. The view outside the castle windows was breathtaking. I could see a well-manicured lawn and trees along a path. It almost looked like our view from Nicholas Drive. I was very happy.

In the last dream of the night, Mark and I were living in a country subdivision. One of the neighbors was having trouble. She had four children and her husband had left her. I knew she needed my help. (Even in my dreams, I help people!) When I went to see her and console her, she gave me a check to help us out.

As I was waking up, I could hear her prophesying over me. If only I could remember her sweet words...

The next morning, my nephew called who had a root canal done the day before. I inquired about how he was doing. Ibuprofen and acetaminophen were getting him through all the soreness such a procedure placed on a body. He also had a request to make of us. He was in need of a truck and help. Would we mind helping him out with our truck? We were more than happy to be of assistance to any family member who needed a truck and hauling.

Mark came home from work under spiritual and emotional attack.

His mood was coarse and surly. I asked if I had done something wrong.

"Yes and no."

"Clarify."

All his feelings and fears came out about building a home on his income. We were ready to build, and I still did not have a job with a consistent income. I was putting everything on his shoulders. How could I do that to him?!

I assured Mark that I had no intention of putting it all on his shoulders. I was putting everything on God's shoulders.

We sat down together, anointed each other, and asked for strength to go on. Peace came as we prayed together. Now we were smiling.

Mark and I got ready for an evening at Ben and Amanda's. Of course we were greeted with smiles of appreciation of all that we had helped them with lately. While there, Ben had developed a cough, drainage and a sore throat. I checked him out with a pen light and said it looked to be a common cold; treat the symptoms.

When we got ready to leave, I thought Ben felt like he had a fever, so I told Amanda how to treat him with natural medications. We left without praying for him. I received a text from him on the way home. It read as follows:

"Mama, you take it back. Your anointed mouth has my ears closing up. You pray me well by morning over there. From Ben."

Well. I was surely put in my place. Ben was right. I did have to be careful about what came out of my mouth.

I called Ben immediately. I repented and went into healing prayers as Mark sang praises.

"Thank you, Mama."

When we got home, Andy had called. He had the same junk that Ben had. We called him back and prayed for him the same way we had prayed for his big brother. We just knew we would hear good reports in the morning.

After all, they are "the twins!"

ACTS OF GOD
(Jan. 29th)

Through the night, I received a word about a friend's illness. I felt that if I called her for reassurance, she would be just fine.

When I awoke, I did just that. Obedience in bringing good news to people is a joyful part of doing the Lord's work.

While making the call, I heard another call beep in. It was Andy, so I called him back.

"Momma! I have two praise reports for you! Both Ben and I were much better this morning after being prayed over last night."

I could hear him smiling over the phone.

What a lovely way to start the day.

We were excited to see our friends Larry and Marilynn. It was our turn to have them over for dinner and fellowship. We had a nice early afternoon meal together. After brunch, we sat in the living room to catch up on each other's activities. In the meantime, Marilynn and Mark remarked about achy knees.

We started praying for Marilynn's left knee. Larry went into praying in tongues while I got out the anointing oil and anointed the area that hurt her. Instantly, she felt something move and go back in place, and the pain ended.

Next was Mark. Now all three of us came and prayed over him. I anointed his knee, and it didn't take a few seconds before he also felt something go back in place, and his pain ended too.

They both jumped up, praising the Lord!

In Jesus' name, we had told their body parts to line up with the word of God, and they did.

That totaled two miracles and two healings in one day. The day was not yet over. What could the evening hold?

At 6 p.m., the four of us left to go to Believer's Fellowship. Our friends went in their car, and we went in ours.

We arrived at the large home as people were going in. We took up one row in the middle, and I got out my notebook for notes on the sermon of the evening. I wondered what word the Lord had given Pastor Schuppert for our small congregation. After all, Fred was not known to be shy with the word of God. As we settled into our seats, Fred settled in to preach.

A FATHER'S INSTRUCTION
(Jan. 29th)

Believer's Fellowship
Pastor Frederick Schuppert
Corydon, IN

"A father does not forget his children or their needs. He knows what you have given up for him. You can't serve God and mammon. Let God do what you need done. Let Him bless you. God is able to bless us even when we doubt and have unbelief."

Pastor Schuppert was already on a roll. He instructed us to turn to Matthew 6, verses 24-34. The flipping of pages was heard through the church as everyone prepared to follow the reading of God's word.

Matt 6:24-34 "Take no thought for your life. What you eat and drink. Your Father in Heaven feeds the animals. He will surely feed you. He has made you, and He will help you. We will not be cast into the oven with the dross. Your Father knows you have needs. God will take care of you!"

Pastor Fred looked at me and said, "Seek first the kingdom of God and His righteousness, and all will be added unto you. It works every time! When people come and hurt you, may God bless you according to the work of your hand. Woe to those who come against God's anointed; who come to steal from you and destroy you! God will give you 100 times more than what they took from you. God has it covered! He is in the midst. God will give us peace and no worries. He will supply all our needs for us who are in Christ Jesus."

The good pastor stopped for a moment to see it all sink in to us and his fellow believers. He took a breath, he took a drink and went on with his sermon.

"It is the others that will be cast into the fire: the ones who don't depend on God! God takes care of those who believe on His Son, Jesus Christ. God takes care of us in impossible situations. He is faithful, and He does not deal with us according to our sin. Halleluiah!" That brought a big "Amen" from our crowd!

"God delights of making a show of you in the presence of your enemies. You are free! God will make a way where there seems to be no way."

Thank you Lord that you had Pastor Fred write this sermon just for us. How did I know it was for us? At the last line, Fred stood in front of me and looked right at Mark and I. We knew it was for us.

Then Fred went into prayer for all of us:

"God, you know our needs. Let your kingdom come. Your will be done. Thank you for bread, forgive our debts in Jesus' name. Lead us not into temptation but keep us from the evil one. All is yours, Heavenly Father. "

His prayer went on, "Supply all our needs, physical, spiritual, mental, providence, providing all...."

Then Fred stopped and listened to a voice we could not hear. He said, "This is from God. Don't worry. It will be alright. The wealth of the sinner is laid up for the just. Ask; God's got it. You feel forgotten, forsaken and overlooked. No! These are vain thoughts! God said, 'I shall never leave or forsake thee.' He will set you on the right path."

Fred listened again, and God told him to say,

"God has seen those who have purposed to destroy you. He will raise you up! You will stand up and come with joyful laughter. God said, 'How foolish to come against my own.'"

Fred went on, "Evil shall be defeated. We believe in Jesus! We are raised with Him! Know this; Fear will come, but it is not from God. Resist it! It is not from God. You have power and a sound mind."

Now Mark and I are counted among the healed of the day. Me, from the attacks I had suffered as of late from others who had come against me, and my husband from fear of going forward.

We saw seven miracles, including healings and deliverance from spirits of fear and oppression, in 24 hours.

FREE LUNCH
(Jan. 31st)

I received a call from Mr. Epperson with Corydon's Chamber of Commerce. He had read my children's Christmas book and wanted me to read at *Light Up Corydon* in November. He loved the book and the fact that I was a local author. I had good news to share with my husband later that day!

My lunch was scheduled at the Snyder house. Meredith set a lovely plate with healthy foods that looked very appealing. Meredith and Peter, her husband, work from home in an office downstairs. They run a medical company, and she brought me up to date on their work and how business was going. We talked about her husband's health, his back, how much he works, and their children in college. Then she asked me what I had been up to. Was I working yet?

"No. I have applied at several companies, two of whom I am uniquely qualified to work for. I have heard nothing so far. It almost feels like God is sitting on me. But spiritually, it's flowing like a river!"

Meredith responded quickly, "Tell me! Tell me girl!"

I told Meredith the story of the anointing oil and how it had come to me at the Olsen's church. I spoke of all the miracles we had seen happen since then. Meredith watched and listened with special interest. She stated, "Deb, Father Bernie has prayed over Peter's back. He is not yet healed."

"I'm sorry."

"But I've watched Peter. He listens to you when

you talk. Would you pray over him?"

"I sure will!"

Then Meredith had words of wisdom for me. "You have been on my mind so strong lately. I don't think God's going to allow you to get a job. But what's a job? We are here to win souls for Christ! That is all that is important."

Meredith was preaching to me. I agreed with her.

"It is the most important thing." I whispered.

Meredith continued, "Deb, I don't think you telling me any of this is a coincidence. I think it's like Fr. Bernie says, it's a God setup."

"Me too." I responded.

We finished lunch and made plans for Mark and I to come back over for dinner the next week. I would bring the anointing oil for Peter and a good diet for her.

When I arrived back home and checked my computer for any correspondence, there was one. I had a reply from the place I had requested to work for. You know, one of the ones I was uniquely qualified for and had ten years' experience in.

"No thanks. Good luck in your future."

After the lunch meeting talk, it was not an extreme surprise.

But, I wasn't sure how I was going to tell my husband that we were supposed to build a new home with me out of work in the business world. As it looked Mark would have to carry the entire financial load as it looked.

"Give me the right words, Father, so Mark won't be afraid."

NICE THINGS
(Feb. 1st)

Some days are counted by the number of nice things that happen to you.

Like this:

The first nice thing — The bank called us and canceled our fees for that month and the last month.

We usually walked such a tight line that even those few dollars looked big to us. At least a nice help out of nowhere.

Second nice thing — Mary Dow Smith e-mailed me and said our new website for "Miraculous Interventions" was up and running.

Third nice thing — (For my husband) I put in ten applications on line. (All were to no avail as Meredith had said, but at least I tried.)

Fourth nice thing — my friend Clare came over. She was in town and dropped by for a visit. She had a problem. Clare's ear was stopped up and hurting. Would I please pray over her for a healing?

"Sure, let me go get my oil." I was always happy to oblige my friends in Christ Jesus!

Clare sat down at the kitchen table, and I stood next to her. I put anointing oil on both of my index fingers, then I put them in her ears and prayed a prayer of healing faith over her.

During the next few minutes, Clare's ears popped and opened. There was no more ringing or hurting.

Then I got a word to pray over her internal organs, which I did in obedience. We would look for the good report on that too. We thanked God for her healed ears.

While there, we talked about the classes she was taking. Clare had another problem. She needed a medical dictionary. Where could she get a medical dictionary that wouldn't cost her an arm and a leg? Did I possibly have one she could borrow?

I giggled as I nodded my head yes. I happened to have one of the best in the business. I told her to please feel free to borrow it for the rest of her course work.

"Thank you!"

We laughed about it being a "one stop shop" for all that she needed for her day. I thanked God for using me as an obedient vessel.

Fifth nice thing—at 11:00 that evening we heard from Fr. Mike and Patti Olsen. They had made it home safely from their vacation-turned-funeral for his mom. We were glad they were safe and sound. Weary, but home.

As we were falling asleep, Mark told me of a dream he had recently.

"Don't be afraid. Everything will work out just fine."

It was a comforting dream.

I dreamed California left the continent; that it shifted away. Lord may that one never come about.

DON'T LEAVE HOME WITHOUT IT.
(Feb. 3rd)

Mark was off that day, and we had lots of errands to run together. Over breakfast, we prayed God's blessing over all we wanted to get accomplished.

The first stop was the bank. "We'd like to make a deposit, thanks."

The next stop was the post office. I was sending my monthly tithe to Pastor Ivie in South Carolina along with a sympathy card to another friend whose momma had just passed away. Then off we went to file our 2012 federal and state taxes.

"Good grief! You mean we only ended up getting $11.00 back after paying to file it all?" What a blow that was to our pocket books.

We had made just enough the last year to bump us up into a new tax category.

"Welcome to the middle class."

That was *not* the start to the day we had prayed for.

After a little while of moping on the way home, we shored up each other's spirits. When we came home, I made us a fun lunch. After all, we still had more errands on our plate. With our tax papers in hand, we went to a lender to finish filing for our home construction loan. We all checked the paperwork together.

"Hmmm....Things look in order."

Things were looking up. We met all the guidelines. In three weeks we were due an answer. We praised God as we left the building.

We stopped by our friends, the people who had

bought our original home on Mathis to give the wife the good news. Our new home was to be directly behind their home. We had a nice visit out on their front porch overlooking fields ready to be planted that spring. We all dreamed together about being neighbors.

We had a few more errands to run before we went to the Horne's for dinner.

As we were headed out of town, we decided to stop at a new little Bargain Supply store. We had heard Christians owned it. We thought it would be a short visit to see what they had in their isles. After all, with the fiasco of our tax return, we had little money for groceries. How much could we buy for $40.00?

To our surprise, an hour later we came out with a big box full of items we needed. The good Lord even cared about our grocery bill.

We were quick off to Rick and Lisa's for an evening meal after a busy day.

Mark and I arrived at a busier home than ours, with four little children and lots of new conversation that went on. Lisa and I chatted non-stop. Mark and Rick looked all around the new addition and the plans they had for it. It looked good to us.

After a nice meal of beef noodles, and vegetable lasagna, we were served ice cream for dessert. The adults sat around the kitchen table and caught up with all our busy lives. We even had a little Bible study on the computer. It was during that time my tooth started to ache, a lot.

I finally called out for prayer. Rick, Lisa, Mark and Alex, their oldest boy, all gathered around me to pray the intrusion away.

"A little bit better thanks." It was tolerable, at the least.

Yet, not a half an hour later, the attack came back so badly from two teeth that hurt, I turned to Mark in tears. I asked him to take me home quickly, so I could take Ibuprofen.

Lisa cried out, "Debbie! The devil is just trying to stop our prayer time!"

I knew she was right.

"Please, someone bring me my purse. It has the anointing oil in it."

For the first time, it was to be used on me. I was going to experience what everyone else had experienced. Megan fetched my purse, and Mark stood up to receive anointing oil on his fingers to touch me.

I started with my familiar prayer, "Thank you, Lord, for your provisions."

I placed oil on Mark's finger. He opened the prayer and touched me in the area that was experiencing pain.

Immediately, I felt warmth enter my skin to the inside of my cheek. It passed through to the hurting teeth and the gum area around it. The nerves stopped firing up, and all the pain ended. Nothing but warmth. I could get used to that.

Now this minister of healing had been healed as well. I started to laugh and smile and praise God. Our Bible study resumed.

Lesson learned?

Anointing oil... Don't leave home without it.

LET THERE BE LIGHT.
(Feb. 5th)

It was a nice, lazy Sunday morning, and we needed it. It was very rare for me to have a sleepless night. You could count them on one hand for all my 53 years. Everything was on my mind. My spirit and body were restless. Over the course of the night, I had two "smells" come across my senses. One smelled like a cross between baby powder and sugar cookies baking. That was around 11 p.m. and it stayed several minutes. I believe it was an angelic visit.

Then, between three and four that morning, I smelled a type of smoke. I imagined it as a fireplace. I hoped it was a premonition of things to come in our next home.

At noon, we skyped our dear friends from England, David and Dianna Gething. For an hour, we visited back and forth until it was time for us to go to a birthday party. It was for Tyler, our son Andy's best friend. We went to help celebrate. Happy 22!

During the course of the festive afternoon, my lack of sleep caught up with me. I asked my husband to take me home. We excused ourselves, and by 5:30 p.m., I was sound asleep. Mark went to church for the evening services.

When he pulled back into our driveway after church, I had a meal waiting on the table for him, with me feeling much better. Sleep is good. After dinner, we relaxed with a family movie. All in all, it was a nice day.

As we were retiring for the night, our phone rang.

It was Fr. Mike Olsen. He had a vision at St. Columba about us, and he wanted to share it.

"Please impart knowledge." I cried.

Fr. Mike saw in a vision many angels rejoicing, dancing, and praising God on our homeland. This was three days after we had turned in our final paperwork to build on Nicholas Drive. Praise God.

Mark got off the phone and cried out, "He saw angels."

Then Mark got very serious. He looked at me closely and said, "I have something I have to tell you."

"Oh my. Shoot." I was all smiles.

"This morning, before we got up to fix breakfast, I saw something. I'm not sure what it was. It was already day light outside. I heard no cars coming down the road. But I saw from our doorway, lights in the living room. Bright lights. It was moving back and forth."

He waited for my reply.

I smiled, "I believe you. Angelic lights," I said. "Angels while we live here for now, and angels on our home property."

Now we were both smiling.

MATTHEW 6:33
(Feb. 6th)

We got up early to do a good deed for Fr. Bernie Weber. Mark and I were to show up at Deb Grimes home to help move 30 cases of blessed candles from her basement to their driveway. Another helper would join us later that morning. Mark got an early start and moved cases by himself. Deb and I got an early start and caught up with all the news from our lives.

The other helper arrived in time to move the last few boxes from upstairs out to the driveway. Shortly afterwards, Fr. Bernie showed up in his truck. Mark left for work, and Dave and Fr. Bernie placed boxes in the truck for transport to the mission field.

Debbie and I sat in the living room while we waited for the men to finish loading up. When they were done, Father Bernie and Dave came in. We talked amongst ourselves until time for the men to leave. As the morning came to a close, Fr. Bernie stood up and asked us to stand for a blessing. The good priest prayed over us and thanked us for doing God's helper work. He asked that God prosper us and our households.

Lunchtime called as I walked through my living room door. After a relaxing meal, a relaxing nap was in order.

I awoke to two phone messages. My husband called to see how I was. He, himself was very tired. Forty minutes later Kelly called. She wanted to come by and pick up a children's book for her cousin.

"Okay. I'm up."

I was sitting and trying to catch up my writing

when she rang the doorbell.

I welcomed her in, and we sat on opposite couches to catch up as I handed her the requested book. The little cottage she and her father were building together was almost finished. I squealed with delight. Kelly showed pictures of her progress.

"Oh Kelly! It's beautiful! I can see me packing up your dishes sooner than we expected." Our housewarming gift to her was a set of great grandmother dishes. She had always admired them.

We spoke of how busy Kelly was now that she had gone back to being a massage therapist. She told me that everything was coming together for her. We praised God for all her wonderful blessings. Then I told her everything that had been going on in our lives since October—all the miracles that had been happening since the first of the year.

Then Miss Kelly Riddle prophesied something I saw in my spirit almost ten years before. I had never told anyone, not even Mark. She said to me, "I see you with long white hair. Your hair will turn white because of a miracle that comes through you. Not grey, white. It's beautiful."

Yes indeed, my friend is a seer in the God way.

Kelly went on about the New Year. "I also see April as a very busy month for you. It's the start. I see three contracts coming for your books. Maybe as many as five books."

"Wow." I had not counted on writing that many in the series. It looked like Kelly was a listener too.

Kelly offered to come with us to a hardware store to shop for items for our new home. Her father used to buy supplies at a discount there.

I spent what was left of the afternoon writing two books at once. I wrote until I ran into dinnertime. And we still had mass at Mt. St. Frances for the charismatics that evening. I served a quick meal, and off we went to another church service.

We arrived in time for song and praise. There was a very nice turn out of people. The readings and homily were exceptional. Mark and I clung to every word the priest spoke about why we were really here on this Earth. We are all to actively participate in spreading the love of Jesus. We are to be His hands and feet. I must admit, we smiled at each other and knew we were doing that very thing, that very calling.

After mass, a prayer team assembled to pray over people with specific needs. I was in the back of the church speaking with people when one of our prayer group attendees came up and grabbed me by my arm. Off we went towards the prayer team at a very hurried pace.

I cried out his name, "What are you doing?"

As fast as he dared, he was pulling me towards the altar! He stated matter-of-factly, "Deb, you are going to pray over me."

"Oh. Okay."

Social graces were not his strong point. He walked right up to the prayer team and said a few words. Prayers began in earnest. I stood in back of him ready to catch him if needed. A few minutes later, the job done, he was once again off and running.

Before I knew it, the ladies prayed and prophesied over me. That was when I was given Matthew 6:33, "Seek first the Kingdom of God and His righteousness, and then all will be added to you." A second time in that season, the same verse was given to me.

Mary Lynn spoke first, "How beautiful are the feet of those who bring good news...."

Mary Dow received a word, "Deb, this is for you. You will be bringing good news to many needful souls." Mary Dow spoke of the greatest gift which is to be able to love deeply and touch other's lives.

Billie spoke words of wisdom over me, "kindness, gentle, goodness, helpful...." She was extolling my virtues to the Lord. I received it all.

Unaware to me, my husband had slipped in behind me to join us in prayer. I could hear his prayer joining the others. It made me smile. I thanked God for all the members there that night, especially the four assembled around me.

Thank you God Almighty for Heaven on Earth.
So be it.
So be it.

HEAT
(Feb. 7th)

Well, (laughing), sometimes good deeds just can't go unpunished.

The good work that Mark had done for Fr. Bernie the day before, moving all those cases of blessed candles up and down the hill, caught up with him. By that evening at church, he was limping with pain all through his right foot.

At 7:30 that morning, I had told Mark something had been going on in my head for over a month. My head, skin and skull, all of it, felt like it was hot on fire from the inside out. Not like encephalitis or a fever, but Holy Spirit hot.

When I told Mark of this, he asked me to please pray for his foot because it hurt to stand on it.

"Bring it out of the covers." We had not yet gotten out of bed for the morning.

I wrapped both of my hands around the bottom of his right foot and prayed the way I felt led in my spirit. In a few minutes, I felt heat radiate from my head, down my shoulders, into the palms of my hands, even into certain fingers that were holding his foot.

Mark felt warmth spread over the bottom of his foot, and he smiled. All the pain ended. He started to shout.

"Thank you Lord! Thank you Lord that you have given my wife this gift!"

Later that morning, I called a local radio station to leave a message for their DJ. I had a story to tell him. I called and spoke to their secretary. As I started to leave a short message about the healings and miracles we were experiencing, I could tell she was a born again, Holy-Ghost-filled believer! She took down my name and number and said he would call me. I felt particularly urgent to meet with him as if this was to be an appointed time from God.

Unfortunately, this meeting never took place, and I take full responsibility for it. Even after all I had seen and witnessed myself, I did not take the authority I was walking in and go heal the DJ. I missed an opportunity to witness for the Lord. Shyness does not bless God when you are being called out of it for His name's sake!

For the rest of the afternoon, I wrote notes until my tape player gave out.

That evening, Mark and I went to separate prayer Bible studies. When we arrived back home later that evening, we caught each other up on our notes and got ready for bed.

As I came out of the bathroom, I heard voices coming from the back bedrooms. I checked each, finding nothing in there. I called for Mark while still able to hear them, and he came and listened. Mark asked me what it sounded like.

"I hear two men holding a discussion—plans of a sort, I think." I wasn't afraid nor did I feel any evil presence.

Angelic forces were at work.

SIGNS AND WONDERS II
(Feb. 8th)

I knew when I woke up that morning, and the Lord gave me a title for the day of "Signs and Wonders," He was sending spectacular events. I was not to be disappointed.

Mark and I had planned a day of fun with Larry and Marilynn Crosier. Larry and Mark had known each other from their youth, but their wives didn't get a chance to meet until my first book came out. Marilynn, while in the bookstore, felt compelled to buy it. When she showed the book and its back cover with our picture on it to her husband, Larry said, "Mark Peyron! I know him! He's my friend!"

The fall of 2011, we found ourselves invited for a dinner to the Crosier home. Long into the night, we held conversations that rang throughout their home and started a lasting friendship.

So for us, this day was a catch up day. Fun in the sun so to speak. On the way to their home, while I was driving, suddenly, I had a piercing headache out of nowhere.

"It just attacked me!" I cried.

As Mark put his hand on my forehead and started to say, "Dear God..." it left as suddenly as it had appeared.

"That's it! It's gone!" I cried with exuberance.

"You stopped the attack with your faith. Thank God."

We pulled up to the Crosier's home and were met with warm greetings.

Once inside, we went into praise reports. Think of it as the opposite of gossip. We told all the good and Godly in our lives.

The Crosiers had a tape of angels singing they wanted us to hear.

"We're for it."

As we were listening, to the singing Marilynn's face clouded. When the tape was over, she spoke about what had just occurred. She began, "Did anybody hear voices coming from the kitchen?"

The men queried, "Like singing?"

"No. Voices talking." Marilynn replied.

"Male voices." I interjected.

Marilynn got excited. "You heard them."

"No," I replied. "I heard them last night. They were male voices."

We all agreed there were angels among us.

We thought that was the highlight of our day and decided to take pictures around the room. Out came cameras from everywhere. Mark, me, Larry; the scene could have been paparazzi! We laughed and all lined up to take pictures of the girls together, the guys together and, a picture of all four of us with the help of Mark's long arms. Of course, we all wanted to see them.

As we began to look at the pictures, we noticed white orbs of light around us or on our clothing on several of the cameras. Angelic lights had been captured on our cameras.

On one particular picture of Marilynn and myself, by my left shoulder, a golden orb was seen as plain as day.

Marilynn asked, "What does a gold orb mean?"

I replied laughing, "Oh Marilynn, it must be

God's gold. It can only mean good. I've never seen a gold orb show up on camera before."

After lunch, and before we set out for the day's adventures and fun events, we prayed over Marilynn for her neuropathy in her feet. I felt the Lord's touch as I was sent to the top of her head and not her legs. Between my medical knowledge and God's direction, I told her, "It's a neuron problem from your brain. It's not just your legs. I'm starting prayer at the top of your head."

We also prayed for Larry's vision.

We looked for the good report for all these things because we knew if God would send unseen voices and orbs of light, He could send healing as well.

The rest of the day was spent in merriment. We all went into town and went bowling. And I am very glad this is a written book and not so much about pictures. When I am the one with the highest score of the bunch, 133, (my weight should be so good) there is something very funny going on. And I mean ha ha.

We had dinner at a local restaurant that was very relaxing. The whole day had been a present from the Crosiers to us. What a blessing they were. No matter where we went, our money was no good.

The last stop of the day was at a Christian bookstore. Larry wanted to get a movie for us to watch as a relaxing way to end the day.

"Oh boy! Look everyone! It's an after Christmas sale for Christmas and Thanksgiving items." I can smell a sale as soon as I come into a store.

Marilynn just had to buy me a candle, and I just had to buy her an angel ornament. Our men smiled.

There in this same store, was the most beautiful

clock in an oval shape with mahogany wood trimmed with a gold outline. The inside was laced with Syvorski crystals. The icing on the cake was it played on the hour, Christmas Carols, church hymns, or classic symphony pieces. As an anniversary present to his wife, Larry left the store with it under his arm.

PRAISE REPORTS.
(Feb. 9th)

From the time we left them later that evening, our dear friends saw the blessings of the Lord fall on their house hold in the form of healings and monetary blessings.

The healings started with Marilynn. The night before, she had hardly gotten any sleep. The day we prayed for her, Marilynn felt 85% better and had a good night's sleep. When she got up the next morning, even her knees felt better.

Larry felt much better the next morning as well.

Wherever they went, they had monetary blessings go in front of them.

At a department store they liked to frequent, there was a substantial discount on a machine for her health. Marilynn was also looking for a housecoat and found one in her size for $11.98. It was the only housecoat in the building that was in her size, and she received another 30% off.

Yes, God cares about what we put in our cart while shopping. He knows our smallest needs to the greatest before we know them.

I was so glad to hear they had such a nice day.

At Bible study that night, I told several of the men in our group about all that had happened since January 1st. It was getting to be a longer and longer story. They both said, "God has honored you for your love and seeking of His heart."

A DINNER INVITATION
(Feb. 10th)

I had a long day ahead of me. Writing was on the order of the day. That evening, Mark and I were invited to a dinner at the Snyder's home. We looked forward to catching up with their activities and talking about the real reason we were going over; the looming back surgery for Meredith's husband, Peter.

Meredith had prepared a meal fit for a king. Well, at least an evangelist. The conversation was lively from the time we entered their house. We talked about everything from politics to religion at their kitchen table. In our minds, we cured the ills of the world.

After dessert, Meredith and I adjourned to the living room while the men talked politics in the kitchen. She and I discussed the dietary changes I had brought her.

Then the discussion turned to the healing of her husband. I asked Meredith to tell me everything that had been diagnosed. It was a composite of all that could go wrong. Even arthritis was beginning to set in. He was in constant pain.

"Bring him in."

Meredith called the men into the living room, and they sat down all smiles.

Meredith started a general conversation. It eventually got around to Peter and his predicament. I started my testimony with the healings of my mother's back in December, the occurrences of January 1, and all that had happened since. Then I asked him if I could pray over him.

"Yes, please!"

I anointed Mark, Meredith and myself. We all laid hands on Peter's back. As we were praying, the Holy Spirit fell and we all felt heat in the affected area.

In less than two minutes, he smiled with tears in his eyes.

"Wow. I felt heat!"

"So did I!" Meredith chimed in.

I excused myself to the bathroom. I went in, closed the door, got on my knees and thanked God for the healing that often comes with heat.

Unfortunately, I learned later, Peter's pain did not go away.

LISTEN WELL
(Feb. 11th)

At seven in the morning, I was awakened with a revelation. The Lord took me back to the night Lee and Anne Schwarz came to our home on Mathes Rd. Anne said, "Lee's hands are anointed like the apostles of old." Then God took me back to January 1, 2012, when the little miraculous vial overflowed in my hands I too, had been anointed by God! God wanted me to know when I pray what He tells me and shows me to pray, God will bring it about. The fire will fall. I woke up singing praises to the King of my flesh!

I wanted to thank God from all my heart for the incredible, indescribable gift he had bestowed on his humble servant. I thanked the Holy God of all the Universe for the season I was walking in.

"May it last as long as You will it, Lord. So be it."

I knew from then on, my head, hands, heart and mouth must be used as God would have them used in times of anointing with each prayer. I was to turn away from sin and follow God.

Now, how did I mean this? God had already dealt with me and healed my heart about the stain of sexual sin from my distant past. I thanked God for the release of everything from being molested and raped to willing before I met my husband, Mark. Oh, I was not a "rounder" or "easy" by any means. But any sin is sin! Even our thoughts have to submit to the Holy Spirit, or we are in disobedience. Yes, our thoughts too. All these things I had wrestled with at one time or another were being left at the cross, and I was not to look back.

The Ancient of Days also dealt with my thoughts

of doubt and worry.

"Clean it up!"

This one took longer than any other! I tell you it was just as grievous before God Almighty as the other sins I had wrestled with. The same with you dear reader, when you wrestle with fear or unbelief, we must all have the mind of Christ. Jesus never doubted! He knew where He came from and whose He was and is!

This is a very good reason to memorize scripture verses. Literally, the word of God from your heart that comes out of your own mouth, will protect you in any situation.

How?

Because God is bigger than anything that we will face.

For example, when God healed my heart of hate, all my pain and suffering left me. I thank God that I did not have any alcohol or drug curses to overcome. My sins had to be looked at differently now in the Holy Spirit.

I was not to give in to, or entertain, fear or doubt.

No oath was to come out of my mouth.

I am to do what God tells me to do at the time of anointing when He tells me to do it.

Obey Him every time.

Don't be shy when under His orders.

The lack of sin is in the obedience to God.

Just like one of my favorite songs, "Be bold, and be strong! For the Lord thy God is with thee!"

By the time Mark woke up at 8 a.m., I had been up an hour writing my new commandments. I went in to see about my husband.

He remarked, "My head hurts. My neck hurts."

"Ready to pray?" I responded to his need.

"I'm always ready to pray!"

I wrapped the back of his head with both my hands and went in. Two minutes later, the attack was canceled and he felt better upon rising.

"Thank you Lord!" Praise came out of Mark's mouth.

All the day's plans unraveled by early morning. The meeting we had planned with friends was canceled due to illness and fatigue on their parts.

God had planned an entirely different day for us. Mark came home after work, picked me up and we did our weekly grocery shopping together. While there, it occurred to Mark to make a pot of chili that week. It occurred to me for him to make it right away that evening. I would make a nice dessert and sweet tea.

"Okay. Why?"

Out of my spirit came a reply, "Company's coming, and they will be hungry."

Mark's eyebrows went up. He nodded his head in compliance.

When we got back home, Mark did indeed make a big pot of chili while I made tea and a nice chocolate mousse for dessert.

We finished it at last, and Mark turned to me and smiled. I could read his thoughts, "Well, where's the company you spoke of?"

Smiling back to him I said, "Wait for it."

It was not two minutes later, there was a knock at our door. Friends stood in our doorway. They had been out shopping, and had not had any dinner yet.

"Yes! We would love to have a meal with you. Thank you for asking us."

Once again, my helper ministry had come to me.

MORNING TO NIGHT
(Feb. 12th)

Mark and I started the day with our friends at a local church. They had brought in a visiting pastor to give the sermon. He spoke on the need for Jesus for the sinful man.

"You never know when your last day is. You could die today! Get your unsaved family members to the nearest church!"

He told funny to poignant stories to get his point across. Many of them brought tears to my eyes.

We came home for lunch and a movie, at least we thought we did. We got halfway through when we started to receive calls for prayer. Would we mind?

By the late afternoon, everyone who was supposed to go with us to Iona in Louisville, ended up cancelling due to family illness of one kind or another. It would be just us for the evening. We wondered if maybe that was God's plan after all.

At Iona, the praise and worship reached an extraordinarily high fever that night. Fr. Mike had been prepared in his spirit the day before. He was told angels would be everywhere, and they were. Mark and I took pictures all around during the mass. There were lights in almost every picture we took.

After mass, the men went to one side of the altar and the women went to the other side for prayer. Patti asked me to come up and pray with her. As I stepped up next to her, she instructed me not to touch anyone unless the Lord specifically told me to.

"Okay, fine."

While praying for one particular lady, I received a word about her illness.

Now, in the natural, I didn't even know she was sick. In my spiritual ears, I heard, *"Paranoid Schizophrenia; big demon."*

"Demon?!" I cried out in my head. Before I could stop it, I spoke in the spirit, "In the name of Jesus, come out of her!"

Patti came right up beside me with support prayer. Mark was behind the lady to catch her in case she fell.

Instantly, we smelled something foul come out of her and go away from the people. Patti and I both backed up at the same time.

Patti said, "Give it room to get out!"

In my head, I was hollering, "Waaaa! How did I get in the middle of an exorcism?" But I tell you, it was not me, but the Holy Spirit inside me that cast the unclean spirit away!

As if coming out of a daze, she blinked and looked at Patti and I as if to say, "What just happened?" A calm spread over her face and she smiled. She asked, "What do I do now?" We instructed the lady to fill her memory up with scripture verses so the evil one would not find her an empty shell.

It was after 8 p.m. before the congregation left. The Lord had put on our hearts to take Mike and Patti out to dinner somewhere nice. We had three gift certificates from Christmas for Red Lobster and were ready to use them. We felt in our hearts this wonderful couple needed a blessing. I had just enough money on me to pay the bill and to leave a nice tip.

Between the two offerings at the two churches and the dinner, we were down to zero dollars. We had blessed with everything we had, just like the widow's mite.

What more could God ask of us?

*The next week, she again came up to me and thanked me for the peace that had filled her being. There were no more voices haunting her. It was my pleasure to tell her that God never leaves us empty.

WEARY
(Feb. 13th)

I was expecting a client that morning. I had already ordered her medications and prepared her paperwork for the last prescription needed. Her bill came to $40.00 for my time. This help was just as needed on my side of the fence as it was hers.

The next day was Valentine's Day, and this was my last shot to make any money to get Mark a card or gift.

My client called at 7:45 a.m. and told me she couldn't make it. Something had come up.

"Can you come tomorrow?"

"Sure."

In my heart, I knew I should send her the last of the paperwork. I had already ordered all her other medications. I also knew not to count on the money coming in. All I had was $1.28 in the bank. If I closed the account, it would be just enough stamp money to send her the paperwork. I wouldn't have enough left over to get my husband a Valentine's Day card.

With a heavy sigh, I put this lady first. I called her and told her I would send her paperwork out. I closed my account and mailed the paperwork to her.

"Surely my blessing will come in from somewhere, sometime, somehow." I said to myself.

After all, I had just given the last of my earthly money to bless three people.

I kept up prayers for the sixteen people that had called in the last several days for their intentions in my heart, throughout the day. I sang praises when I could muster it up.

I thought, Lord, I am weary. I could use being on the blessing list myself.

As the day wore on, more requests came in to pray for people in far worse shape than my weariness. I had to get over my flesh in order to go on.

That evening, Mark and I went to dinner at Mom Peyron's. We arrived promptly on time. Mark greeted his Mom with warm hugs, kisses and a Valentine's Day card. His sister Dana was there too. She said to us, "Don't get too close, I've got the flu." Dana did not look good at all. Her eyes were red and glassy, her nose was red from blowing, and a deep cough came from her chest.

Dana and I sat in the living room and talked while Mark and Mom went in the kitchen and finished the meal preparations. I prayed a gentle prayer in my heart for Dana as we waited for dinner.

And what a lovely dinner it was! Mom had fixed ham, green beans, sweet potatoes, and two kinds of salad. Dessert was in order for later. It was a beautiful berry pie with ice-cream on top. The conversation was just as good as the food.

After the meal was over, I cleared the table, and Mark did the dishes. Then we adjourned into the living room for more conversation. During this time, Mark and I looked at each other and knew it was time to pray a healing prayer together over Dana. She was ready for it too.

I anointed Mark's hands, mine and Dana's. Together we anointed Dana's head, sinus, and chest. I was compelled to pray for her health, her steps and prosperity. In Jesus' holy name, I asked. Mark joined in with scriptures and thanksgiving. Shortly after this, Dana had to run an errand and hoped we would still be there when she got back.

We stayed another hour with Mom until we were all tired. As we were leaving, Dana drove up. She looked, sounded, and felt much better.

"Thank you Lord!" There were smiles on all our faces. Dana had news to tell us. Two of her friends had biopsies lately. Could we remember them in our prayers?

"Yes ma'am! Let us know if you want us to go lay hands on them and anoint them with oil."

When we arrived home and got ready for bed, I asked Mark if he would be in agreement with me to pray over one-another for wisdom, understanding of dreams and visions to come to us in the night.

"Yes."

We requested direction and monetary help.

That night Mark dreamed of being a teacher. I believe it! A teacher for God.

Then I dreamed. It went like this:

I saw me helping and healing everywhere I went. I was loving without boundaries. I could hear people saying, "Loving, kind and compassionate." I heard from an unseen source, "I escheweth evil."

I woke Mark to tell him of the dream and he said to me, "Yes, because of your great capacity to love."

At 4 a.m., we both awoke with sinus congestion and sore throats. We fell back to sleep in prayer for each other. By 7 a.m., when we woke up for the day, we were healed!

VALENTINE'S DAY
(Feb. 14th)

All through the night, giant snowflakes fell and blanketed the yards, homes and cars. I had planned a quiet day of writing and a nice meal of leftovers for my husband and I since I had no money for a card, present or groceries.

Mark had texted all our family and friends a "Happy Valentine's Day." I personally called all three of our sons to wish them a "Happy Valentine's Day."

Our youngest, Andy, upon seeing our number come up, shouted at the same time we did, "Happy Valentine's Day." We had a long conversation about his work hours, and maybe he could squeeze us in for a visit in the near future.

Our other two boys called us one after another. There is no lack of love in our family. Wonderful conversations engulfed an hour of the day. We loved it!

For the rest of the afternoon, I wrote until time to get up and fix us our leftovers. My husband was due home any minute. As I turned on the oven, a call came through. It was our friend, Gail. She had a question for us.

"Deb! What are you doing tonight?"

"Nothing," I answered. "What are you doing?"

Gail replied, "Mike is taking me out to eat at Olive Garden. Do you and Mark want to go as our treat?"

I knew this was in response to my cry out for a blessing!

"That would be great! Thanks for thinking of us."

When Mark came through the door, he told me we

were going out to eat with Mike and Gail. Gail had already called him. Mark also brought in a beautiful, wrapped package.

I inquired, "What's this? We said we weren't spending any money this year?"

Mark smiled, "I didn't buy it. I won it!"

Yet another blessing for us from God.

The Lord knew my heart and form. Mark had won an all-weather radio just in time for the mean season of spring.

Olive Garden was crowded but well worth the wait. There was so much food and so little time. After prayers at the start of the meal, one crazy conversation after another left us all in stitches throughout the evening.

The ride home was quiet. I must confess, it was because we were all too full to hold a complete conversation. On our ride home from Mike and Gail's, Mark and I talked about the double blessing God had secured for us. We were not aware at the time who else's heart He had touched to be good to us!

JEREMIAH 33: 9, 3, 14
(Feb. 15th)

Early that morning, I felt in my heart to get out my King James Bible.

"Really?" I usually used my Complete Jewish Bible for a word.

"Okay."

"Open it where the marker is." A still, small voice had instructed me.

"Okay."

"Jeremiah! Oh boy! I love Jeremiah! Where?"

"33, 9 then 14, in that order." More instructions came down the pipe.

This is how it read:

"And it shall be to me a name of joy, a praise and an honour before all the nations of the Earth, which shall hear all the good that I do unto them and they shall fear and tremble for all the goodness and for all the prosperity that I procure unto it! Call unto me, and I will answer thee, and shew thee great and mighty things, which thou knowest not. Behold, the days come saith the Lord, that I will perform that good thing which I have promised unto the house of Israel and the house of Judah."

Let it be known here that when scripture speaks of Israel it is in reference to the seed of Abraham. Gal.3:29 *"And if ye be Christ's, then are ye Abraham's seed, and heirs according to the promise."*

"I believe it! I believe it Lord!" I cried out in happiness. We were being remembered. In the middle of my living room, I loudly proclaimed in Latin and in English, "Behold the cross of the Lord! Fly all hostile powers! The Lion of the Tribe of Judah, Root of David,

Hath Conquered! Alleluia! Alleluia!"

The Holy Spirit fell, and tears of joy came. I knew without a doubt blessing had entered into our atmosphere. We would eat the fruit of this.

What a wonderful start for a busy day.

The first stop was a woman's business luncheon. At my turn to speak, I told of all the hats God had given me to wear. I spoke of being a patient care advocate, a nationally certified wellness consultant, and an author of books about miraculous occurrences. Because I had limited cards and bookmarks, I asked all who were interested to raise their hands. I had just enough to go around. Of course.

When Mark came home after work, he had a card in his hands. He said it was from our good friends, the Crosiers. The Holy Spirit had told them to send us a card with monetary help. For two days in a row since I had cried out for help with a weary soul, we were being remembered hand over fist.

BILL
(Feb. 17th)

For four days, since Monday of that week, I was besieged in my spirit to pray for our friend, Bill Best. Bill Best. Bill Best.

"Okay! I get it. I'm on it."

Thursday night, on the way to Ben's birthday party, Mark told me he had heard on the radio that Bill's mom had just died.

There it was.

I went the next afternoon to gather food and supplies and took them to the funeral home as an extension of our shared grief. I wondered if I would meet Bill there.

I pulled up to the funeral home and saw two women struggling to gather supplies out of their car. I jumped out of my car quickly and called out to them,

"Wait! I'll get those heavy things for you. Let me help!"

"Oh, could you? Thank you! You came just in time." Imagine that. I was getting more and more used to hearing it.

Well, the first person I saw when we walked through the door was Bill Best.

"Deb! Now you know why I haven't called you." Bill cried out.

We had been trying to contact him for a bid to build another home for us.

"I know! We understand fully." Hugs were exchanged. I brought in the rest of our donations. I told Bill and his wife, Tammy, that Mark would be over after work.

Bill reintroduced me to his daughters, all grown up, no more pig tails and shy smiles that hid behind Daddy. The oldest, Brooke, remembered me from the time when Bill built our home on Mathes Road. We talked about Bill's Mom and Dad, family life and our shared memories. We talked of things to come.

One good deed done, I still had more to do before the end of the day. Mark was waiting for my help with a Bible study meal. And I was late! That time around, I only had three hours to help.

I arrived at our friend's in a rush. The wife grabbed me an apron as I pulled my hair back into a ponytail. The cooking commenced! While we were busy cooking in the kitchen, I told her, "We may put our home on the market soon, so we can start building later this year. Is the offer still available for us to come and stay in your basement while we build?"

Her answer came quick, "Yes! You are our best friends. You'll stay here."

I was not able to stay for the Bible study and left as people started to arrive. We had company coming to spend the night with us. Within a few minutes of arriving back at my own home, Kelly Riddle pulled up in the driveway. She was to spend the night with us and catch up on each of our undertakings. Kelly was building a home too. We were all going on a journey the next day together. We were looking for supplies to help our builders with the building of our homes.

Mark arrived home late from work. He had been to the funeral home to see our friends and give his condolences. I had brought us all a meal from the Bible study. The three of us ate together, held conversations until a reasonable hour, and made our way to bed.

The next morning had an early start to it.

AGAIN! AGAIN!
(Feb. 18th)

I awoke earlier than the others that morning in order to cook a hearty breakfast for our little troop. Mark and Kelly were both very grateful. Mark made coffee. Everyone was very grateful for that.

We set off, coffee travel mugs in hand, to our first destination 150 miles one way. Scenic highways and a river dam were passed on that cold, winter weekend to end up at the little hardware store that we were sure could help us, due to their low pricing, build our homes. We needed ideas.

Three very productive hours zoomed by. I wrote down everything from paint supplies to blank Disney keys (which I bought), to all the big stuff and everything in between. Three pages of notes and 20 pictures later, we were ready to head back to Indiana.

On our way home, my right ear, jaw and teeth started to ache. We figured it must have been from being outside in the cold air for so long looking at doors and windows. I didn't really care why, I just wanted it to leave. While I drove, Mark and Kelly prayed over me for the pain to cease. Unfortunately, when we stopped to buy gas, I was still in a considerable amount of pain. I asked Mark to hand me the anointing oil out of my purse. Quietly, I anointed myself and asked God in the Spirit how He wanted me to pray.

I was given the answer immediately, and I prayed it. Within two minutes, back on the road I was once again talking up a storm. My healing had come. Mark and Kelly laughed. She said, "When she's talking, she's

111

healed!" I laughed too.

As a thank you to Kelly for spending the day with us, we took her to one of her favorite restaurants uptown for dinner. When we finally arrived back in Corydon, she bid us good night and went home.

When we went inside, I noticed Mark did not look very well. I inquired, "What's wrong honey?"

Mark replied, "I guess I just need a nap. I don't feel well."

After our nap, Mark did not look any better. I took his temperature, his blood pressure and his heart rate. All three were up! Before I could react, the phone rang. Our brother in Christ, Bill Mauck, called and asked for our help the next day. He was going to preach at Potato Run (yes, it is a real church), and he wanted us to help with a song he would be doing.

"Sure. Fine."

Bill Mauck showed up a couple of hours later for our practice. As Bill unpacked his guitar, I told him Mark was feeling ill. Bill promptly stood up and laid hands on Mark as he led us all in prayer. A few short minutes later, Mark was fine. The temperature left him, and everything came back down to normal. To God be the glory!

Two healings in one day.
One for each of us.
What a nice way to end a very busy day.

CALLED TO STEP OUT

Don't tread water, walk on water!
(Feb. 19th)

The next morning, Mark and I arrived at church a few minutes after Bill. We still had time for a couple more practices of the reading before church started. When Potato Run started to fill up with people, Bill started to play. The song went well, as did the other songs, and Mark and I sat down to hear the man preach.

Bill did a wonderful job officiating the service. He spoke a blessed word about healing scriptures and how to make them your own in your daily life. He asked Mark and me to come and lay hands on all the ill along with him. We felt the healing power flow through all of us.

When the services were over, Mark and I came straight home. We were having company for the afternoon. Our friends, Larry and Marilynn came by with a cake prepared for Fr. Mike's wife, Patti, for the mass that night at St. Columba. We closed out our visit at 4:30 with prayer, and we all hit the road for our respective churches.

At St. Columba, during the praise and worship time before mass, God's Shekinah Glory fell over the congregation. A beautiful purple hue, engulfed the inside of the church. On the camera, we saw multi-colored orbs, purple and blue, gold and white. Words of wisdom came from two sources.

"Don't tread water, walk on water!" This came from one of the associate pastors.

Towards the end of the mass, the weighty presence of God was felt in the atmosphere. Fr. Mike received a word of knowledge. He spoke these words, "You're doing what you feel like you are supposed to do. You have asked yourself where God is taking you. You want to hear clearly that you are on the right path. You are in confusion. Confusion is leaving you! God will confirm it. It will be confirmed. God is saying, "This is the direction, follow me. Watch me provide, and watch what I do."

We felt this was straight from God to our hearts.

BY THE WASHING OF HER FEET
(Feb. 20th)

All afternoon, I cooked Mom and Mark's favorite dinner. I packed it all up in a box, and when Mark got off work, we went straight to Mom Peyron's. The table was set, and she was ready when we arrived. We were met with warm hugs and kisses. Mark led us in the dinner prayer. He blessed the hands that made it, and I blessed the hands that bought it! The meal commenced.

Salad and chicken pot pie made from scratch were served and enjoyed. Afterwards, Mark and I did the dishes while Mom spooned out ice-cream for dessert. We adjourned to the living room.

A while into the conversation, Mom talked about how her feet had been hurting lately. Mark and I looked at each other as if to say, "You bring the vial?"

"Yes, sir."

We asked Mom if we could pray over her feet.

"Of course!"

Betty took off her shoes; I prayed silently while Mark led us in spoken prayer. Then I anointed her feet and blessed her in the holy name of Jesus. I obeyed what I felt I was told. The rest was up to God.

We looked for the manifestation of that miracle.

A SIGH OF RELIEF
(Feb. 21st)

Writing can take up a lot of time in a person's life. So can helping a friend buy a home. I worked on that a good portion of the morning. Anything I could do to help.

Mark and I still had a revival to go to that evening. He came home late from work. Mark had stopped on his way home to give blood. He seemed a little concerned as we sat down to dinner. They said his blood pressure was high. I got up from the table determined to prove them wrong.

"I'll take your blood pressure."

"160/110."

"Oh boy!"

"Oh, boy."

We arrived at Grace Tabernacle right on time. The Crosier's had invited us to hear a traveling missionary at their church. Pastor Greg Carter welcomed us in.

The Crosiers were right. It was an amazing night. The praise was excellent. I saw the Shekinah Glory fall as a mist over the congregation. I smelled Heavenly incense as it filled the air around us. Then the preaching began! I took page after page of notes. Pastor Carter introduced his long-time friend, Pastor and Evangelist Keith Taylor. He had recently been to Africa and wanted to share his experiences with his friend's church.

Pastor Keith spoke of how he happened to be invited along with other pastors from America to go deep into the jungles of the dark continent of Africa.

There was a man of God there and a prophet of God who had warnings for the churches in America. They each had a story to tell. Keith told amazing stories of miraculous events that happened at their 24 hour church services. He spoke of 8 hour praise and worship, followed by 15 hours of church preaching and miracles right out of the New Testament! We sat mesmerized by the man's words. I had never been so happy to be in the right place at the right time.

Then God started showing Pastor Keith who needed prayer and what for. The man went all over the church with words of knowledge followed by prayer for each individual. When there was a demonic presence felt in a person, Pastor Keith went after it with gusto! Chairs flew! People ran the aisles! Deliverances were had in multitude. In all my days, I had not seen so much in one place!

When Pastor Keith came around to our area, he looked right at Mark. He stated firmly, "You need a healing."

Before I could stop it from coming out of my mouth I said, "Yes, he does. He has high blood pressure."

Keith put one hand on top of Mark's head. I raised my right arm in prayer as I stood beside them both. The good pastor canceled the devil's attack on Mark's health. God had work for Mark to do.

"That's right." I agreed. Then Pastor Taylor took my left hand and slammed it against Mark's heart! Immediately, I felt power come out of my head into my hand and cross into Mark's body; his heart.

Mark felt a jolt go directly into his heart! It almost knocked him off his feet. We both knew he was instantly healed. That was when we knew why we were really there. It was all for Mark.

Pastor Taylor turned and looked at me. I knew he was from God and could see into hearts. I knew he would see me as I am. I stood ready to receive any word that came from his mouth.

Then Keith did the most extraordinary thing. As he looked into my eyes, he bowed to me.

To me!

My knees almost gave out. With tears of gratitude, I bowed back to him.

We arrived back home late that night. I immediately checked Mark's blood pressure. It was 142/98. Better. Praise God! The battle had begun.

The next morning it was 138/94.

We both breathed a sigh of relief.

Total healing had come in less than 10 hours.

HAPPY BIRTHDAY MARK!
(Feb. 22nd)

The attack started early; 6 a.m. There were family members splitting up. Our hearts were aching. From this, there were physical repercussions. I suffered nausea, and Mark had a bad headache. Calls went back and forth from both our homes until noon. People took sides. Tears flowed. And that was just in our home!

By noon, I had lunch on the table. The wind was out of our proverbial sails. Going out and having fun did not have the appeal it did the day before. By now, Mark had a full-blown migraine with nausea. It was not one of his better birthdays. He ate and went back to bed. I took his blood pressure again. It was still better, but I could tell he was sick with the migraine.

I looked at my husband lying in bed so uncomfortably.

"Would you like me to anoint you and pray?" I volunteered.

"Yes!"

I pulled the anointing oil out of my purse, centered my prayer thoughts and started. As soon as I took the top off the bottle, but before I could turn it over for the oil to come out, oil overflowed all over my hands from a bottle held straight up! As I ran my anointed hands over Mark's head, he was instantly healed. All nausea and a "10" headache left in less than two seconds!

Mark smiled and pulled up his shirt and shouted, "Pray over my heart!"

I asked God for the right prayers, and they came that quick. His heart rate and blood pressure came down even more. Then Mark fell off to a deep, peaceful sleep. When he awoke later that day, I once again took his blood pressure.

"128/76"

Every symptom was gone, and Mark was back to his normal self. He was so tired that he could tell he had been in a battle for his life.

We praised God, and thanked Him for another victory in Jesus!

ALMOST

Ben and Amanda, our oldest son and his girlfriend, spent the night with us. Unbeknownst to Ben, he was having a surprise birthday party the next day planned by his sweetie. I was the decoy.

Miss Amanda was to go "off to church" with a friend that morning, and Ben and I were to stay in Corydon. Ben helped me with several projects for upcoming books. It was a wonderful ruse. It worked so well, we were late getting back to Ben's apartment for his own party! Ben thought we were to finish up working on my project at his house. Well, it was sort of the truth. Getting him to his surprise party on time was my main project of the day.

Until the phone rang as we were going out the door.

"Wait Son, I'll catch this call."

"Hello?"

"Deb?" It was my friend Gail.

The tone of her voice sounded anxious.

"What is it?" I asked. I felt a need coming through the phone line.

"Deb, do you have anything to drive at your house?"

"You mean like my car?" I stifled a giggle.

"Yeah."

"Yes." I replied.

"Mike's not back from running errands, and I have to meet a lady in twenty minutes who wants to buy my Dad's house. I don't have a car to drive right now."

"Oh my! Okay. Ben's here with me. I'll come right over, and he can pick me up from your store in his car. When you get through, drop the car off at the house and put the keys under the mat."

"Thanks, you're an angel."

An angel now late for a surprise birthday party! How do I keep getting myself into these situations? Chuckle, chuckle. With a little help from my dear friends.

We arrived at Ben's townhouse to lights out and no cars in the driveway. All was quiet until he stepped through the door.

"Surprise! Surprise! Happy Birthday, Ben!"

Mission accomplished.

"Whew!"

For anyone out there who thinks there were no angels involved in any of this, I say to you, try keeping a secret, getting your grown son out the door on time for "no reason, Mom", do another good deed in the process, and still have everything work out just fine.

Man, I was tired.

I was pretty sure, so were my angels.

COOL HAND JIM
(Feb. 26th)

Not that we would ever have considered resting on our laurels, but it sure sounded like a nice idea when the alarm went off early the next morning. We had to get up and go to another party. This one was for our friend Kelly Riddle. Her mom, Sharon, was throwing her a Pampered Chef® housewarming party for the cottage she and her dad were building together. Kelly's cottage on the family farm was expected to be finished by later that spring, and it was time to get the things she would need.

Coffee in hand, Mark and I headed out the door once again. This day would begin and end miles apart. Our first stop of the day, was 30 miles west of our home. Kelly's dad, Larry had done a wonderful job building his own home and his daughter's. We always liked going over to see what new project he was working on.

When we arrived at the Riddle house, the first site to see was Kelly's cabin. The walls were up, and the doors and windows were in. From the outside, it looked almost finished. Of course, we loved it. From there, we went to the main house for fellowship, and we ordered the latest kitchen gadgets. Another mission accomplished.

By the afternoon, our travels took us 100 + miles to the east.

We arrived at our friends Jim and Ann Carter's house just in time to go out to dinner with them.

The four of us settled into conversation at a comfortable little diner near their home. What a treat it

123

was to be with this lovely gentle couple. They exude warmth and grace and love as if it were from Jesus Himself.

After a delightful meal, we arrived back at their home ready to have a night of fun and playing cards together. At least that was what we had planned. It seemed the Holy Spirit had a different idea!

I had brought the anointing oil with me. We talked of the amazing occurrences we had witnessed lately. Jim and Ann also spoke of wonderful gifts God had bestowed on them too. When they both spoke of prayer needs, we knew in our hearts it was time to go to work.

First, we anointed Jim and prayed over his eczema. We cursed the power of it and forbade it to come back in Jesus' name. I could feel hurt and sorrow pouring out from Ann, so I anointed her too. Our husbands shifted to pray over her.

Then Jim began to speak. As he prayed, we felt the Holy Spirit join us in that room. The air around Jim's hands became cool. We could feel a breeze around them. Jim prayed over my eyes. I felt the pressure in my left eye change. I knew the astigmatism I had had all my life was gone! Jim then prayed for our resources; for God to send what we needed to accomplish His goals in our lives.

MARILYNN
(Feb. 28th)

Marilynn arrived early the next day to finish her stories for their portion of the new book. We were so engrossed in our talk that we forgot to eat lunch! When we finally settled down to eat a proper meal, I was not feeling so well. I had a headache, an earache, and my jaw and teeth ached all along my right side. It felt like the beginnings of a sinus infection.

I was under attack, and so was Marilynn. On Marilynn's left leg, she started to have pain and a charley horse. What was all that about?

We went into prayer for each other. We canceled all attacks and pled the blood of Jesus over us and our afternoon together. All was healed in ten seconds!

Marilynn and I walked into the living room, rejoiced and praised God for His goodness. I sat on the couch, and Marilynn settled down into the recliner. As she was talking, and I was writing, Marilynn noticed a mist forming in the room.

Marilynn simply said, "Debbie, do you see it?"

I looked up and smiled. I saw and felt it. The Shekinah Glory of God came down from the ceiling and into the room. We started singing praises and welcomed the presence of God into our midst.

BREAK ITS BACK AND
NEVER COME BACK!
(Feb. 29th)

Again, illness and tornadoes were approaching our area. Mark was two days into an antibiotic for a sinus infection. With every pill Mark took, he took it in the holy name of Jesus. That morning, I was not feeling so hot myself.

I spent the morning helping out a gentleman with paperwork for his doctor's office. And in the late afternoon, I had a couple that came for prayer for the husband. Mark arrived while we were praying for him, and he joined his prayers with ours.

While making dinner, I felt so poorly I had to sit down. My temperature was starting to climb over 100 degrees. I called and canceled my meeting for the night. Even though Mark was still sick himself, he took over. Mark did the dishes and took care of me.

When we went to bed that evening, Mark got out the anointing oil and prayed over me for a long time. I felt something give in my sinuses, and a big "goop" came out. My temperature broke, and I rested for the rest of the night.

I was healed just in time! We had friends coming over to visit the next day.

CALM BEFORE THE STORM
(March 1st)

I started, early that morning, cooking a fragrant beef stew. The Crosiers were coming for an afternoon of fellowship and Christian movies. Mark watched the meal simmer while I ran an errand. When I got back, our guests had already arrived and blessed our household with a freezer full of meat!

Over lunch, we talked about my healing the night before and about Mark's healing from his migraine. We thought when I was given the miraculous oil it was to be used for the benefit of others. As we found out over the course of months, it was as much a hedge of protection and blessing for us as it was for anyone else. Boy, were we grateful!

The four of us enjoyed movies, popcorn, and desserts made by Marilynn, as the afternoon worked its way into the evening. But every little while, I got a gut feeling of impending disaster. I asked in my spirit, "What is it?"

The reply came quick, *"Pray for your region! Region! The region!"*

Larry had set my all-weather NOAA radio for us just that afternoon. My stomach churned that night as we watched the local television stations' weather forecasts. I packed two boxes of children's pictures and keepsakes, and a box of all my notes and information for the two books I was working on. Mark packed a satchel full of important papers that we would need if anything happened. We both packed an overnight bag. We prayed ourselves into an uneasy sleep.

FATALITIES 3/2/12
(March 2nd)

The next morning, I awoke with the words ringing in my ears, *"Pray for the region!"*

"Yes sir! Yes sir."

I called Gail McCullum at her home early that day.

"Hello?" She answered her phone.

"Hey, it's me."

"Deb. I was expecting a call from you. What time are you coming over?" She had been watching the weather reports too.

"We're all packed up. I have a couple of errands to run, then I'll head your way. Need anything from the grocery before I leave town?"

"No," she responded, "just get here when you can."

"Will do. On my way."

I made a couple of phone calls and left messages for family and friends and informed them that we had bugged out. I told Mark to meet me at Gail's that night after work.

I arrived at her home within the hour. We turned the television onto local channels, and busied ourselves with housework. By lunchtime, Gail made us grilled cheese sandwiches. We sat in her living room and watched every local television station pull out all the stops to keep everyone safe. The *perfect storm* was headed right for Indiana and Kentucky.

Even the National Weather Service had a bullseye directly over our region. Region! Just like the warnings from the night before. Southern Indiana and Louisville, Kentucky, were going to take a direct hit!

Gail called her husband, Mike. He said not to worry; he was working in a basement and should be safe. She then called her daughter, Melissa, and told her it was time to come over. Melissa packed up her baby and headed our way.

I called our oldest son, Ben. He was at a coffee shop with his brothers in Louisville, Kentucky.

"Momma," he started. "Don't be spreading fear."

Gail heard Ben's answer and asked for the phone. I handed it to her, and she very calmly told him this was a serious situation. They needed to be informed. She handed the phone back to me.

"Momma, we are pulling up the national radar right now on our laptops. It looks like it's going north of us. We will all stay safe. Take care of yourself."

At least I knew they were informed and all together. Then I called my husband and begged him to come to Gail's. He also said, "Honey, we will go into the vault if need be."

Once again, my *Rock of Gibraltar* said to hand her the phone. I did.

"Mark, you know I don't get excited unless it's necessary. I think this is a big enough weather event, we need to be together." She handed the phone back to me.

"Okay," Mark said, "I'll call Jim. He's not here."

One by one, our family members showed up. Gail and I were joined first by Melissa and her baby. Barry, Melissa's husband, showed up when his office at Ft. Knox closed due to the oncoming weather. Mark left Corydon as the sirens were going off to take cover. When he arrived at Gail's, I ran out and jumped into his arms with relief and cried. He kissed me like he meant it! The last one in was Mike, Gail's husband. He was two minutes behind Mark. We were all very glad to be together to weather the storm.

At the height of it all, in late afternoon, we watched as the trees around their home started going around and around in circles. We knew it didn't mean anything good, but we would have none of it! Mark went out onto their back porch and rebuked the winds in Jesus' name. I went to the open kitchen window and pleaded the blood of Jesus over their home and land. Gail prayed at the other side of the house.

Gail said, "Okay, we've all prayed. Now it's time to have faith in God."

We watched the radar as we saw the tornadic storms go north of us. Our sky cleared, and the sun came out.

By 6 p.m., it was all over for our area. We thanked Mike and Gail and went home. The first thing we did when we got home was call our friend and builder, Bill Best, to see if his family was all okay.

"Bill, you guys all right?"

"Yeah, you?"

"Yes. Do you still want us to come over and draw up plans for our home?"

The question hung in the air.

"Come on!"

What a day it was! During our drive to the Best home, I heard clearly in my spirit the word "**fatalities**." I cried out, "Oh, Mark! There are deaths! Many deaths!" We prayed all the way to their home.

GOOD DEEDS DONE DIRT CHEAP!
(March 2-3rd)

We found out overnight about the EF-4 that severely damaged Henryville, Indiana. The tornado that hit Henryville started at the south side of Fredericksburg as an EF-1. By the time it hit Palmyra, it had ramped up to an EF-2 and was gaining speed. It was snapping trees and power lines as it graded to an EF-3 and cleared Airgo Industries factory to its foundation slab. By then, the width of the path was 1/3 mile, and tragically, five people lost their lives. As it reached its peak at 170 mph, and almost a half mile wide, it straddled the Washington-Clark County line. When it crossed over Interstate 65, it seriously damaged homes and the Henryville Middle and High School with children and teachers still in it. That cyclic vortex narrowed just west after the Henryville-Otisco line. The tornado had traveled a 49 mile stretch taking 14 lives in Indiana. The same storm spawned another cyclic vortex from Marysville all the way to the Jefferson-Scott county line. It became once again an EF-4 with three more deaths as it crossed the Ohio River into Trimble County, Kentucky. The death toll in Kentucky was 22 bringing the total from both states to 36 deaths; 41 for all the states involved.

Saturday morning, we were grateful to have only a couple of sinus infections to complain about. Shortly after Mark went to work, I received a call. It was from Erin, Mary and Mitch's daughter. She called to make sure we were all okay. Yes, they were fine as well. Mitch, who had a military background, and his son-in-law Chris, went up to Henryville as soon as it was safe to take coffee and water to the first responders.

When they arrived and got off the exit, they were greeted by police and asked to state their business in the area.

"We are bringing coffee and water to the first responders." They replied.

"Coffee? You got coffee?" The boys had made a new friend.

I asked Erin, "Are they going up again anytime soon? I know a couple of people that would like to donate supplies. Including us."

Erin called back and said they were indeed planning another trip that very afternoon. Could I get supplies to them by 2 p.m.?

"Yes, I can!"

Bed covers went flying as I jumped out of my sick bed to go to somebody's rescue! I gathered up funds from us and several friends and went shopping with the list of needed items Mitch gave me.

I tell you, the Lord showed me every place to go and what to get at each store. For $120.00, I filled up my trunk, back seat, and front passenger seat. When I pulled up to Mary's and asked Mitch to help me unload supplies, he came out of the house and said one word, "Wow."

God had moved mountains.

I did not stay long. I still had to go to the grocery and finish dinner for friends that were coming over that evening. One of them, a truck driver, had a story to tell when they arrived at our house. She told me that at the height of the storm, she was crossing the bridge back to Indiana with an empty 18 wheeler. It jumped all over that bridge! She finally got off the first exit and parked by a large two-story building and rode out the rest of the storm there.

As we were enjoying fellowship after dinner, the phone rang. It was our brother in Christ, Bill Mauck. He noticed how hoarse I sounded and offered to come over and pray with me. He did. We all enjoyed each other's company until time to go home. It had been a very busy two days for all of us.

A WORKMAN IS WORTH HER WAGE
(March 5th)

I called that morning to make an appointment to see a doctor. Healing had not come to me supernaturally. I felt lousy. And for the fourth time in two months, I gave away my services for no charge to help clients with paperwork. I obeyed God when He said to do it.

With the last money we had in the bank, I mailed her paperwork to her and charged nothing.

With sorrow in my heart, I went to the doctor and picked up a prescription, all on a credit card.

Broke and sick, I cried all the way home.

FASTING AND PRAYING AGAIN
(March 7th)

I will be the first to tell you that my husband likes to eat. He and his tummy are very close. When Mark heard the Lord say to fast and pray for Pastor Fred, he knew it was serious.

As he fasted at work, Mark remembered Fred in his prayers all day long.

I was recovering from a sinus infection, but from my bed, I joined my husband in prayer. I sang songs of faith to shore up our brother in his time of trial. I asked God personally to remember the number of Fred's days. I tried not to cry. I knew Fred was in a battle.

VICTORY FOR VICTORY!
(March 8th)

After a couple of days off for R&R, I was ready to catch up with the world again. Several pre-blessings were in the works for us. I needed to catch up on my side of the paperwork.

I had been contacted by a bank with a request to fill out an application for a position. I worked on it all day, the day before (7 pages) and I was ready to fax it over. I was also contacted by a church over in Louisville to come and be a part of their health fair. I asked if I could bring my books and my editor.

"Why sure!"

Our loan papers came in showing we were applying for our home loan. It showed how much our anticipated payments would be and such as that. I asked them how long it would be before they had any answers and when building could start.

"Five weeks out."

"Oh my goodness!"

I was not emotionally prepared to hear such good news. I could hear her laughter as I was putting the phone down. I had much to tell Mark when he came home from work before Bible study.

Dinner was small that night. We had to leave room for dessert after the study. Mark and I were the first to arrive at the Schuppert home. I asked Fred how he was, and he looked me squarely in the eyes and said, "I am healed and whole."

Mark and I sat down and listened as Fred

recounted the word he had been given by one of his sons.

"God sent my son to tell me what was wrong with me and what to do about it. He reminded me of all the miracles I had seen; all the things God has done for me and my family. I need to stop letting the devil push me around! What am I doing? This is not going to take my life! And God Himself will tell me when my time here is over."

Fred spoke with authority in his voice and victory in his spirit. When everyone was finished arriving, we went in for Bible study with thanksgiving in our hearts. We all went to our knees and fervently asked God for answers to our deepest prayers.

EMISSARY I. M.
(March 9th)

By that time Mark and I were on the mend physically. I felt like doing the dishes and laundry all in the same day, much to my husband's relief.

I took the last papers into our lender for our home construction loan, and I faxed the paper in to confirm my attendance for the health fair.

On the computer I consoled two gentle women's broken hearts and spirits. The Lord led me to words of comfort for them as I ministered to their needs. I believe, because of this, God sent a man of God to me with a good word for us from the Lord. My tears over being sick and broke ended. Brother Dennis spoke powerful scriptures over us and our household.

It seemed, over the instant message, we were both emissaries of Christ Jesus.

But the day was not over. While I was fixing our dinner that quiet afternoon, a lady called me and asked me to a revival. I thought in my head, "Another one, Lord? I thought we had the night off."

When Mark came home, I informed him we were going out again to another church. Bless God.

We arrived and found our friends near the front of the church. We sang for a while and then welcomed the travelling evangelist.

The young man preached a good sermon on the river of living water.

"Jump in the water!"

After he was through preaching, he was ready for prophesying and healing.

Well, the first people he signaled to come up to

the altar were us! We didn't know each other from Adam. The Lord led him to us. He called us again to the altar. We walked up with questioning looks on our faces. The young pastor joined our hands together. Then he spoke these words to us, "I heard in the Spirit, God's Spirit is upon you. You have questions, and you have been praying with all your heart. God has heard your prayers. Restoration is upon you. God is restoring you!"

When he started speaking in tongues, I started speaking in tongues as well. Then he blew on us the breath of God, and I went down to the floor. I was slain in the Spirit. A man caught me and laid me on the floor. Mark sat beside me until I was able to get up. Sounds and feelings faded away from me as if on cue. For a brief moment, time stood still and the peace of Jesus settled over me like a warm blanket. I am sure I was smiling.

PHILIPPIANS 4:13
(March 10th)

"I can do all things through him who gives me power."

I got up early with my husband as he got ready for work. Shortly after Mark left, I felt a drawing in my spirit, **"Come talk with me."**

I sat down with my Bible before me and simply asked, "Where would you have me look?"

Immediately, in my head came Philippians 4:13. *"I can do all things through Christ who gives me strength."*

"Is that it?"

"Go to your Jewish Bible."

"Yes sir."

In the Hebrew, it spoke volumes more. *"I can do all things through him who gives me power."*

Then quickly, I was taken to Philippians 4:19, "My God will fill every need of yours according to his glorious wealth in union with Messiah Yeshua."

Right after this I got very sleepy very quickly. I laid down and slept a sleep of peace for over an hour.

I was awakened by a phone call from Ben. He had my video ready and wanted to upload it to my computer. After an hour of wrangling with it, success was had.

I was able to see his finished product of a video of myself on camera reading a story from my first book called *Jesus*. It was set to beautiful soft music and a nice background.

At the end of the video, Ben quoted Philippians 4:13. It was my confirmation for the scripture given to me earlier that day.

I sent it out to 117 Facebook friends.

I thanked Ben and Amanda for their help throughout the morning, and we promised to see each other soon. I got ready for the day and took off for the grocery. I still had to cook a roast for dinner for all the guests coming later that evening.

Mitch and Mary Smith arrived right on time as well as Deb Grimes. We sat down to a nice meal served on good china with stimulating conversation.

Later on several more friends dropped by to add different opinions to the ongoing conversation about God, Jesus and truth.

The last person left at 1:45 a.m! Our little impromptu Bible study had been a success. Church arrived early the next morning.

BELIEVING
(March 11th)

Six hours later we were up and at it. We headed to church in Clarksville, Indiana. Our family members, Tom and Bridgette McCullum were expecting us for church and then lunch.

This was another place that, when we took pictures we saw angelic orbs all over. Having known Tom since his youth, it did not surprise me one bit.

After a gracious welcome and a bit of breakfast, we all entered into the sanctuary for service, and it was wonderful. People gave their testimonies, they showed films and prayed together.

At the end of the two-and-a-half-hour service, we went to a local restaurant for lunch and fellowship. Tom and Bridgette blessed us with the meal. Tom said we have to be able to receive as well as give. They were words of wisdom from a wise man. I thanked him for that reminder. Tom said it keeps one from getting weary in their walk. Amen to that.

From there, we went straight over to Mike and Gail's. We had planned to spend the rest of the afternoon with them playing cards and hanging out. It almost went like that.

When we arrived, Gail informed us we were going to church that night at our church. It was to be a night for prayer and healing. We were the first ones to arrive at the Schuppert's. Fred was feeling under the weather and had been for a while. It was time for all of us to get into deep prayer for his healing. And it was our Gail who led the prayers over him.

BLESSINGS ABOUND!
(March 13th)

I was up late the night before, working with Mary until almost midnight.

So, when I was roused up in my spirit to get up and pray at 6:30 a.m. I truly felt the scripture, *"The spirit is willing but the flesh is weak."*

I complied.

On my knees, Bible in hand I asked, "Who is it that needs prayer so early?"

"Fred Schuppert and your son, David Merk!"

"Got it."

I opened my Bible and looked for prayers for Fred's body and David's emotional heart. Mark joined me with prayers and supplications.

Prayer time ran right into radio time. I turned on our radio to WOCC to listen to my "live interview." Mark wanted to hear it too. The interview went well and Mark got up to start his day. He kissed me goodbye as I snuggled back into our oh-so-comfy bed.

I awoke at 10:30 a.m. to the sound of the phone ringing. Did I have time to see someone today?

"Why sure! See you in two hours."

With last night's dishes still to be done and a bed to make, it didn't take long to stir me up and get me going. Covers went everywhere!

I got all accomplished with relative ease, sat at the computer and caught up before my client arrived.

I had a heart to heart with the Lord.

"I love working for you. But every time I put out effort, the money goes to other people. I love you, but we need help too, would you start paying me, even if it's just until our books take off. Please, please help me!"

I looked down at the computer and saw we had three e-mails from the department store Mary and I were trying to sign up with to be a vendor for our books.

"We're ready for the next step." I said to no one in particular.

Before I could open them, my client rang the doorbell. Then during our visit, my phone rang. It was for a phone interview with a credit union to work for them.

After my client left, and the interview was over, I received another e-mail from another company requesting I come in for an interview.

Yes, I felt the Lord had heard my lunchtime prayer. When Mark arrived home later that evening, he had been praying the same thing for me.

And the day wasn't done. It was on my heart to take Pastors Tom and Bridgette a copy of my miracle book. We called after dinner, and Tom gave the go-ahead to come by.

We intended it to be a short visit, but God our Father had all sorts of other intentions.

I had known Tom and Bridgette since 1979. Tom even re-baptized Mark, me and our youngest son, Andy shortly after our marriage. We went to their church several times over the years. They had helped us out a couple of summers in a row when we were first married when all the boys were young and we needed food. For some reason, we had never sat down and had a heart to heart talk about Jesus in our lives. Until then.

After a few minutes of talking with each other, I

told them a little bit about my first book, and we realized that we were all on the exact same spiritual page. They had the same stories in their lives as well.

"Glory!"

We had found another brother and sister. Family once again. Our twenty minute stop turned into a two-and-a-half hour visit.

TYPING
(March 14th)

I had set aside almost all that week to finish typing book two in the *Miraculous Interventions* series. The only thing I ended up doing all week was dodging thunderstorms.

I had too much work to do to fool with turning the computer off and on all day long.

So, I prayed.

"Dissipate! Dissipate!" I cried out.

And they did.

Now what do you think about that?

How big is our God?

Just that big.

A LITTLE GOOD NEWS
(March 15th)

Some days, while we are quietly working, things are happening all around us for our benefit. Isn't it good when God remembers us?

It was another day of typing at the computer when I got an e-mail. It was from Tonini's Church Supply. They were asking for more copies of my first book. I called Mary, and she called them and made arrangements.

Did you ever feel like your own prosperity was emerging as a chick hatching from an egg? Just a little at a time? I still said, "Thank God!"

When it happens to you, remember to thank God too.

As the day unfolded, requests started to come in for landscaping jobs. Over the next several days, they started adding up. I kept a list. "1, 3, 4, 7 -14, 20."

When could we start?

I told them we would watch the weather and see.

I thanked God for opportunity.

AN ODD DAY
(March 16th)

I awoke early that morning, groggy due to all the storms during the night. I thought I had an interview to go on. Somewhere in my sleepy brain, it occurred to me to call the business I was going to just to make sure they didn't have any trouble with their power. That was when I found out our internet lines were down, and I couldn't pull up their phone number. Somehow, I couldn't shake the nagging feeling that I was wasting my time. Our telephone was out too. Ominous was all over the day.

When I arrived at their office, they looked perplexed at why I was there. Did I not get their e-mail? And they even tried to call me, but it seemed my phone line was down.

"Sigh. Tell me."

"Please don't come in for an interview. This position has been filled."

"Thanks for at least trying to reach me."

I called my husband as I walked out of their office.

"No interview, they already filled the position. Oh and we have no phone, or internet. I sure hope the rest of this day gets better."

There was sorrow from one end of the phone line to the other.

"Do you still want fish for dinner?" I inquired of his request that morning.

"Yes, please."

"I'll pick it up at the store. Love you. Once again, sorry." I felt dismal.

"I know, Honey. It'll be okay. Love you too." My husband sighed heavily.

I went to our local grocer where we are known by everyone. I picked up three items, one being fish for that night's dinner and got in line. When the clerk added up my total, it was $8.00. I swiped my card and it read, "Not available."

"What? No, wait. I just put in $20.00 Monday morning. I haven't touched it." We tried again, and it came back the same. The clerk sent me over to the front desk. They tried it. It still wouldn't run through. I called Mark, and he couldn't explain it.

"Go see your bank. They are just across the way." They suggested.

"Good idea, thanks."

I went to our bank and walked in with a smile.

"Hey, you guys! My card won't run at the grocery. Can you check our account? I just made a deposit Monday that should cover $8.00 for our dinner just fine." I was still smiling as they pulled it up on their screen.

"Your balance is $.07."

"What??? Somebody get my husband on the phone." What the heck.

"Albin Jewelers, this is Mark."

"We have $.07 in the bank. Why?" You could have hung icicles on my tone.

"Uh, oh! I forgot! I took out $20.00 Tuesday to give an offering to another church."

That was the third offering that week. We had simply tithed ourselves out of even one night's worth of groceries.

"Oh Lord." My sigh was heavy.

Mark's paycheck wouldn't go in until midnight that night. I stood embarrassed in the bank line. The grocery store was still holding my groceries. I had to go tell them I didn't have enough to buy us even one meal.

Let's recap. No job, no interview for a job, no phone, no internet to look for a job, no money and no dinner. Yep. I had to look up to see the floor I was standing on. My heart was so heavy I couldn't even pray a little prayer for help.

Then the bank teller spoke up, "Debbie, we know you and Mark here. We know he put his paycheck in. We'll allow you to draw out $10.00 for your dinner. Go get your meal."

"Thank you. God bless you."

I got home with my $8.00 of groceries and two dollars in my pocket. I put it away and got on my face.

"Alright Lord. I repent. I'm sorry for whatever I did. Is this a punishment? Because, even if it is, I love you anyway." My heart hurt.

I sang praises the rest of the day. I couldn't muster a smile, but I could at least praise God. After all, in all circumstances, we are supposed to praise Him. I finished typing *Miraculous Interventions II* to send to the editor.

Even though weary, somehow, among all the circumstances that day, I still felt peaceful that night, even on an odd day.

MODERATION IN ALL THINGS
(March 18th)

Spring came a whole month early that year. There had been no sign of winter practically all winter long. By mid-March we had gotten requests for over 20 landscaping jobs. What an early, busy start to the season!

I woke up with an instant word of knowledge.
"Moderation in all things."
"Got it! Thanks."

I received the message right away. I called out to my husband.

"Honey. I just got a word from the Lord. We have to pace ourselves today. No overworking at the start of this season." I waited to hear his reply. He was in agreement. We agreed not to push each other.

"Deal."

Mark packed the tools in the truck while I packed our lunches. With everything ready to go, we took off for a full day of landscaping. We tackled the big job first; my cousin's yard and all four of her flower beds. Big flowerbeds! We did indeed pace ourselves and the day went well. By the end of the job, as we packed our tools up to go, we were very glad to get it over with first.

Dirt and all, we climbed back in the truck to go load more dirt into the truck. On the way back into town, our builder called and asked if he could change our meeting to the next night. As bad as we smelled at the time, we thought it was a better plan than going straight to his house that night.

We loaded down the trailer with another four

tons of dirt and brought it back to our home. I came inside to put things away while Mark moved the dirt from point A, our truck, to point B, our driveway. This was to be used for other landscape jobs later that same month.

While I was inside, a call came in. One of our many friends asked us over for dinner. I thought, "Gee, work another four hours or relax with friends over a nice meal?"

It sounded like moderation to me!

I went outside, all smiles, and told Mark the good news. He was overjoyed to be off the clock for the rest of the evening. Between us, we finished moving the last of the dirt quickly, showered, and went to have a wonderful dinner with friends.

ADVERSE EVENT
(March 21st)

The attacks that day came in hard and furious! And not only on us but those we loved as well. We found out a precious friend passed away in Florida, Pastor Ivie, whom we had known for ten years, had cancer invade her body once again, and our pastor in Corydon was fighting his own battle with an unknown illness. And then, there was our battle out of the blue.

I was sent to a women's business meeting during the afternoon. I came home and made dinner for us, expecting to have a nice evening with my husband after such an unsettled day.

Mark came in the door, and he looked upset. I thought it was because of our friend who had died the day before. I am sure it added to his emotional state. He set his briefcase down as I hugged him hello. I let Mark know about Pastor Ivie and her recent diagnosis. It surely was a hard day.

Mark sat in the kitchen while I was making our dinner plates. He spoke quietly that he wasn't hungry. Problem. Trepidation filled my spirit.

"What is it?" I asked.

Trouble spoke out of my husband's mouth.

"I got a call today from our lender. They don't believe we can build our home for what we say we can. The underwriter wants us to have $16,000.00 in the bank to cover any overages, or they'll deny us." Mark took a breath and spoke.

"The underwriter said I'm not worth enough to

build a home."

At that point, Mark broke down, visibly sobbing. He cried to me, "I'm sorry, I'm not worth anything!"

I held my husband.

"I am sorry they spoke such lies to you!" My warrior shields were up and I went to war! They had hurt my husband, and I was not going to stand for it. But I could not cry with him. God immediately put in my remembrance about the last time we had devastating news.

"Do not cry! Praise me!"

"Mark, I feel like I need to praise God and see what happens."

I started singing love songs to the Lord. Soon, Mark joined me. The longer we sang, the stronger the conviction on our hearts that God would set everything right. Satan would not be allowed to steal from us again!

Mark finally agreed to eat a meal with me.

Our Father, in His infinite mercy, sent a friend, Kelly, over to see us. We told her what had happened and how it hurt Mark. Together, we all went out to the land. Kelly smiled.

"It's coming anyway. I hear reward. God will reward your faith."

EXPECT THE UNEXPECTED
(March 25th)

That day, we divided and conquered. Mary and I went to a health fair that I was asked to bring information and books to. Mark went with Larry and Marilynn Crosier to see a Pastor from Tennessee speak in Berea, Kentucky.

Mark would not be back until late that evening, while Mary and I would finish early in the day. We decided after the health fair, we would go back to her house and work on the children's book together. Ours was the easy day. Mark, Larry and Marilynn had the anointed day.

The health fair went well. I did lots of Body Fat Analysis', took blood pressures and pulses, gave out fliers on good health habits, and people seemed genuinely interested. Mary set out our three books that had been published by HCAP, Home Crafted Artistry & Printing, Mary's business that she had started in order to help me. At the end of the day, we only sold one book. Being the optimists that we were, we figured it was lunch money.

When it was over, we did indeed go back to Mary's and work on the new children's book. As it got late in the evening, I packed up and came home. I had not been there long when three very excited travelers showed up in our driveway. I could hear them shouting for joy from inside the house. I ran outside to see what all the commotion was about.

Mark, Larry and Marilynn had an anointed day as evidenced by their jumping up and down as they got out of the car. I started jumping with them and I didn't even know why yet.

"Please come in and tell me your news. Do you have time to stay and catch me up on the events?"

Could they stay? They practically ran me over to get in the house!

They came in all aglow and took off their coats, and we all settled into our seats. I waited with great anticipation! I love stories with good endings, and I knew the one coming would be a doozey. I offered coffee and tea.

"Yes, thank you."

The conversation went back and forth between Marilynn, who started the story, to Larry who interjected from time to time, and then to Mark, who just bubbled. It went something like this:

"Well, when we got there, Pastor was just getting ready to be introduced. We all clapped, and he started preaching. About halfway through his sermon, he stopped. He got a funny look on his face. He said this had happened only a handful of times in his 35 years of preaching. The Lord was changing his sermon right in the middle of it! And, the Lord wanted him to do something out of the ordinary."

Larry picked up the story from there. "He said someone here needs a financial miracle, and they needed it now. He said this person had been a giver and a tither and a helper. Now's the time for them to receive an unexpected blessing. He cried out for us all to believe for the unexpected. Expect the unexpected!"

The Crosiers and Mark could not believe what they had heard. It fit both our families to a tee. All of the meeting was recorded on a DVD and a CD and could be ordered the next week. Yes, both couples ordered one. Now, back to the meeting.

Mark jumped in, "Pastor asked everyone who needed a monetary blessing to stand up and come forward. I ended up right in front of him. Believe it or not, the whole group did not go up. It was only about a third of us. He then reminded us of our covenant with God. He asked each person to take a dollar bill out of their wallet and fold it four times until you could see the words "In God We Trust" on top. I showed him mine, and he said I did it right."

Marilynn jumped back in to the conversation. "We were right next to Mark. He looked at ours too. Pastor had us all hold up our dollars as a reminder to God about the covenant we have with him. Then he went into deep prayer and spoke in tongues. Then he asked God to anoint each family that was asking for God's divine intervention."

"Wowwww!!" I felt as if I had been right there in the room with them. Excitement crept through my whole body.

Larry finished the conversation, "Pastor said at the end of the segment to believe God for the unexpected blessing. Don't stop reminding the Lord until something happens."

Mark spoke in awe as he said, "He even spoke over my money for it to expand supernaturally."

I believed every word out of their mouths.

As it happened, our good friends did come into unexpected money several times over the next 18 months, and were able to be a blessing to the house of the Lord.

»» INTERMISSION ««

HIGHER THAN BLOOD

"Oh, Debbie! You are just like a sister to me!" I could feel Lisa smiling over the phone. I had just read her the story about the prophesy that was handed down in her family. Now it would belong to the world. I felt love flow through the phone.

After her call, I pondered how good God had been to me after all. What he had not sent me through blood relation, He had sent me in a higher form.

Some people, when you meet them, you know they are there for a purpose in your life. They are destined somehow to become family. For someone who had only two friends most of her young life, it was quite humbling to watch God fulfill a small child's wish; His design of what plenty looked like.

God sent higher-than-blood sisters through Christ Jesus.

Shall I name just a few?

There are my big sisters, Anne, who has gone on to be with the Lord; Debbie Grimes; and Mary, before she was my publisher she was my dear friend. And then there are my little sisters: Crystal, and Lisa coming in as the baby. (She'll love that, she is my editor. See if this makes the final cut.)

Just like in the flesh, I am the middle child. Well, at least it is a role that I am familiar with. It is not that I don't have other female friends through church or categorized as second mothers like Vicki Sampson, or cousins once removed like Gail, I love all the ones the

Lord has sent to me to encourage me in my walk on this planet. But I would like to tell you a little about some of these women.

Anne Schwarz, my oldest sister now with the Lord, was once upon a time my chemistry teacher. Before the end of our second class together, the Lord spoke to the Schwarz' hearts and said, "This one shall be special." That was me-special. That was them-special to me. Please see the "Christmas Story" in book one of *Miraculous Interventions*, and in *Miraculous Interventions II*, see the story called "The Road to Seattle" for some of our adventures together.

About the same time, I met Mary Smith at St. Mary's prayer group in Lanesville, Indiana. Little did we know, almost 20 years later, we would be partners on a mission for the Lord. The year God gave Mary the aptitude to publish her own book, my orders came down to write. Our destinies were locked in place. To print my books, Mary had to start her own publishing company. After a prayer to God, she named it HCAP — Home Crafted Artistry & Printing. Now, Mary has many authors that have come to her company. I was just the first. Along the way, her three daughters and my three sons became each other's siblings of the heart.

Debbie Grimes, the second oldest in my growing group, is a giver unparalleled. She never ceases to amaze me. She is sweet to a fault, thoughtful, and a hard working soul, no doubt about it! It was a blessed day when Fr. Bernie told me that there was someone he wanted me to meet, and it was Deb.

The first time Ben met Lisa, the youngest of us all, he turned to me and said, "Momma! She looks like she could be your daughter." A compliment for sure. Family relation was set. But, if Lisa called me sister, then sister I am. And I am grateful for it. Intelligent and thoughtful, she was the perfect editor for two of my books. Like I have said, one day I will have to pay her.

The last one so far to come into the sister-fold, is Crystal, aptly named. For years Crystal had wished for a big sister. She was tired of carrying the burden of being the oldest and wisest. She knew it was an odd request, but she had set her heart on it. Even though she never asked God for this, with one phone call and ten minutes into it, He answered. There we were. When we met at my first LCW meeting—Louisville Christian Writers, of which Crystal was the president, she knew me on site. And the first time she and her husband David set foot in our home on Dutch Street, she knew it was a perfect home for her. A year later, they bought it.

We all lift each other up, love unconditionally and support each other's endeavors.

I do not know if there are any others out there, but I bless God for all the beautiful souls, male and female, that have touched my life.

I am overjoyed!

Season II

Blessings, Wonders & Prophesy

2 Samuel 23: 5 "For my house stands firm with God —
He made an everlasting covenant with me.
It is in order, fully assured,
that he will bring to full growth
all my salvation and every desire."

Given to me in my spirit on my 53rd birthday.

By the last days of March, I noticed a slowing down of healing miracles.

The call for them dropped, and I wondered what the rest of the year would look like until I spoke to my friend, Karen, and she had wisdom for me to consider.

"Deb, maybe this year is about all types of miracles, not just healing."

"I hadn't thought of that." I was already pondering her statements.

"Look around to see what starts showing up at your door. Blessings and miracles can take many shapes, you know."

"Thanks, I'll look for it."

Well, she is a pretty sharp cookie.

PULLING A MIRACLE OUT OF A HAT
(March 26th)

Mark and I were to meet later in the day with our builder. I did not know how he would receive the information we had to tell him.

During the day, the Lord pressed on several people's hearts to stop by and see me. It was on their heart to shore me up. Without my having said a word, they knew I needed encouragement. But everyone that showed up that day came with the same message, "If I come into a lot of money, I will remember you and your husband."

I thanked them all for their many kindnesses and thoughts.

"Big money, Lord."

We were quiet on the way to Bill's house. Half way through our meeting with him, Mark told him what had happened with the underwriter and how hard our local manager had fought for us at the lending institution. Surprisingly enough, Bill was not upset. He had seen this kind of thing before. Once, while working with a bank to do work for them, he had to send his bid in with every detail and amount specified. All the way up to, and including, the scanner numbers of the products. He told us banks don't understand. No one else does the quality work he does for the bid he makes. He said, "Lending institutions are used to contractors taking their heads off. We just have to show them this isn't one of those times."

Bill was so cool and confident. Then he started doling out our homework for the next week until we could meet again. Our assignments were to go and get specific bids and their prices for building supplies. He would go get other bids on the main construction project part of it.

We would meet again in a week to hammer the whole thing out.

THE START OF THE HARVEST
(March 27th)

Bill was so sure everything would be all right that we agreed to meet the next morning at 8:30 a.m. on our homeland. Mark and Bill walked the 10 ¾ acres parcel to stake where our home site would be. I pondered in my head which rooms would be where, how all our furniture would be accommodated and what else there would be to buy at the end of the process. It was a good start to a busy day.

I watched as the wind ever so gently swayed our field as if to a rhythm only the sky could hear. Peace engulfed me from my head to the soles of my feet. I felt I was seeing a long-awaited event unfold before my eyes. This was the closest we had been to seeing our dream come true. Thanksgiving went up from my heart to God. We had reason to hope again.

As they drove a few stakes in the ground for an approximation of feet, all was done for the time being. We shook hands and planned to see each other in a week.

Mark and I got back into our truck and headed straight for our first landscape job of the day for Miss Vicki Sampson. Vicki was a regular customer of ours over the last four years. Our job was to spruce up her existing landscape and make it all pretty again.

"Sure. Fine."

I had known Vicki for almost 38 years. I figured the fall of 2013, we could hold a 40th friendship anniversary. We are BFFs, as the kids would say!

"Sure. Fine."

Vicki was all smiles when she saw us pull up next

to her house. She walked out onto the porch and gave us instructions before she took off to go on her daily walk with her youngest son, Gary. At 80 + years old, she was still as healthy and lovely as the day I first met her — at least in my eyes.

It was late afternoon before we were finished at her home. Vicki inspected all the grounds, and with a smile, paid us and we were on our way to the next job site.

On the other side of town, across the street from my mother, was Momma's best friend, Kathleen, who we had known over 47 years. It was our next job site. As a widow, Kathleen needed help sprucing up her yard too. Within a few minutes of our arrival, she was ready to feed me. Surely I was hungry. Some things never change.

Mark cleaned out her gutters and trimmed bushes. I walked along behind him with big bags and a rake to clean up the mess. It was well past dinnertime when we called it a day. Of course she had to feed us again. Mark and I sat at her kitchen table where she served us a grand meal like we were her own children. Kathleen caught us up on her life and what her children and grandchildren were doing. She asked about us and ours as well. We all visited well into the evening hours, and with fond farewells, we promised to see each other during the summer.

YOU HAVE TO PREPARE TO MAKE MONEY
(March 28th)

The week before, I was minding my own business, when I went into my husband's work to ask him a question and heard my name called.

"Debbie! When are we having a yard sale together?"

I laughed and called back to Lana, the young lady who had worked with Mark.

"When do you want it to be?" I figured I would get at least a couple of weeks' notice to prepare everything. After all, those things take a little time to get together.

"Thursday."

"Yikes! That's one week."

"Okay. Where at?"

"Your house." Lana smiled when she said it.

"Oh boy!" I realized at that point I was out-numbered and out-gunned.

"Okay. Put an ad in the paper, and I'll get things ready to go."

Mark whispered to me as I was leaving, "What do we have to sell?"

"I guess now is as good a time as any to find out. I'll start cleaning out our closets."

My work was laid out ahead of me. Now, not only did I have to go around and get estimates in the next week, but I was also having a yard sale!

While I was getting items ready to sell, Pastor Ivie from South Carolina called. As usual, we had a very fond conversation. I brought her up to date on our home situation. She reminded me of what she had seen in her spirit, in a vision, that our money was not coming from a bank. God was going to send a person to help us. When she prayed over us at the end of our phone call, she reminded God of what He had shown her over two years ago and asked Him to bring it soon.

It was the day before the sale, and we had stuff stacked all over the living room. Since we had planned on putting our home up for sale in the next month, we thought it would be a good way to make some extra money, clean out closets of items no longer needed or willing to take with us, and put out a little advance advertising of our home.

By the end of the day, I realized, you really do have to prepare to make money.

YARD SALING
(March 29th)

By the time the lovely, cool morning dawned, Lana and I were hip-deep in customers. Trinkets, glassware, clothes and kid's stuff found new homes as we busied ourselves from one customer to the next. But I have to say, the most enjoyable part of the day for me was in the afternoon, during the quiet times. I had the privilege of really getting to know the young lady that my husband had worked beside my husband for over 14 ½ years. I always knew she was smart and pretty as a picture—but I hadn't known the depths of her heart until she shared with me.

Lana is a thoughtful person with a seriousness about her. Outnumbered by two sons and a husband (I resemble that as a mom with three boys and a husband), her time was not her own. All good mothers know the lament of not having enough hours in their days.

And talk about sons! As soon as we were to tear down this event, Ben and his sweetheart, Amanda were coming over for dinner and an evening sunset out on our homeland.

Mark arrived just in time to help with the cleanup. The only evidence left was the money we had.

Ben and Amanda arrived a short while later for a quick dinner together. They had plans for us! There was still more fun to be had.

We all went out to our homeland of four plus years armed with a Frisbee and a football. The four of us dreamed of what was to be there. Home plans in place, we were sure in our hearts to be building by mid-April. Mark and I could hardly wait. Memories were already being planned.

Some of our neighbors drove by and stopped to chat for a while, or walked out their back doors for a visit. We just wanted to have a porch to put them all on.

A KIND WORD'S PERFECT TIMING
(April 3rd)

I believe I have decided that there must be 365 busy days in a year — especially if there is work to do for the Almighty — even a kind word.

Words of knowledge were seeping through my daily errands. For example, I knew in my knower we were to go to Easter Sunday services at my cousin Tom's church.

"Wonderful!"

Tom and Bridgette are charismatic Christian Ministers, and we loved to worship with them. Their church was called *The Edge*.

God works all for His purpose with or without our understanding.

The person I was to meet for lunch canceled at the last minute. No problem.

I could eat by myself... maybe.

An elderly lady was a table across from me. She too, sat all by herself. She was dressed as though she had been to church. She looked quite proper in her long skirt and hand embroidered top with tiny flowers. Her hair was up in a neat bun on the back of her head. I did not know it, but she watched me pray before my meal.

In my spirit, instructions came quickly, *"Be kind to this lady. She's lonely."*

"Got it."

"Address her."

"Okay." I spoke out loud to my unseen visitor.

"Hello! My you look nice today in your skirt and top!" I smiled at her.

"Why thank you!" The smile came back to me.

"Are you eating by yourself?" I inquired of her.

"Yes." Short reply.

"Me, too." Now we were in agreement.

Conversation picked up.

"I noticed you prayed before you ate. I wanted to say something to you then, but I am too shy." She smiled once again, and her words verified the call I had been given.

"So you are my Christian sister?" I already knew the answer but thought it polite to ask anyway.

"Yes I guess I am!" The sweet little saint brightened up like a light bulb.

I moved closer to her side of the table. We talked about the Lord and how good He had been to us and our families. I allowed time to pass as she shared with me some of her adventures. Wherever I had needed to go, it could wait.

This little sweetheart was reveling in the moment. During the conversation, I took the chance to take out my business card and hand it to her. I wanted her to know I was a Christian author.

Just the look on her face was worth the telling of this story in print.

Now she will be remembered.

If only I had thought to get her name...

5:30 a.m.
(April 4th)

It was 5:30 in the morning when I was shaken awake, spirit and body. My eyes opened, my mind already alert, I heard in my spirit, *"Do not worry! I may only use you a little now, but there will come a time when I will use you greatly!"*

I had gone to bed that night with a pain in my middle, right side—I was uncomfortable.

I heard again, *"Would you rather Me heal you or go get medication?"*

Before I could reply, my feet had already hit the floor, and I was running to get the anointing oil! Mark awoke and asked what was going on. I told him that the Lord had come to heal me. Please lend a hand.

Now there were two wide awake people in the bed. We thanked God for His provision, and I watched the oil come out richly and quick as Mark rubbed oil on my side, my heart and my back. The little vial overflowed more and more. Healing came instantly! God was in the house!

I anointed my husband as the oil flowed freely from an upturned bottle. Then I ran and anointed Mark's wallet, my books, our home plans, and each of our son's pictures. I did not want to leave anything to chance. I went back to our bed and anointed our eyes, teeth and Mark's head as well. We anointed our ears to hear a rhema word from God.

Then, we both fell to the ground and worshipped God our Father for ten minutes non-stop. We held hands and said the *Our Father* together. Through closed eyes, we both saw bright colors exploding before us. We were led to a Bible verse that stated, *"Adonai will reward you!"*

What a way to start a new season; with the Lord at the helm! We praised God once again for remembering us.

A HARD NIGHT'S DAY
(April 7th)

Once again, the first words I heard as I awoke were from the Lord God.

"Listen to me."

My spirit was on high alert!

During that same morning, I put a call in to a family I had yet to meet. I represented Jesus to them. They were going through a great loss and strife in their lives. I listened to the mother for an hour and a half. Then, I comforted a child of seven and gave kind words to help her heal over the loss of her best friend.

When Mark got off work that afternoon, we started out to finish a landscape job so it could be done by Easter, the next day. Right before leaving the house, Mark presented me with my Easter card and candy. He smiled patiently as he waited for his gifts. Surely, I had not forgotten the season. I smiled uncomfortably.

"Honey, can we stop by the store on our way out of town?"

"What?"

"I need to pick up something. It's important!"

"Okay, but hurry. We only have so much daylight."

I thought to myself, "Self! How could you forget your husband a card and a gift? Sheesh."

But the good Lord had something entirely different in mind for me when I arrived there.

I ran in quickly and looked for a card and some of Mark's favorite candy. Although, at the time, anything would do. It was obvious the cat was out of the bag; I'd forgotten my husband on Easter.

As I stood in line, I heard a lady speaking to the cashier, "Remember, the next person who comes in and asks for a job, we're hiring them."

"Oh, my gosh! That's me! That's me!" I jumped up and down as I realized why I was there. It was for a job. What a gift I could give my husband. A job one mile away from our home. The prayer I had prayed on the second of April had been answered.

"When can I see the manager?" I was breathless.

"Tomorrow." She laughed.

"Easter? You mean Easter?"

"Yes, go online, print an application and bring it in with you." She smiled.

A thousand thanks escaped my lips as I ran toward our truck.

"Mark! You won't believe it! I just got a job interview!"

He laughed and asked, "When?"

"Tomorrow."

"Easter? You mean Easter?"

"Yes. By the way, Happy Easter. Here's your card and candy. I'll sign it later."

Mark shook his head with a smile. "That's my baby doll!"

A JOB ON EASTER SUNDAY
(April 8th)

At *The Edge* Christian Church, services were wonderful and long. Pastor Tom spoke volumes on how *Resurrection Day* was every Christian's resurrection day

He quoted Romans 1:1-4, "Paul, a servant of Jesus Christ, called to be an apostle, separated unto the Gospel of God. (Which he had promised afore by his prophets in the Holy Scriptures.) Concerning his Son Jesus Christ our Lord, which was made of the seed of David according to the flesh; and declared to be the Son of God with power, according to the spirit of holiness, by the resurrection from the dead."

Tom went on to explain, "The eternal halls of justice declared with honor and power, prophesy was fulfilled by Jesus, raised from the dead. In Jesus' resurrection, we are separated from cults and false religions. Jesus was declared by the Holy Spirit to be the Son of God! Death couldn't hold Him!"

Our dear friend was just getting warmed up, and he already had half his congregation up on their feet.

As things quieted down, Tom went on, "If you believe in the *Shroud of Turin*, the energy that it took to make that impression must have been atomic! It was not only a demonstration but a declaration of His Spirit of holiness. Now, what does that mean for us? The holiness of Jesus is a qualifier. In 1st Corinthians 15:13-20, Jesus took our sins away. Right then and there, He equipped His saints. We must be born again in spirit and the blood of Christ. The requirements from us is repentance. John 5:28-29 and I quote, "Marvel not at this; for the hour is coming, in the which all that are in the graves shall hear his voice, and shall come forth; they that have done good, unto the resurrection of life; and they that have done evil, unto the resurrection of damnation." It was a sobering message. You better be about one, or you will be about the other.

Pastor Tom continued on, "People, we are called to the resurrection of life! Jesus delivered us so not to face the crisis of life or death. He gave us hope. The evil heart has unbelief. Without faith, it is impossible to please God! If you want to move Jesus, you have to have faith. The Spirit of Holiness allows us to hear, *'Well done, my good and faithful servant.'* Don't let anything get in your way!" The good pastor was emphatic. He was begging people to get this message. This was important. It was not a sermon to sleep through. Pastor Tom posed a question to the crowd, "How do we walk in holiness?"

I could feel people putting on their thinking caps. Tom answered for us simply, "Escheweth evil." Had I not heard that very command in my spirit? Tom's questions started going deeper.

"Are we loving something over Jesus?" He watched his congregation closely.

"Stay close! Don't wander. Live in His shadow. Where your treasure is, there also is your heart."

Mark and I walked out with a message of hope. Before we got home, I asked to be taken over to the store to speak to the manager. I felt important decisions were ahead.

I was greeted warmly as I walked through the doors. "Welcome to our store!"

I smiled at the cashier and asked if the manager was in.

"Yes, she's putting a display together in aisle 8."

"Thanks."

I went to the assigned area, and there she was finishing up a display with two other employees.

"Hi! My name is Debbie Peyron, and I live a half mile from here. I heard last night you all are hiring, and I would like to work here." I stopped to catch my breath.

Without looking up, she said, "I know who you are. Fill out an application, and bring it back to me."

I thought she didn't understand the urgency of my request. I spoke again in case she missed it. "Uh, I'm a Christian, and I've been praying for a job in this area. I knew when I heard your employee speak about hiring, I knew this was my job. I'm supposed to be here." She was following the conversation just fine. I was the one with the problem.

Again she stated, "I know who you are. Fill out the application, and bring it back to me."

"Okay."

It was a long and detailed application. I worked on it for over an hour and a half. By mid-afternoon I was back in the store, application in hand. I handed it to the manager who turned it over without so much as a glance and asked me if I had time to take a short test. I had to pass it before I could be hired.

"Please, take your time."

Forty-five minutes later, I was a fledgling employee, still to go to their website and fill out the rest of their paperwork and take more tests. I had never done so much to get a job that paid so little! And all I could get was part-time. It was all they allowed. Something at the time was better than nothing.

I was sure this was another key to bringing us closer to building a home on our land. Gainfully employed, I looked forward to helping with the household groceries and payment of bills. I felt in my heart that some help was better than no help. It was, at least, a start.

A PROPHET'S MANTLE

(April 10th)

This day was set aside as a day of help for our pastor and his wife, Fred and Jeanne Schuppert. Mark did all their yard work — which was formidable — and I made them dinner. I even made them an Easter basket with only Christ-themed candy in it!

I arrived to find a busy household. Mark was still diligently working in the yard, and Jeanne was teaching music as I brought in their afternoon meal. I had just set it all on the kitchen counter when Pastor Fred walked in. He looked tired and weak but happy to see me. I showed him what I brought for their dinner and their Easter basket. Fred chuckled over receiving an Easter basket at the ripe old age of 64. It figured it would come from me! I asked if I could talk with him for a few minutes, and he nodded yes and sat down to listen.

I had a vision back in the middle of March. I was taken out of my body and shown God's will for our pastor's life — what was to be. I knew the time to share had come. I started the conversation.

"Fred, you know how you've told us to talk to God as a friend, and He will answer us?"

"Yes, that's right."

"Well, I did that back in early March. I asked the Lord a simple question. I said, 'Lord, what are we going to do about Fred?' Immediately, I was not in my body or on my couch anymore. I have only had a handful of visions in my life and only when they are important. When they happen, I try to pay close attention."

"Yes, yes, go on."

"I saw you standing in front of me. You had on a prophet's mantle. It was white. You looked strong and determined. You turned to the side, and there was another man standing there. I think it was your oldest son. You took off your mantle and put it on him. Then, you turned back toward me, looked at me one last time, and then turned and walked away. I knew I would never see you again on this Earth. Immediately, I was back on my couch. The only thing I am not sure of is this; if you are going back to Illinois or going home."

Fred was quiet for a moment, then he spoke up, "I have been waiting for someone to come and tell me this."

I thanked God I had been given a chance to speak the prophetic word. I thanked Fred for his ministry and told him that we loved him very much. He said he loved us too. And, just like in the prophesy, Fred gave his mantle to his oldest son, and I never saw him alive again after that.

MINISTERING OVER THE PHONE
(April 11th)

It seemed everyone and their brother needed help on that particular day. Fortunately, most everything was taken care of over the phone. Ten calls came in for prayer or consultation, and God allowed me to have the right words for all of them.

Questions about health, hearts on the mend, and others who just needed to vent, took up hours of the day. I was grateful to be of service to God and to His children.

Mary came over that evening, and with diligence, we finished editing *Miraculous Interventions II*. We made sure the stories were sequenced in proper order.

By the time we finished it, like its predecessor, it had 55,000 words and just over 260 pages.

TRUDY TO THE RESCUE!
(April 13th)

Sometimes, when our spirits are down, God sends resources to bolster us back up so we can move forward. That was exactly what happened on this morning. Trudy didn't realize it at the time, but she was following direct instructions from God and was an answer to my prayer.

The conversation started out as a nice gesture and went up from there. Trudy is naturally effervescent, and she has grown markedly as a mature Christian since I met her eight plus years ago. I am not usually on her call list, so when I heard her voice, I made sure all was well.

Trudy wanted me to listen to a pastor on the television. She felt his words were for me. I was very grateful to have been remembered, and we ended up being on the phone for an hour. It turned into an excellent Bible study! Good thing. The news in the next few hours was not as joyful.

Later that day, I heard from several sisters in Christ. Attacks were on the horizon! Clare's physical heart was having serious trouble, cancer was invading Pastor Ivie, and Fred was worse than before. How could three pillars in Christ be called to bear such heavy burdens? Was it to show the rest of us what a real faith-walk looked like?

I had already received a word for Pastor Fred. I was to leave his condition in the Lord's hands.

Yet, I was approved in the Spirit to pray and

request direct intervention for Clare and Ivie. God was not yet done with them here on this Earth. There was still work for them to do.

Fiat.
So be it.

FINISHED!
(April 14th)

When you start a project, watch it grow and develop, you look forward to the finished product. The same with Mary and I. *Miraculous Interventions II* was coming to a close. It was our last day to work on it. Pages were numbered; each piece of the puzzle fit together nicely. We were grateful and sad at the same time.

We like our productive visits and fellowship. Mary has been all along what I had missed my whole life — a sister closer than blood to me.

By 11:00 that night, Mark and I were preparing to watch a video we had borrowed from a friend about a pastor preaching on a Cherokee Reservation. It was a direct home run in my heart! He spoke of the Cherokee Nation and their lineage. How they and two other Indian Nations had direct ties to the Hebrew Nation!

The fruit of this?

All the gifts of the Holy Spirit that poured out on their people (your young men shall see visions and your old men shall have dreams) — are theirs too.

The minute the words were out of his mouth I knew with our Cherokee heritage, that was my mother, myself, and my sons. I had wondered all my life where these beautiful and unusual gifts had come from.

Now I knew!

It was through my very ancestry coming forth with power and fruit from the vine! I cried and fell to the floor with my husband joining me!

Mark and I danced and sang when the praise group came forward. It was a mix of Native American and gospel music, and I loved it as if it were my own! My feet danced beneath me! I felt the Holy Spirit join us as we called out His glorious name.

Mark had the good sense to grab our camera and take a picture. Just like he felt, all over the picture, "angelic orbs" could be seen joining us in our praise.

You see, our praise was so sincere it had called them down from the Heavens to see what we were about.

KEEP THE LORD'S DAY HOLY!
(April 15th)

From midnight to midnight, Mark and I were in praise and worship. All had been explained to me in one fell swoop. I and my family are of the Truax clan, of the Cherokee Tribe.

One is a warrior — Ben

One is a healer — Andy

Two are visionaries — my mother and myself

Words of knowledge come quickly about our little clan to share with each other.

Mark and I barely got seven hours sleep before we set off for a revival at a local church known for their worship and monthly revivals. Two hours later, we were at our local grocer to pick up a few things.

As I was getting out of the car, I was given a word of knowledge about an 81 year old woman in the parking lot. Knowledge was shared as I helped her up to the door.

That afternoon our good friends Larry and Marilynn came to go with us to Iona to hear Fr. Mike preach. The day kept getting better and better. The miracle healing service at St. Columba was almost three hours long. By this time, Mark and I had already spent 17 hours straight in the presence of the Holy Spirit wherever we went.

Father Mike spoke on Acts, Psalms 133 and 1st John 1:1-2. It was all about the fellowship of Christians together. We are the witnesses for the light of life. Fr. Mike said we are to testify and be light! We are to confess and be cleansed from all sin.

As usual, Father gave prophesy over his congregation one at a time, including me.

"Your finances are not a problem to God! Trust God." He continued over my husband, "Mark! Finances are coming. God is answering your prayers now."

Everything Mark and Larry asked was answered. Father Mike saw a vision for us.

"Wherever you go, I see a stream of multi-color and blessings."

Father went on with words for everyone, "Where there is fear, you lock doors. God won't move in fear. God is for you and not against you, even through locked doors. Jesus wants to come in. Don't live in fear. Peace has come. We are sent. We have a calling in life. You are equipped with all you need! Jesus breathed on the apostles and they received the Holy Spirit. We make it so hard. With God, it's easy. God wants us to release people. Don't ever give up on anybody! Be expectant! Look for miracles, signs and wonders. Don't doubt but believe! Belief opens doors. Today is the day of salvation. He can use us right where we are. Believe for greater things—even the impossible! Have faith to trust for the impossible."

The good priest stopped to take a breath and let it all sink it. His words were pregnant with the power of the Ancient of Days. How marvelous are the feet of those who bring good news!

"Rise up!" Fr. Mike exclaimed. "We need to be known as people of faith. Blessed are those who have not seen, yet believe. God does what He pleases. He makes a way for us in the wilderness, when we believe God, He moves through us. Take God out of the box!

Be willing to be used. Ask God, 'What do you want me to do today?' When you live in His name, it will energize you! Take what you, have and take it to the streets. This is breaking lose all over the world. Watch for dreams and visions. Revival is here!"

By the end of mass, Fr. Mike prayed over me again and said, "God is getting ready to bless you all so big that it is going to knock your socks off!"

Right after that, Mark and I both felt the floor shake beneath us. We asked at that time, "Lord, what does this mean?"

After mass, and people were leaving, it was decided for all to come back to our house for dessert and fellowship and prayer until midnight.

We spent midnight to midnight in prayer.

Amazing!

Even miraculous.

A POSSIBLE DREAM
(April 20th)

A word of knowledge came between 6 and 7 a.m., and it came in the form of a dream. I saw gold falling from Heaven all over me and another lady. It sparkled all over us, and we were joyfully happy. I wondered "Who is this sparkly lady?"

(April 14th, at a resource meeting for *Louisville Christian Writers*, a woman named Susan, president of *Women Who Write*, was in attendance. She took down the phone number for LCW.)

I showed up that Saturday at *WWW*. My topic of miracles did not fit in with the secular writers. Two days later, Susan, who had not been in attendance at that meeting, called me and gave me the phone number of the new organization she had just been introduced to. Susan did not realize it would come in so handy so quickly. Of course, I called.

Over the phone later that day, I met a wonderful woman that would generously influence my life. It was Louisville Christian Writer's President, Crystal Murray.

I left her a message with my name and phone number and within two hours, she called me back. During that period of time, Crystal had looked me up, looked up my books, and anything else she could find out about me. Armed with information and ready to talk, she called me back that afternoon.

Crystal started out all business. But within ten minutes, I knew I had found a friend.

Over the phone, Crystal was amazing! She knew

everything and all at once! Gifted, smart, whatever; I was a fan. And it seemed from what she said, after learning about my books and me, she soon became a fan of mine as well!

Crystal referred to herself as an empath. She asked if I knew what that was.

Her question brought back memories of a conversation held 30 years before. I had lunch with friends, and one of them spoke up and said, "Do you know you are an empath?" The only reference I had for that term at the time was the one on a popular science-fiction show of a lady empath who could feel other's feelings as deeply as her own. At the time, I replied, "Cool."

I smiled as I responded "Yes." I realized I had gifts of empathy and could feel others' emotions. I told Crystal that, other than myself, I had never known anyone else with that gift. It was nice to meet a sister. As we hung up, I looked forward to meeting her in person. We planned it for her next upcoming meeting of Louisville Christian Writers on May 12th.

MONETARY BLESSINGS
(April 23rd)

Some days, you just have to stop everything and clean. Spring cleaning is not called spring cleaning for nothing! By late afternoon, I was satisfied enough with my progress to sit down and write. Words were always beckoning me to paper. I knew it was old-fashioned, but one day, I reasoned, it would mean a lot to our sons.

Mark came home at dinnertime to a pleasant surprise, but also brought one in himself. We had received an unexpected check in the mail from our escrow account. It was $1,100.00 worth of monetary blessing.

Thank you Lord! Money in our house is always appreciated!

Mark came in again the next evening with more good financial news. Our house payment had dropped by over $100.00 a month. It looked like Karen's words were coming true right beneath our noses!

During that time, we were getting our little home ready to put on the market. We had the owner of a local carpet cleaning service come by to clean the carpets for us. He was such a nice man! We paid him to clean two rooms, and he was not satisfied with just two rooms.

"No! Look around!" He ended up cleaning a whole other room for free.

"Thank you, kind sir!"

By the end of that day, we got another check in

the mail. This time is was for $35.00. It was enough to pay for Mark's needed medications.

Even the tiniest details were being taken care of. I felt the path was being laid open for us, and all we had to do was walk into it. By then, we were giggling and wondering how long all this good fortune could or would go on.

Once again, $80.00 out of the blue.

One of our prescriptions had been filled wrong, and I took it back. Do you know it saved me another $8.00, and I got the better medication?

Icing on the cake—I got my first check for working in almost four years. $61.00 never looked so good!

Well, to celebrate our week of good fortune from the Lord, we decided to take Mom Peyron out to dinner to her favorite restaurant, Red Lobster® .

Hold onto your hats, dear readers. Three hours before we left to go out to dinner, we got in the mail, a $60.00 gift certificate for Red Lobster® .

I am not kidding! Don't you think that free food tasted even better?

Is there anything too small or too large that the Lord can't do? For us? For you?

And is there anything too small or too large you or I can do for him?

PEACE, BE STILL
(April 30th)

I recognized in my spirit, as my hands touched the door of the Harmony and Health in Corydon at 9:40 that morning, I was needed.

A lovely lady named Dianna, who waited on me, needed prayer for a situation, before 10 a.m. I had been called out to pray. And on their counter was a daily log, with my favorite verse in the whole Bible.

Psalm 46:10 *Be still and know that I am God.*

I fulfilled my role as an intercessor, and she blessed me with a discount on my product.

I believe, as a thank you from God for obeying; Tonini's Church Supply in Louisville, Kentucky, called for a renewal of my first book, and they wanted to see the proof of the second book to approve selling it as well. Thank you, Lord for kissing me on the head.

That night, I spent the night at Momma's. We were heading out early to go to Frankfort with my little brother Ron to take care of her retirement business. Back at home, our middle son, David called and talked to Mark for a long time. Mark got to be Dad for a while — without Mom calling any shots.

The door was once again opening on our relationship with him. David had gone through a struggle in his life and was finally coming out on the other side. He was ready to talk to us again.

Our prayers for him were being answered.
Peace, Son, peace.

STANDING ON THE WILL OF GOD
(May 3rd)

I awoke that morning to another word of knowledge. I heard a eulogy being prepared. To make the matter more apparent, later, a church member called with concern that our pastor was much worse. I did not know what to tell her. She wanted me to call his house, and see if she could go over and pray for him.

So, I called.

They had decided as a family, they were "standing on the will of God."

I was in total agreement, but around me were sorrowful hearts.

Fiat.
So be it.
Us too — the will of God.

TO HEAL THE BROKEN HEARTED
(May 4th)

Have you ever been in the right place at the right time, not for yourself, but for others, over and over again on the same day? It was a very interesting day and it went much like this...

It was mid-morning when I arrived at my little brother's house. I was doing book deliveries for *Miraculous Interventions II* in his area and stopped in to say hello.

Ron had just opened his mail and found out he had been laid off from his job. He greeted me this way, "Deb! I'm glad to see you! I'm going to be a full-time writer now."

"Wonderful! When did you make that decision?" I innocently asked.

"When I got the notice five minutes ago that I was laid off."

I hugged and consoled Ron as we spoke positively of his plans for their future. I could not stay all morning as I would have liked. I was due to meet a lady and hand-deliver her copies of my newest book. What I did not know at the time, I was again walking into a situation where I was greatly needed.

I arrived at Ray and Rae's to sorrowful faces. Just the day before, all was well, and we were looking forward to meeting.

Now tears were on their faces. Their beloved dog had died a few hours ago. Rae was practically inconsolable. What could I say?

God gave me these words in my heart, *"I have sent you to heal the broken hearted."*

"I got this." I spoke aloud.

I found the perfect words were the ones coming out of *their* mouths. I listened. I patted hands and wiped a few tears away from even myself. A family member had passed away. All I could think of was "I love you all and I am sorry for your loss." I met some of their children (they had 16 between them) and I got to read to them.

I was still on a deadline. I had to go to work that afternoon until close. On the way back home, I wondered after such a day, "What could be in store for me there?"

I entered work to be greeted by one of my favorite shift managers.

Annette was all smiles. Her personality was bigger than life. A buxom blond with a ready smile, she seemed glad to see me.

On Friday nights, we stayed pretty busy and all kinds made their way through our doors. I always greeted them with, "Good evening! Welcome to our store! Can I help you?"

As customers would leave, my last response to them was always, "God bless you."

In my head, Annette was always cheery and had no surface problems. By the end of that evening, I found out how wrong I was.

As we were closing up shop, Annette got very pensive and said to me, "Before you came, I hated my job. Now I look forward to work every day."

"Gee, thanks."

It showed me, once again, why God had me working at a dollar store for minimum wage. I was to console this lady and give her hope again.

By the end of the day, I had a clear insight on why I am on this Earth, "to heal the broken hearted."

Blessed be the name of the Lord.

Whose heart have you helped heal lately?

ICING ON THE CAKE
(May 5th)

Kisses from God can come in ways we aren't accustomed to seeing. Call it a verification of "you are on the right path." Keep going, keep coming to the Lord. And then, there's icing on the cake!

That was the way Mark and I felt when Fr. Mike called us and asked us to a Derby Party. Our friends, the Crosiers, were welcome to come too. Since we were not usually on people's "A" lists for Derby, but it was Fr. Mike and Patti who asked, we thought there just might be a blessing in it.

The party was held at a beautiful home in an upscale, well-established neighborhood. Larry and Marilynn, Mark and I traveled together. Marilynn had made a beautiful set of cake pops — bite size cakes on a stick with different flavored icings.

We were cordially greeted and ushered inside the beautiful, spacious home. Those at the party were very social as we all got acquainted with one another. My husband is wonderful at this kind of thing. I, myself, am a wallflower of a sort — not particularly outgoing. It's once I get to know people that it's hard to shut me up! (This is your one and only warning!)

It was soon time for the race to begin. The people there had a draw pot going around the room for others to pick a horse and put money in for the winner. This kind of game is a long-standing tradition all over Kentuckiana for the Kentucky Derby. Mark smiled and put in the only money we had. I thought to myself, "There goes our grocery money—keep smiling and maybe they won't know." We knew nothing about the two horses' names we had drawn.

"And they're off!" The announcer started his commentary as the horses ran around the track. What did we know? Mark and I cheered for them all! We had no clue whose was whose much less whose was ours! We clapped our hands when the winner crossed the wire.

"Whose horse won?" We asked.

"**Yours.**"

"**Ours?!**"

We could hardly believe it! Nobody else could either. We left their home with six times more grocery money than we had come in with. God knew.

The icing on that sweet cake came a little later. That Derby Party turned into a two and a half hour church service with prayers, praise, singing and the joy of the Lord! Who knew?

God knew.

*** Please note again, this story is not to condone gambling. But this author also knows God can send little kisses, like extra grocery money, any way He sees fit!*

MARY'S HEART
(May 8th)

All during the process of writing these books, I wondered if I was to become a pastor myself. So many of my friends were clerics. I talked it over with several of them, and they offered to write me letters for ordination—which they all did and I have on file—somewhere.

Then I spoke with Mary Smith, my publisher and dearest friend for over 20 years. Mary grew quiet and had no response, but I knew she would pray long and hard about what I was considering.

The next time she and I were together for a meeting, Mary spoke from her heart.

"Debbie, God has called you to be an evangelist and a messenger. But, if you become a protestant minister, you will lose the ear of over one billion Catholics worldwide. Be happy being what He made you—evangelist and author."

I allowed her words to settle into my heart and head. Slowly, I responded, "Of course, you are right. Thank you for listening to the Lord and then telling me."

All my pastor friends agreed. Mary had indeed heard from the Lord. I was grateful the Lord had sent her to speak to me.

Do you listen when God sends messengers to you too?

FROM DYING TO LIFE
(May 11th)

We received a call from Brother Bill that our pastor was soon to go home to be with the Lord. Fred's kidneys were failing. We called out to many people in our prayer chain to pray for him and his family.

When I called Fr. Mike, he had just been thinking about us. The Lord had put us on his heart. He said, "Deb, I'm so glad you called. This morning, God showed me something. I saw helper angels being sent for you and Mark right now."

"Thank you Father Mike."

I asked him for prayers for our pastor and his family. Could that have been what the angels were for?

That evening, when Mark arrived home from work, he brought in several rolled up papers.

"What are those?"

Nonchalantly, he replied, "The blueprints for our new home."

I squealed just before I kissed him!

Mark smiled as he unrolled them, one by one. We sat and looked at each detail as if it were already built. At the time, we had no idea the project would still be another year out.

LOUISVILLE CHRISTIAN WRITERS
(May 12th)

Mary and I attended our first Louisville Christian Writers meeting that evening. We arrived almost on time. I brought some of my books as Crystal had suggested.

LCW always opened with a prayer from one of the members. Crystal asked the Lord for a name of who should pray, then asked that person to open the meeting. Next, Crystal's husband, David recited scripture and gave a small sermon on it. For a quiet man, David became very animated when he spoke on the word of the Lord!

Association business was next in order, and anyone who had questions for Crystal, she would answer to the best of her ability. Then she introduced their guest speaker, Maureen Morehead, Poet Laureate for the state of Kentucky. Maureen gave wonderful examples and notes about poetry in general and how to get started writing.

Maureen read from several of her books, and we all got to try our hand at poetry.

After the meeting, a few people came up and asked who we were. Mary and I introduced ourselves, and a few of my books were sold that evening. Mary and I could hardly wait for the next meeting.

When I arrived home, I told Mark about the wonderful couple that had come into my life!

What would be next?

HAPPY MOTHER'S DAY!
(May 13th)

After a jam-packed two days, Mother's Day stayed the same course—busy on top of busy!

We spent the night at Mom (Betty) Peyron's to make it a day of blessings. I awoke to the sound of my husband preparing breakfast for Mom and myself. I thought what a sweetie I had married—and a good cook, I might add. We didn't even have to do the dishes. And, Mark wasn't the only man that cooked for me. Ben, our oldest son, was on track to make us lunch. His duplex was the next stop of our day together.

Before we left Betty's for lunch, Mark and I prayed over Betty for her stomach distress. We laid hands on her, and she said she felt heat inside. She felt markedly better before we got out the door! We would see her again later in the day for dinner.

Mark and I arrived at Ben's to a buffet set up and a family movie at the ready. We were always greeted with warm hugs and kisses from our oldest son. Enjoyable conversations were held. We caught up on lives and stories were shared. The movie was great fun, (Disney®, of course.) and before long, we headed back to Mom's for a light meal. Our youngest son Andy called me twice from work with loving wishes.

That evening, we met David and his girlfriend at the movies. The last of our sons to visit, I got to sit next to him and had an enjoyable time. I was glad that, the next day, all I had to do was go to work! A regular day; every once in a while, I need one of those.

I'M ALIVE!
(May 15th)

I awoke with a great start! My heart pounded in my chest! My eyes were wide open, and alert. I sat straight up in bed at the sound of the familiar voice as it shouted with awe.

"I'm alive!"

I knew without a doubt, our pastor had just moved from our three-dimensional world to a world with no limitations. Fred had gone to a world that he was so fond of saying, "under the spout where the glory pours out!"

That same morning, I heard from Pastor Ivie Dennis. Ivie called to tell me she had seen it all happen in her spirit. She saw Fred pass from this life to the next. Of course she had.

Later that day, the news was verified by different church members that called our house. But Ivie and I, already knew.

It was time to go to work. I called friends for provisions to send for his family that would come back to our area.

A local church was most gracious to hold services and agreed to supply a good portion of the meal.

BUSY DAYS AHEAD
(May 16th)

Funerals take organization. The family, along with the church, had all that in order. Funeral food also takes organization. Calls were made back and forth from one church member's house to another.

"What are you bringing?"

Women outside of our church group volunteered to make food, and friends and family alike pitched in.

This was our mission:

"To boldly make sure no mouth was left unfed."

"Could you make a little extra to send back to the house with the widow?"

"Surely, we could."

"GET IT RIGHT!"
(May 17th)

Mary and I worked all day long on *Miraculous Interventions I and II.* Since we had met Crystal, we realized the writing of the stories needed a little tweaking. We had to make sure all the paragraphs were in agreement with each other.

I asked the Lord, "When are you going to bless this work?"

I heard from God, "**Get it right**."

"Working on it Lord. We're working on it."

Are you working on getting it right too?

WEARY TO THE BONE
(May 18th)

I cooked all day until time to go to work late that afternoon. Even then, at the end of my shift, my day was not over. There was still another function to attend. With fatigue that came on fast, I drove over to our dear friends' house for dinner and to help clean up from their Bible study earlier that evening.

Mark met me at the door with a hug. Something in his eyes didn't look right. I attributed it to the loss of our pastor.

The elderly gentleman who had given the gospel message that night had stayed until I got there to give the message again to me and my husband. The Lord had given him the message personally, and he wanted to share it with us. He spoke as I sat with my meal in my lap.

The pastor had spoken on despair. I knew immediately it was for us. Yet at the time I did not know the whole reason why.

"Don't let satan's attacks discourage you! Don't give in to it." He balanced it with scripture and spoke of promises. We left their home after midnight and felt uplifted.

After Mark and I arrived home and got ready for bed, Mark pulled out a letter from the people we thought were just days away from starting our new home. They would not take our appeal with the prices we sent to them. And the place I had just gone to work for would not count as income. It actually hurt us. They looked at it as just a menial job. It was not in the field I had trained for. It was not a position consistent with my education.

It read, "You are denied."

Shock slowly settled over me. I apologized to my husband, and he to me. Hot tears ran down our cheeks. If it had not been for the gospel message against despair, given directly to us that evening, we would have given up. Instead, we went to bed and prayed ourselves to sleep.

The day ahead was not to be any easier.
The troubles kept coming from all sides.

FUNERAL FOR A FRIEND
(May 19th)

Mark and I sighed heavily as we got up early that morning to prepare for Pastor Frederick Schuppert's funeral. We imagined how his dear wife, Jeanne, and their family were doing. Prayers went up for all of us.

Everything went beautifully. If God allowed Fred one last glimpse of those he loved here on this Earth, I am sure Fred was very well pleased. The eulogy was given by a local pastor Fred had befriended while in the hospital. Their church welcomed us with open arms and more food than we could all eat.

One last time, our truck was used in service for Pastor Fred. Mark and I had the honor of hauling Fred's flowers from the funeral home to the church and back to Jeanne's.

Now, this is just this author's opinion. I feel Fred is not resting in peace. Surely God did not call him up early just to have him rest! Not Fred - but to be of greater service in the Heavens by God Himself? That I would believe. After all, it was God that called Fred a prophet with a mantle. The only thing that changed was the location of his duty.

By three that afternoon, we were back home to once again less-than-fortunate news. We had received a card in the mail from a lady I had known since the boys were very small. When my hands touched the card in the envelope, I knew her husband, Stanley, had died. Dorothy apologized for having sent us notice five months late. Stanley had gone to be with the Lord back at Christmas.

There was a message on our recorder. It was Mary Smith, who was due to come over and meet with me. Her old, white, barely-held-together-with-duct -tape car, had also finally seen its last day. Mark went and picked her up in my car.

Later on that evening, as we worked on the last revision, Mary told us of trouble in her household. One of her daughter's marriages had failed. Of course, as mothers, we take the success and failures of our children personally. Hugs and reassurances of better days to come were given. We then told Mary our news about the loss of our home construction financing, the loss of our pastor and of our dear old friend, Stanley. Hugs and reassurances came back to us.

I prayed that night for God to give Mary a car for half the price, just as He had done for me.

WEARY-- PART II
(May 20th)

It had been a long week. Sorrows had trudged their way through our hearts. Mark and I were glad to be in the house of the Lord at Iona, even with heavy hearts.

Shortly after the mass had started, I could not contain my sorrow anymore. I went to the back of the church and cried. My heart was breaking. I felt inconsolable and shaken. I knew we were both hurting on all sides.

Father Mike and his wife Patti had compassion on us. They both started speaking life to us! Words of knowledge came down from other church members too. I felt a word of knowledge come over me, "The joy of the Lord is upon you!"

Father Mike stated, "There is a new day of restoration coming down upon you."

Patti joined in, "Enter in by faith. Manage all doubts and unbelief! Join Heaven with your brothers and sisters. Sing praise to the King! Be worthy! You are freed from sin and its yoke. The curtain has been rent. Enter into God's presence."

Deacon Paula stepped forward, "I see a blue gray thread being woven by God. It is a beautiful tapestry for you both. Stop worrying! God is working everything out. In everything praise the Lord! He alone has the power to save."

Father Mike said, "When we grumble or complain, we set up the enemy's camp. Instead, be thankful. It creates new wine. Be bold! Have a thankful heart."

"Be careful of persecutors. Look for angels, signs and wonders. This is the glory realm. We are seated with Christ in Heavenly places. We are supernatural beings with dreams and visions. They translate up like Philip—when we want what God wants! Angels will assist the heirs of salvation."

Father Mike told the church that two prosperity angels had been to see them that very week. By then, Father Mike was on a roll. The Holy Spirit had taken over and words of wisdom came for all of us. "Get God out of the box. He just might bless you. How? Do your part. Believe He is a rewarder who rewards His children—those who diligently seek Him."

Then God spoke through Fr. Mike, *"Don't you know who I Am?"*

He went on, "Jesus has been appealing to Muslim Imam Leaders through the supernatural realm. Exercise your spiritual senses. See, taste and touch the Lord—then miracles will happen! When you allow God to be God, anything can happen. All is possible! Spend time with the Lord. What a resource, power and anointing He is! We are called to walk in the supernatural. Weep before God for others. It is in the glory realm that the angels are released. Pray for our angels on assignments. Speak about the glory and it comes."

A breath taken, a minute for the priest to gather more thoughts, and Mike went on, "Watch your words create an atmosphere. It is not hard. Just speak it out. Speak what you want, and angels will attend to you when what you want lines up with what God wants. Then it comes quickly! Angels bring the message of "I care" from God. Praise until the glory comes, and then stand with the Lord. Watch signs, wonders, miracles and clouds of glory move. New heights will be achieved. Participate and be in agreement with Heaven. Believe the word of God! God will fill you up so you have more to give away. "

"There is no mountain so tall, He cannot move it.
Sorrow so deep He can't soothe it.
He will carry you."
Father Mike quoted scripture, "Come, all who are weary, and I will give you rest."
At the end of the mass, this was said for our benefit.
"Someone is worrying. Stop! Don't doubt! I have already taken care of it."

The last word of knowledge for us was again about the thread and the tapestry. It would all come together.
Now, if we could only believe!
At one point, I smelled the fragrance of God three times in a row. Then I went into a vision. I saw me being taken up in a chariot.
I said, "Lord! Show us what to do that pleases You most. Stay or go?"
The reply to this eager request?
Wait.
Wait on God.
So be it.

TO THE RESCUE!
(May 21st)

Early that morning, our son Benjamin called.

"Hi, Momma! I love ya!"

"Hi, Son. I love you too! What's going on?"

"Momma, there is a family here at the hospital with a daughter who is actively dying. They have called out for prayer. Her name is Bonnie."

"I'm on it Son!"

"I knew you would be! Thanks Momma."

"Keep me informed."

"I will."

Immediately after I got off the phone, I asked God who He wanted me to pray with over this. The answer came quick.

"Bill Mauck!"

I called Brother Bill right away. Of course, he picked up his phone.

"Bill! It's Debbie Peyron. Our son Ben just called about a young lady, Bonnie, who is actively dying right now! Her family has called out for prayer. I asked God who I should pray with, and He said you."

Bill jumped in with both feet! "Okay, Debbie! That's good enough for me."

"Please lead us."

"Dear Father in Heaven, we ask that You shore up Bonnie's heart. Your word says that all we ask in Jesus' name will be granted. Your ear is not deaf to our prayers. We are in agreement that with Jesus, she will live and not die! What is bound on Earth is bound in Heaven. Lord, we bind in Jesus' name, the Spirit of death that hovers over her and ask that instead the

Spirit of life enter her. We thank you Lord, that this will be done speedily, and even the doctors will call it a miracle! In Jesus' holy name, amen."

"Amen! Thank you, Bill!"

"Whew, Deb! Did you feel Holy Spirit bumps? I believe she is being healed right now!"

"Yes, I felt them too! Let's look for the good report."

THE 28 CENT JESUS
(May 24th)

I had been at my new job almost six weeks and had gotten to know some of the regular customers. My boss was very tolerant as I blessed each person in my line as they left the building. I tried to treat everyone the same — even the lady who was short on her balance.

"I'm short 28 cents."

"Oh, hold on! I believe I have change in my purse. I'll look." I offered assistance.

"No! You don't have to do that. I can put something back."

"But you need everything you're buying." I countered. "I don't mind. What would Jesus do?"

I looked in my change purse, and there was exactly 28 cents. My God of just enough had come through again!

That was when she looked at me and said, "I see Jesus in you."

That sweet lamb saw Jesus in me just because I gave her 28 cents. All I did was fill a small need.

After she left, I cried. I talked to the Lord, "Lord, I just treated her like she was one of my kids, the same way you do us, Lord. And she saw You in me." How humbled I was.

I got home after 9:30 that night. It was on my heart to call Andy. It wouldn't leave me. I called, but, before I could speak any words, I heard him crying! He had broken up with a girl for the last time. He was tired and couldn't take the rough relationship anymore. We offered to come over right away, but he told us no. Just please pray for him!

As Mark and I prayed for Andy's heart to mend quickly, we received a call from Ben, our oldest son. He had a praise report for us! And we could sure use one.

"Go ahead, Son."

"Do you remember the young lady I had you pray for a couple of days ago? The one that was an hour from death?"

"Yes."

"She is still alive and getting better! Please keep praying for her!"

We told Ben we were in the middle of prayers when he called. We would add her to our nightly prayer chain, and prayers of thanks for Bonnie's healing!

PRAISE REPORTS GALORE
(May 25th)

Have you ever felt inundated by needs for yourself or others? You put up prayers continuously and then wait for the praise reports to come in.

Then, when you think you can't take anymore, all of a sudden it is as if a spiritual dam has broken. Prayers are answered, burdens are lifted and made light, and peace abounds. Just like on this day...

Phone calls started early that morning and drifted in though out the day.

Our brother in Christ, Bill Mauck, who is an early riser, called with the first good news.

"Good morning, Sister Debbie! If you have a few minutes, I have a praise report for you."

"Of course I have time for a praise report! Please go ahead."

"I have had a growth on me, and I have been praying for it to die and be removed from me. This morning it did! It fell right off!" Triumph was in the air.

"Yay! That's wonderful, Bill. I'm happy for you."

"I just want to give God the glory for answering my prayer."

"Amen! I believe with you."

I hung up the phone and thought what a nice start to the day that was.

A little later, I received another call from Ben, to keep praying for the young lady at his hospital. Things were looking very hopeful and the family was giving God the glory.

Later that afternoon, Andy, our youngest called. What a word from God he had to tell us!

God had sent angels through the night to comfort our son in his hour of need. The peace of Jesus confounded the ache in his heart and sent it away. Andy gave God the glory for his healing. Then Andy spoke of prophets and the archangels and deep things of God.

From Andy, it did not surprise me one bit.

By that evening, Andy got a little kiss from Heaven. His brother, David, our middle son, offered him a free upgrade for his phone.

THE UNKNOWN ANGEL
(May 26th)

A friend came into the store where I worked. She had a bad back. Cheryl couldn't stand up straight. She depended on the cart to hold her up as she walked the aisles.

In between customers, one of my responsibilities was to put back merchandise people didn't want. I walked up and down the aisles until my mission was accomplished. At the time, I did not realize I was but a few minutes away from my real mission for the day.

I was walking up behind Cheryl, on the way back to the register. She was hunched over her basket picking up a few things from the store. As I walked up to her, I knew in my spirit exactly what to do. I touched her back and started to pray in tongues.

"Ooohhhh.....!" Fire fell.

The Holy Spirit entered the situation. Cheryl stood straight up with no pain!

"What do I do?!" She cried out.

I answered her with a big smile, "Raise your hand and say thank you Lord."

Cheryl did just that. She left the store with praise and thanksgiving on her lips!

A while later, another lady came in the store; a woman unknown to me. As I checked her out, I said to her, "God bless you."

The unknown angel replied with a prophesy, "God be good to you and bless you every day of your life."

I stopped in my tracks and said, "I believe you, and I receive this message."

God never forgets the desires of our hearts.
Blessed be the name of the Lord.
What other is there that is like our God?
None, I say.

I did find out later that Cheryl's pain came back.
Keep her in your prayers.

LADY IN BLUE
(May 28th)

My husband's and my fathers served in World War II, as did many of the fathers of the "sandwich" generation. That is, those of us who help our children and our parents. This is a tribute to Daniel Peyron and Earl Aubrey.

Daniel Louis Peyron was born in 1925. Earl Gilbert Aubrey was born one day behind him in 1926. That made both of them eligible for the draft on different fronts. Daniel was sent to the European Front and Earl was sent to the Pacific Front. Timing was everything.

The war on the European Front was still going hot and heavy when Daniel set foot on the shores of France and Italy. It was up close and personal. His father was originally from France, near the Alps. It was probably Divine Providence that sent him back to his original homeland to help defend it and kept him safe. When Daniel and his troops landed on the beach in France, there wasn't an enemy to be seen. First miracle. So, they started their march towards Italy. While on their way, they found a burro along the roadside. They were able to coax it with food, and when they ran out of that, cigarettes (eaten, not smoked), to carry a load of their supplies on its back. Second miracle. When they arrived in Italy, they encountered the Germans and took on casualties. Daniel was wounded, but not mortally. Third miracle. He was not captured and not mortally wounded. He took shrapnel in his left knee and shoulder.

Dan was shipped to a hospital in England for a long recovery. He was awarded a purple heart, and I thank him for his service for our country.

As the war on the European front wound down, things heated up on the Pacific Front. After the Atomic bombs were dropped and peace declared, we were still a large presence over in Japan and the Philippines. That was where my Dad, Earl, came in. He was drafted and sent over as an MP — Military Police.

If I sit and calm my mind, I can still recall his stories of the events of that time. One of Dad's main orders was to ride the trains through that area. It was his duty to stop the Japanese from throwing the Filipinos off the moving trains! It sounded like a pretty important job to me and my little brother when we were seven and nine years old, sitting around the kitchen table on a Saturday afternoon waiting for Momma to come back from the beauty parlor.

Earl and Daniel are buried in different Catholic cemeteries across the Ohio River from each other — which is what brought us to this story.

Mark and I were at my dad's burial plot saying a prayer when Mark saw her.

Standing a short distance from us was a lady with a blue mist all around her — and then she was gone!

"Did you see that lady in the blue mist?!" Mark said excitedly.

My head had been lowered in prayer. I knew I

had missed a supernatural event!

"Nnnooooo!!" I cried out with a longing for the missed vision.

But that night, I had a dream.

It was of a friend who had passed long ago, Ralph Sampson, sent with a comforting word to let me know I was not forgotten. Our circumstances of desiring a home on our land were still in consideration and progress.

"Don't be afraid."

If only, he had not said "if" in my dream.

THE MESSAGE
(May 29th)

No matter how hard we tried to go through banks, we could not catch one break. Our own bank wanted $10,000.00 down to start a home construction loan. We could not come up with all the money requested.

It didn't surprise my good friend and sister in Christ Jesus, Pastor Ivie Dennis. She had been saying for four years, God was going to send us a private lender, just like He did for her and her son, DJ.

I have to admit, we didn't know anyone with that kind of money that would loan it to us; at least at that time. I thought it would be impossible for her prophesy to come true, yet I knew it would take a miracle. Even though Ivie told me to look to God for the funds, I tried over and over with different banks in our local area. Her message had not gotten through to me.

That particular evening, toward the end of May, our good friend Jeremy Ward came over to assess how much our home was worth and whether or not he could sell it. Jeremy's news was mixed. Our home would appraise at $93,000.00 with no problem. But he could not sell it.

"Why?" we asked.

"You can't sell it for a year, or you have to pay back the $8,000.00 you got when you bought it. And, even if you wait and I sell it, it will take most of your equity." He replied.

Big road block. Sigh. "Oh."

When Jeremy left, I went straight to God and asked, "What are we going to do now? Because if this house doesn't sell, I don't know what we will do!"

Immediately, the answer came like a bolt of lightning! God thundered a reply,

"I have already sold your home."

One would think I would have been very grateful to have heard from the Almighty; that He was ahead of us and for us. Not so much. I was not in a calm, happy mood. I was in my stubborn, unbelieving-self mood. And it came out in my reply. Sometimes, I don't even like standing next to me for fear of lightning!

"Well, you better produce them quick because I don't know where to look!"

100TH SHEEP
(May 30th)

While I worked that afternoon and evening, my husband was holding a Bible study at our home. It was our first official Bible study for people from our home church. I was very disappointed that I couldn't be there, but God knows our hearts desire and fulfills them in His time.

Many blessed people came through my checkout line at work that evening. Some were prophetic and prayed over me, while I stood in for others that were in need of prayer and prayed for them. I gave out several cards for my books and where to find them, and for my publisher, Mary Dow Smith; and some for wellness care.

Before I knew it, the day's work was over and I was off. I was concerned the Bible study would be over — but when I arrived, only part of it was. The singing, praise reports and prayer requests had all been done. They had dismissed and gone into the kitchen for coffee, cake and fellowship. I thought I had missed the evening's services altogether. After all, it was way past 9:30 p.m.

When I came into the kitchen, I was greeted with warm hugs and a kiss from my husband. They got me coffee and dessert and a chair. I was told to "take a load off" while Brother Bill caught me up on the evening's progress.

Then, all very naturally, the rest of the evening took a turn. Instead of the evening winding down from a Bible study, it ramped up! The conversation about the deep things of God started in the kitchen. We adjourned to the living room, and people stayed until 2 a.m.! I hadn't missed it at all! God had saved the best revelations and teaching for my arrival. The Holy Spirit had kept the best for last, just like in the Bible when Jesus and His mother, Mary, went to the wedding at Cana of Galilee. The best wine was saved for last.

The real reason we were all there was to search God out and find truth through Scripture and interpretation. How good God was that He saved it all until the 100th sheep (that was me) could be with all the others and glean from the real teaching of the Holy Spirit.

NOTHING BUT RAIN!
(May 31st)

While I had been at work the night before, I was very worried about a coming storm in our area. Tornadic activity was headed our way. It was wreaking havoc all across the west and aiming straight for us!

God knew my heart and sent two sets of people to tell me everything was going to be okay.

"Have no fear."

They said that no matter what the people on the television said, it would be nothing but rain.

Well, there was a party scheduled that day at Mark's sister's house. I called and asked Sandy if we could spend the night instead of driving home in bad weather. Of course the answer was, "Yes."

We packed up overnight bags much to my husband's disapproving "sigh." He had no fear of storms or tornadoes.

The party went well, and as nighttime approached, so did the storms. We hunkered down in the basement. We watched the front roll in on Hunter's "supersized" television. Prayers started up. Just as I had been told the day before, the weather dissolved before our very eyes as it hit the edges of our county. Yes, there had been nothing to fear because it was nothing but rain!

Do you see how my flesh and spirit were at odds with each other? If my faith were as a mustard seed, as it should be all the time, I could have had no worry in that situation.

How many times must God show me before hand,
"things unseen," before I will believe Him every time?
Seventy times seven?

Is this the same for any of you?
Or all of us?
Only God knows.

EARS TO HEAR
(June 2nd)

The morning was spent doing a good deed for someone. It had gotten to be a regular routine almost each and every day. But today, jealously reared its ugly head between family members, I was left crying and with a sore heart.

Shortly after I arrived back home, my telephone rang. God purposed Fr. Mike to call and pray for me. The good pastor had a message to convey. Father Mike acted as an angel of mercy for me in obedience to God. Just as Jesus was King of the angels of mercy, as we ourselves are called to be for each other, even if all we are called to be is a listening ear.

In the afternoon, Mark and I met with friend to go to dinner with them. Conversation was held, and dinner was consumed. Talk eventually came around to Scripture and what a history our Bible had behind it.

I sat and listened to several learned men discuss biblical history, and who did what in each century; one of my favorite subjects.

At one point in the conversation, there was a pause. No one could remember the name of one of the primary translators in a certain century.

As the room grew quiet, while the male brains were considering answers, quietly within me, I asked the Lord for the answer. In less than a minute, the correct answer dropped into my head and out of my mouth.

"Wycliffe!" I exclaimed.

The men in the room, with wide eyes, nodded their heads in agreement. I smiled. Mark smiled his approval at his little sweetie.

Wasn't it funny how it happened? I knew better than to ask my brain. I asked the one that made my brain! It just goes to show you, if the subject is God and His word, He Himself will get involved in the conversation.

If ... we have ears to hear.

SOLD
(June 3rd)

I was very excited! My new friends, Crystal and David Murray, were coming for dinner. They brought Crystal's sister who was visiting from Arizona for the summer. Crystal felt prayer with us would help mend her sister's worsening physical condition.

When they arrived, true to what Crystal had said, they had to help her sister into our home. She was too weak to walk by herself.

Before I served dinner, we sat Candie down in a chair. I got out my anointing oil, and all four of us surrounded her with prayers of health and strength. As the minutes rolled by, Candie felt better.

I had made a chicken pot pie and fruit cobbler for dessert. Dinner went well, and the conversation was lively, sprinkled with intermittent laughter. For the first time in months, Candie was able to eat her whole meal. Everyone at the table was elated!

Mark and I got up and cleared the table to bring dessert dishes in for everyone. While we were away from the table, Candie turned to her sister, Crystal and said, "This house would be perfect for you."

Crystal responded, "I felt the same way when I walked through the door. I can't say anything serious without talking to David."**

The next week, I called Crystal to confirm with her if they really wanted to buy our home.

Crystal talked to David who said he would buy it if he knew for sure it was God's will.

As we got to know the Murray's over the next several months, her husband David questioned me several times about whether this was a God incident.

"Yes. I'm sure of it."

"How?"

The fruit was apparent to me. First, I had heard with my own ears ten days after we moved in, "*Bigger.*" Then again, six months later, I heard it again with my ears, from an unseen presence. I almost packed us up then and there, but I waited for a third confirmation.

When Crystal walked through the front door she said it felt like it could be her home. That was confirmation enough for me. And then there were all the physical signs that told us we were in their home after all.

For example, the sinks that were all too low for me, were just the right height for her. The laundry room cabinets that I hit my head on with regularity, Crystal cleared with ease. And we had the same type of faucets Crystal had just installed in her Louisville house, so she felt like God was saying He had already put in her favorite faucets for her!

That first night we ate together, Crystal already knew in her spirit it was her home. All she had to do was figure a way to tell the family she sat across the table from that we were living in her house!

** Sometimes, when I see in the Spirit, I cannot tell that I am not seeing in the flesh. Crystal and I saw what happened differently. What I saw, I knew was confirmation from what the Lord had already told me.

This is what I saw in the Spirit: Mark and I walked

235

back into the dining room with dessert dishes in hand to give out. Crystal smiled as she addressed us, "Take down your sign. We're buying your house. By the way, how much do you want for it?" She was still smiling and did not appear to be kidding.

We were stunned! Stopped in our own tracks! Mark and I looked at each other as I spoke, "Well, it was just appraised at $93,000.00. But, we like to be a blessing as well as receive a blessing. Would $90,000.00 be all right with you?" I smiled back hesitantly.

Crystal nodded. She knew God was at work!

Confirmed once again.

David and Crystal moved in less than a year later. He did this in obedience to a call others had heard, and he trusted. God knew David's heart and sent him confirmation that it was indeed his home.

One day, while David was outside weedeating his new front lawn, he noticed there were numbers on the fire hydrant. He bent down and read "123."

David sat back on his knees and remembered, almost all the years he was in the military, he was in the "123rd Armor." Only to him would this have meant something.

How many times had we moved in obedience to God's command?

"Go buy land." "Build." "Sell to a missionary." "Sell to the Murrays." We ached for our own happily ever after. All through the year 2012, we asked God, "Where is ours?" We had no idea it would be another year and a half of testing our faith.

QUEEN ANNIE FRANCES
(June 4th)

Being dethroned is an uncomfortable experience at *best*, uh, Bill Best, that is. After all it's entirely his fault, on how it all came about. But I'm way ahead of the story. Let's start at the beginning, shall we?

Bill's father died when he was very young. He was raised by his grandfather who was an architect. That was how Bill became an architect and builder. He may be rough as a cob but the finest kind still.

He and his wife were high school sweethearts. Tammy was Mark's (my husband's) little sister Sandra's best friend all through school. When we decided to build our first home on Mathis Road, we were led by friends to Bill, who had just built their home. Bill's bid was very reasonable, and he was so easy to work with. Besides, he did an excellent job!

Due to circumstances beyond our control (2008 recession, my job gone and a second mortgage due to an injury) we sold our beloved home. We bought the land behind it, and waited for better to come along.

Four years later, things did indeed look up. So it seemed to us, the stars aligned, God nodded His celestial head, and once again we made the trip back and forth to Laconia to see "our brother" about constructing another home for us.

When we met for our first home, we had no idea what we wanted. We started from scratch. This time, we were ahead of the game. Mark had been ordering a certain magazine for two years. He just knew our next home layout would be in their pages somewhere-and they were. We rearranged the second floor to accommodate a bedroom for each of our sons. We handed over our plans and agreed to meet two weeks later.

The eagerly awaited date arrived. As we sat with Bill in his dining room, we heard unfamiliar noises coming from his living room couch. New puppies had just been born. Would we like to see them?

"Sure!"

We walked quietly over, and Tammy lifted a pillow up. There laid a momma and four little, brand new puppies. Two were all curly-haired and wiggly. The other two were different; almost premature. One was a very small, solid black puppy who moved about weakly. The last one, so small it did not move at all.

Four more weeks went by as we met a couple more times to gather our estimates and see if we could make budget and get our project off the ground. We were working with a bank despite Pastor Ivie's misgivings. Everything looked good to go to start our home that summer (which moved into fall.)

While we were doing a final check of expenses and of where everything was to go, Bill and Tammy's girls walked up with the two curly-haired puppies in hand. They were so cute! One had already been assigned to a new owner, but the other one had not. Brooke and Britney smiled at us.

"No thanks!" I cried. "We've only had a house to ourselves for four years. We are not on the market for a puppy." Mark nodded his head in agreement.

Then Bill said something interesting.

"There's another one in this bunch. She's real small and skittish. She hides. Girls, go see if you can find her." Obedient to their father, they went to look for the last puppy.

A few minutes later, Brooke came back holding something small and black in her hands. As she opened up her hands, I turned to see what she had. Instant knowledge entered my brain on several levels. I gasped.

"Oh! She's beautiful! She's just beautiful."

Mark immediately said, "No!"

"I think I shall name her Annie; Annie Frances."

"No way!" Mark sounded a little more frantic.

I smiled. I knew she was mine. The instant knowledge I had received was what I had been promised a long time ago.

After I had my three sons, I felt strongly in my spirit that there was a little girl in Heaven waiting to be born to me. When Mark and I couldn't have any children of our own, I wondered what would become of the little girl that was supposed to be mine. Time passed, and I gave it little thought until the instant I saw that precious little puppy. In her was my promised one.

Mark continued talking as they let me hold her. "Are you out of your mind? We're going to be building a home! We don't have any time for a puppy!"

I held her, gently pulling her up to my face. I kissed her on her head, and she kissed me back on my nose.

Contract signed.

"Oh honey! She loves me! Here, hold her."

I handed Annie to Mark who promptly put her on the floor. I was devastated and started to cry. Mark looked to Bill for help. Tammy came around the corner to see what the fuss was about.

Smiling, Bill said, "Debbie's made a new friend."

They nodded their approval. Mark hung his head low and sighed.

I pleaded, "Just think about it Honey! Please, Bill, don't give Annie away to anyone else!"

Four more weeks went by. Every time Bill's family came by my store, I asked about Annie.

"Is Annie doing okay? Are you calling her Annie so she will know her name? Are you working with her to go potty outside?" All the answers were affirmative.

I cornered them one afternoon in late May and said, "Listen to me. If I can talk my husband into a $200,000.00 home, I can talk him into a two-pound puppy!" The word got back to Bill, who in turn called Mark. What I did not know was that they were all keeping a secret from me. Mark had already agreed on a pick-up date. He was going to surprise me with her. They were all in on it. Their Grandma almost let the secret slip once.

On a Monday night while at work, I tried to call my husband on our home phone and then his cellular phone. No answer.

"Hmmmm..."

After work, I walked into our home and called for my husband. Mark called back from our bedroom. I went in, and he was smiling so sweetly, laying on our bed. I wondered if I had missed a memo about a date night. Then he lifted his hand up.

There on our bed was my Annie! I squealed with delight! Her tiny little tail wiggled her entire body! She weighed less than one pound and was only eight inches long. Her first night with us was spent sleeping on Mark's tee-shirt in a laundry basket.

In my telling time, early the next morning, I dreamed a foretelling:

We were all in bed asleep. Annie was bigger and sleeping between us on our pillows. She sat up and said to me, "Mommy, I'm sick." Then I woke up.

I knew immediately, Annie would be mine for a season only. I vowed to make her the happiest and best- loved baby on the planet.

And that was how Annie got the nickname "Queenie."

That was when I became dethroned.

"Ra"

Now, whatever I did, I always had company. Annie was a very good girl. From the time we got her, she only made booboo's five times total. She was a dream to potty train. To me, she was a dream period. Soon, Mark loved her as much as I did. Annie became his little girl too.

When I had to work, Mark took her with him. The first day I took Annie to Mark's work, he sat her on a towel on top of his bench where she laid comfortably. At less than a pound, she fit quite well there. The girls at work loved her immediately! They called up the steps to Jim, their boss, to come and see the new employee! Jim's own Chloe visited Albin's quite frequently. Now she could have a playmate.

Jim came down the steps saying, "Well, let's get a look at her. Where is she?"

"On Mark's bench."

Jim turned the corner to Mark's bench area and exclaimed, "Oh my goodness! She's so tiny! She's precious! Oh yes, she can stay with us!"

Contract signed.

I called the boys, family and friends to let them know we had a new family member. Everyone said she could come over, as long as we brought a carrier to keep her in. All each person had to do was take one look at her, and they would cry, "Please let me hold her! Don't put her back in the carrier!"

Queen Annie Frances Peyron was her own

Good Will Ambassador. She had her own favorite people too. She loved Grandma Peyron and Grandma loved her. Uncle David and Aunt Crystal were her other besties.

Contract signed.

All our boys came around to meet Annie. They too, instantly fell in love with her.

Annie was nicknamed "Little Sis," and they played with her like you would a child. My own mother, who never met an animal that she liked, allowed Annie in her home. She had permission to explore and go wherever she wanted. Why, Momma even petted her!

Annie went to church with us. No one complained. If the music was too loud for her ears, Mark or I would walk her outside like you would a baby or a small child.

Contracts signed.

I taught her to say Momma. I sat Annie in my lap and pointed to her.

"You, Annie."

Then I pointed to myself.

"Me Ma."

Back and forth, we went through this. After a few short sessions, she got it.

"You Annie. Me Ma."

"Ra?" She cooed back at me.

"Yes! Me Ra!" Communication had started.

From then on, when Annie needed water or food or to go outside, she would climb up to my face, put a paw on my chest and say, "Ra?"

And so it was.

Life was now different. We became better people because of Annie. I am not sure at what point I became a "dog whisperer," but it happened nonetheless. It was, to our hearts, much like having a mute child that you had to learn how to communicate with.

Annie learned how to shake her head "yes" or "no" to questions frequently asked of her. If it was an emergency she would call out "Ra!" instead of barking. Rarely did she bark. After all, Mommy and Daddy didn't bark.

We took her to visit her birth mother, dad and sisters at the Best home on occasion.

Annie would play with them but didn't understand how they could be dogs and she wasn't.

We wondered the same thing.

YARD SALE
(June 8th)

If you ever wanted to get to know your neighbors, go through your closets, your garage and backyard, drag all the stuff to your front yard, put prices on all your priceless objects, get up at 6 a.m., and make lots of coffee. Your neighbors will all come out to see what you're getting rid of at a good price.

My hope was to raise at least a hundred dollars for each family that I had brought together for the four-family event. It would be enough to buy each of us groceries.

Annie Frances and I sat outside with Lana and waited on people. Over and over again, I was told to watch out for Annie. She was so pretty and tiny! At three-fourths of a pound at ten weeks old, our little Deer-Head Chihuahua—the second smallest dog in the world—someone might just take off with her! I kept her close by me.

The nicest thing about the yard sale was that I got to work with Lana again, one of the ladies Mark worked with. She is a hard worker, wife and mom. On that morning, she was a yard sale technician! And she was great! Lana could wait on several people at once. It must have been her experience at the jewelry store that came in handy. She answered questions while she wrapped up selected treasures for customers.

Between customers, we got to talk about being moms of all boys. We caught up on all our children's lives and our future plans for a home on Nicholas Drive.

That evening, we took Annie to visit friends. My friend convinced me to let Annie stay by herself the next day while we went to church together. Annie stayed in the laundry room with her food, water and bed for seven hours. It was the first time we had ever left her for more than an hour. We found out that night when we got back home to her, that all three of us had separation anxiety! Annie Frances was hysterical, which meant I was hysterical! We never left her alone like that the rest of her life.

If we had to go somewhere for an extended period of time, we got a sitter. No more trauma for that baby! And as far as church was concerned, Annie went with us every Friday night and Sunday night. She was accepted and loved everywhere we went. After all, we were "Ra" and "Da."

UNSOUND MIND
(June 10th)

Mark finally confessed to me that he had been suffering from depression for three weeks. The passing of our pastor shook him. Ever since I had the vision of Fred heading into Heaven, I felt peace about his leaving Earth for a better, much better place. Fred now existed forever with Jesus.

But Mark's depression was inhibiting his thoughts. I prayed for answers, and the Lord showed me fear all around my husband. Fear tramples all over faith. They don't co-exist well in any believer.

One evening, we spoke together about this, and I reminded Mark that fear was from an unsound mind. Scripture speaks that God will not move on someone's behalf when they are double-minded.

It was something to think about.

RON
(June 11th)

I am 18 months older than my little brother, Ron. In our younger years, I picked on him something terrible! When Ron turned 8 years old, he stood back and "whopped" me in the nose! I hit the ground like a sack of potatoes. Blood hit the floor! A truce was declared that very day. We have been the best of friends ever since.

Ron and I have both been writers since our youth. He started out better than I, and I am not sure that he is still not the better writer and storyteller.

When I was 16 years old, during a Christmas Holiday break from school, Ron came up from the basement—his man-cave long before man-caves were in vogue—and asked me if I could help him out with a project he had going downstairs.

"Sure."

Ron had started a story he called *An Old Man's Christmas*. He was at the beginning of the third typed page, and he was not sure how to proceed. Intrigued, I sat down to read the fledgling story and fell in love, line by line, as I saw an intricate story form before my eyes.

When I finished what he had written so far, I knew there were many more pages left in the adventure. Ron and I looked at each other with a glint in our eyes and a smile on our faces.

"I'm in!" I cried out.

We joined forces and finished the eight typed pages before Christmas. As a Christmas present, we read it to the family on Christmas Day. We could see in Momma and Daddy's eyes how proud they were of us. We put our collective pens away and never worked together again on a project, until June of 2012.

The words I had heard so long ago came running back to me.

"Hey, Sis! I'm working on a project and I'm a little stuck. It's about our family's five generations in the military."

"Wow, Ron! That's wonderful! What do you need me for?"

"You know Papaw Aubrey's stories better than me. Will you help me write them down?" He paused for an answer he was already sure of.

"Whew wheeee! I've been waiting for 38 years to hear those words come out of your mouth. Another invitation to write with you. Yay."

My yes was apparent.

"Great! I'll call you when I'm ready for his segment. Can you come to my house?"

"You bet! I'll look forward to your call."

As the weeks went by, I reflected on my brother's life in the military and the stories he had told us verbally. I was pretty sure some of those stories would never make it to print! I was very proud of his 20-year service in the United States Navy. At the time of this writing in 2013, Ron's son, Joshua, is now demonstrating his love for his father and our country by serving honorably in the United States Marine Corps. This statement is usually followed by a very loud "Hhooorrhhhaaahhh!"

The day arrived for me to meet Ron at his home. I had to admit great excitement at the prospect of us working together once again. Ron met me at the door with a big hug. We got comfortable in his living room and went to work.

"I'll show you what I've written as a beginning, and then you tell me the rest of the story. We'll start writing from there."

"Okay, Ron."

When Ron had first contacted me about his book, he wanted to know if I had any pictures of Grandpa. I had a few, but I knew where I could get more. I contacted our Aunt Reva from Illinois, who sent me more pictures for us to use in his book. Thanks, Auntie.

I read his introduction to Grandpa Clarence "Joe" Aubrey's life and the beginning of *The Great War*, World War I. Then I turned to Ron and told stories of that tall, handsome Irishman with blue eyes; his strength of a Paul Bunyan, engulfed with a heart of compassion.

I told the story of how Grandpa became a boxer in the military. Joe Aubrey was good too! Until he threw a punch straight into his opponent's chest cavity and he hit the floor and never got up again. Grandpa Joe's compassionate heart broke.

Well, that was the end of that budding career. When Joe got out of the military, he went out for the new sport of baseball. Joe tried out and did very well. He was accepted on one of the earliest teams.

In one of their first games, Joe was in the outfield,

caught the oncoming ball and threw it toward the base with great strength!

You hear this one coming?

The ball hit the runner square in the chest and he, like the serviceman, dropped to the ground and never got back up. Sorrow filled Joe once again.

It was at that point, Clarence "Joe" Aubrey decided to be a farmer. At least, Joe reasoned, if he killed something on the farm, he could eat it.

Clarence Aubrey came back to Shelbyville, Kentucky, to settle down; which is how he met a very pretty Mae Snyder. Oh, at first Mae's parents of German descent did not like the big, young Irishman. So, Joe wrote to her best friend.

"And, by the way, could you please give this letter to Mae for me?"

"Thanks!"

Over the course of several months, it was decided, they would become Mr. and Mrs. Clarence Aubrey.

Ron and I worked on the stories through the morning and early afternoon. When we finished, which was all too soon, I dropped by to see our momma and told her of our work together. Momma hoped well would come of it all.

On the way home, I stopped and picked up a pizza, chips and a cake for dinner. Mary was coming over to work on our project on her birthday! Mark and I wanted to make it worth her while. She was surprised at her three-person birthday party. Mary hugged us over and over!

Laughter echoed through the halls as we settled down to work. I had read through both proofs, and there was just a little adjustment to make.

The goal line was before us. I started the day at the writer's desk, and that was how I finished it. I had excellent company at both ends of the day.

I could not be more satisfied.
My hope; God was too.

PEACE AT LAST!
(June 12th)

The day started busy. Mark and I landscaped at Mom's, no charge of course. We cleaned up after we finished and had dinner with her.

After dinner, our day was not yet finished. We still had a healing service to go to over in Louisville with Fr. Bernie Weber. (For more of Fr. Bernie's stories, please see *Miraculous Interventions II Modern Day Priests, Prophets, Pastor's & Everyday Visionaries*.) It was always a pleasure to be involved in whatever the good priest was involved in.

After joyful singing started the evening, with an overflowing group, Father Bernie gave a wonderful talk on going out into the world and showing the compassionate side of Christ. The last song was sung, and the group was dismissed except for anyone who needed prayer. Those people were to meet Father and his helpers in the church. There, they would be prayed for, for whatever healing they desired or needed.

Mark and I went in to stand in line for prayer. I had brought my books and our house plans to have them prayed over for guidance and blessings. Essentially, any help God would care to send down the pipe, we were happy to receive.

Several others came over to join Fr. Bernie in his prayers over us. As each one gave utterance, the room felt warm, and the air had a different quality about it. Something was going on in the supernatural world of God! Words of knowledge came forth. These saints prayed in the spirit, interpreted and then spoke.

"God gave you that land! I see a vision. You and

Mark are walking on a gold path! A road, hand in hand. It is God's gold!" People got excited.

We thanked those wonderful, gentle, Spirit-filled people for their words of knowledge, comfort and the peace of mind they gave us that we were on the right path. Most importantly, we were happy to know that God would once again bless the work of our hands.

REACHING OUT
(June 14th)

After having worked an early morning and afternoon shift, I came home to the real work I had in mind. I called the office of another pastor who had a book published to request my sending them a letter and a copy of my books. I also requested the name and address of their promotions department of the publishing company he went with to contact them as well. They gladly gave me all the information I had requested.

I called public libraries and asked them to consider carrying our books. I also contacted several newspapers to see if they would do an article on the newest book that was coming out. I did not know at the time that the article the Corydon Democrat would run would change lives down the road.

READING OUR THOUGHTS
(June 16th)

Again, another day of phone calls to promote the *"Miraculous Interventions"* series. I called the Louisville Public Libraries, the New Albany Public Library, (approved), the Harrison County Corydon Branch Library (also approved), and others. I was on a mission. Surely these books were not just meant for my benefit and the benefit of those I knew.

I asked the Lord when He was going to bless the work of my hands. Again the word came down in an instant, *"**Get it right**."*

"Yes sir. Working on it."

When Mark came home from work that evening, he knew we were going to our oldest son's apartment but he did not know the real reason why. He was pleasantly surprised when they yelled "Happy Father's Day!" as we opened the door. All the extended family were there. Amanda, Ben's girlfriend, and her family were there for the cookout. Four generations of family were celebrating *Father's Day* together. Of course, we brought our little Annie. Her diaper bag was full to the brim with her things. I had her milk in a jar with a dropper, her soft foods, snacks, her sweater in case she got all shivery, her blankie, toys and her outside hoodie for when she had to go do her business.

It was Annie's first time to meet everyone. What fun they had holding her and playing with her. After dinner, Ben and Amanda had another surprise. Down in the park, a few blocks from their town house in Charlestown, the town was putting on the movie, *"The*

Wizard of Oz" on a big screen. There was no charge, and all were invited.

We cleaned up the kitchen, packed a basket of snacks and blankets to sit on and took off for the event. *The Wizard of Oz* was one of our boys' favorite movies. We were off to see the Wizard! Mark, Annie and I sat next to Ben and Amanda. As we got ready for the movie to start, Ben started an interesting praise report.

"Momma?"

"Yes, son?"

"Do you remember when I called you for prayer for a lady that was two hours from dying?"

"Yes. After we got off the phone, I prayed and asked the Lord, 'Who do you want me to pray with?' I heard Bill Mauck. I called Bill and we prayed to save her life right away! We prayed away the Spirit of death in Jesus' name."

"Well, I want you to know that she is doing fine now. She got up and is eating, talking, and walking. She has now been alive for over a month!"

"Thank God! How wonderful! Thank you for sharing this news with us."

"You're welcome, Momma!"

Annie slept in her blanket while the rest of our hearty group made a wonderful evening of it.

We arrived home in the early hours of the morning. As we got ready for bed, Mark and I marveled at how merciful God was to snatch the young lady from the jaws of death in answer to her family's and other's prayers.

ON THE ROAD

(June 17th)

It didn't start out to be such a long day on paper, each dedicated task so far from the other. It just sort of piled up. I squeezed in this request and that request, and before I knew it, I was telling my husband about our nine-hour road trip with stops in between.

It went over well. Well, sort of.

"Sigh. Really?" Mark labored his point home with one of those looks.

"It will all work out! We like everyone we are seeing today, and we're getting to go someplace we've never been. It will be an adventure! Kelly will be with us, and you like her. And I *think* you still like....me?" I ended the request with a smile. When Mark gave an over-dramatic sigh and a big smile, I knew all our plans were on!

The day started with a 45-minute drive to a church we enjoyed in Clarksville. I had known Pastor Tom, since he was 19 years old, long before he ever thought of becoming a pastor. I still remember how beautiful he and his wife, Bridgette, were when they got married so many years ago. Now, Tom and Bridgette have grandchildren of their own. Their service was moving as usual.

There was no time to stay after church. We had an hour-and-a-half trip to go get Miss Kelly and take her another two hours to Owensboro, Kentucky.

We arrived on time to Kelly's home. She was expecting us and came out when we pulled up. That was the first time Kelly got to see Annie and meet her.

Kelly laughed when she saw how much stuff Annie had in her diaper bag.

"So much stuff for such a little dog! Debbie! This is your baby!"

"Yes, Ma'am, she is!"

Kelly laughed and said, "When did you become a dog whisperer?"

It was my turn to laugh as I replied, "I think it came with the territory!"

We all laughed as we set off for Owensboro. There were packages to pick up for Kelly and her dad. This was also the store she thought we would be interested in for our home construction supplies that would save us a good amount of money right off the top — and she was right!

After we picked up Kelly's packages, we looked around and took notes on flooring, lighting, and bath sinks. I daydreamed about what our home would look like and when we might move in.

We were an hour late getting to our son Andy's for dinner. And what surprised us, was, Kelly and I were the ones cooking! Andy had everything together, but he had planned on his momma cooking. It did not help that we had gotten lost on the road to his house, and everyone arrived hungry, including us! Kelly and I jumped into service quick! In short order, less than an hour, we had dinner on the table. After prayers, we all talked, laughed and ate — Annie too! As it got late in the evening, we still had to take Kelly home. It was another hour-and-a-half trip once again. We had started the day with lots of conversation in the car, but on the way back to Kelly's home, we were all pretty quiet. We were all talked out and ready for bed.

Once Kelly was dropped off, we still had one last 45-minute drive home—just like when we started the day.

Of course, we thanked God for all our safe travels as we crawled into bed and mumbled our "good nights" at almost midnight.

Sleep was not far away.

THERE'S NO PLACE LIKE HOME!
(June 20th)

Times were hard.

I called twenty banks and lending institutions. Ever since the 2008 Recession, banks were not keen on home-construction loans.

Yes, our credit was good. We owed very little besides our property — and the home we were selling to the Murray's. We were not your typical, average Americans, even on paper.

Almost all the banks said we would qualify — there was no reason to turn us down. The only problem was the high down payments they requested. We had good equity in our land and in the building of the home, yet most wanted between $10,000 and $20,000 more.

My last call of the day was to a bank in New Albany. I gave the young man the same spiel I did all the others. All was quiet on the phone while he ciphered on paper and calculator. Finally, he said, "Do you have $2,500.00?"

"Yes! Are you kidding me?"

"Nope."

"When do you want to get started on the paperwork? I can set you an appointment for this week."

I couldn't believe my ears! Someone was finally asking me to come in and fill out paperwork. They were saying yes.

"Wheeee!! I will see you then. Wait till I tell Mark!"

I was on cloud nine.

My hope upon hope was that Ivie had been wrong, and that with that bank, it would be full steam ahead.

Only time would tell...

SPIRITUAL WARFARE
(June 21ˢᵗ)

Spiritual warfare can take place anywhere. It can be in your mind, or by a family member or friend, even at work. Some days, especially at work.

I went to work early in the day. I was a cashier for most of it. About mid-day, a lady came through my line who seemed rather distraught. Of course, I asked her what was wrong, and could I help?

She said she had a seriously ill child, and she was very concerned for her. I asked her, after she checked out, if I could pray with her for her daughter.

"Oh yes, please!"

In the doorway of the store, we held hands and prayed agreeing together for the health of her child. During the prayer, I went into my Holy Spirit language, the gift of tongues. Afterwards, she hugged me and left.

I turned around, still smiling and singing in tongues, and headed back to my station. I stopped in my tracks! Immediately, I knew my enemy was close by. I could feel him! Standing at my station, staring at me through empty eyes, were two young people. One of them was wearing a shirt that said, "Child of Sodom."

Warrior shields stayed on high alert! I never came out of my holy language! I approached them to ring up their items, talking in tongues out loud the whole time. They said nothing and stared straight past me. The only words I spoke to them in English were "milk in a bag?"

They shook their collective heads "no." They paid and left the building. I jumped up and down and shook off the bad vibes, bad karma, bad spirits. Whatever it was, I did not want it attached to me! I said a prayer over myself and went back to work.

If this ever happens to you, cover yourself in prayer too.

REJOICE!
(June 22nd)

A lady called from the only bank that had said *yes* to our housing application. She said we were just a little short on the income end. Was there anything we could do?

I hung up the phone and said, "Lord, we need more money!"

Not thirty seconds went by when Mark called.

"Guess what honey? I just got a raise! My first one in seven years! Can you believe it?"

"Oh my goodness! Yes! Yes, I can! I just got a call from a lady at a bank who said we needed just a little bit more money each month, and thirty seconds later, here it is!" I called the bank back and told her what had just occurred. It was just enough for us to qualify.

Of course it was, at least for them.

Our new friends and owners-to-be of the home we were living in, had come by. Mark, Crystal and David had spent a nice evening together. They were still at our house when I arrived home after work. They all asked how my day had gone. I told them of the day's events and blessings. All in all, it had been a good day. I smiled at them.

Crystal sat across the room from me and smiled back. I could see her thinking. She had been after me for weeks for us to go with them to something called "Cowboy Days." I already had two events scheduled for the next day that I felt I couldn't or shouldn't get out of. Crystal wanted us to meet her best friend, Joy. She felt it was very important in her spirit for this to happen.

Finally, Crystal spoke to a quiet room. "Rabbi Joy sees angels and demons. She can see if anything is attached to people." Then Crystal stopped speaking. No one spoke. I got up, went into the kitchen, got both calendars and a pen. I came back into the living room, sat across from Crystal, and I crossed off both activities on our calendars.

"How do you spell what we are going to?" I inquired.

With a smile, Crystal said, "Wild West Day Festival by Christian Country Cowboy Church."

"What time does it start?"

"From noon until 6 p.m. tomorrow."

"Got any directions?"

With a nod of her head, Crystal told me how to get there as I wrote it all out for us. I agreed with Crystal. She was right, we should be there right after Mark got off work. Something in my spirit rejoiced!

WOMAN OF GOD
(June 23rd)

Our Annie needed some things. Our tiny little girl, sent from Heaven in a puppy's body, was so small; just over a pound at three months old, we couldn't find a harness to take her out for a walk. I had been told the local Tractor Supply was having a "Dog Days," and they might have what we needed.

We pulled up to the store's parking lot. It was quite full with many people and their pets all running around. There were vendors with dog treats and items especially made for different breeds.

I put Annie in the bag that I carried her supplies in. When we walked past the vendors, Annie popped her head up to see what was going on. Everyone reacted.

"Oh! She's beautiful!"

"What's her name?"

"She's so tiny! How old is she?"

That's the smallest dog I've ever seen!"

"You're so lucky to have her!"

Inside the store, an employee helped us find a harness that would almost fit her; at least she had a chance of growing into it. It was for a bunny. All the dog harnesses were too large.

When we got back outside, people started to come up to me to talk about Annie. Everyone wanted to give her something. Treats, toys, etc., whatever they could think of. I already knew she was tiny, being premature and part of the second-smallest breed in the world, yet I wondered how much bigger she would get. I was told, maybe three pounds. She was at a pound.

Then a woman came running up to me saying, "Hurry! The judging is going on now! Come on!"

"What?!"

"Your dog; she'll win! Come on!"

Off we ran to the front of the crowd. The judges smiled when they saw Annie.

They declared "Annie Frances, the smallest dog award!" Everyone clapped and cheered.

They asked me Annie's name and who I was— owner or family member?

"This is Annie Frances, and I am her mommy!" The crowd clapped their approval as heads nodded with understanding for the new winners. We even had our picture taken. Annie was given a bag of treats and gifts.

How exciting it all was! We had almost gotten back to the car, when once again, another lady came running up to me and grabbed me by the arm!

"Come on! We need Annie in this contest too! She is sure to win the youngest award!" With Annie in my arms, we ran back to the judging table.

"Here's Annie! Here's Annie!" We cried out together.

"How old is she?" the judges asked.

"Three months."

"Our new winner!"

Applause erupted, prizes were awarded and pictures were taken. On the way back to the car, I cried real tears.

"Oh, Annie Frances! We've only had you two weeks, and you are already a prize winner. I'm so proud of you! And look at all this free stuff we got for you! How special you are. I can't wait until we tell

Daddy!"

The sweet little puppy just blinked at me and sniffed at the bags of goodies. As I unwrapped a snack for her, I called Mark, still crying. I told him what happened at the store. Mark hollered to the others in his store (also dog enthusiasts) that Annie had won two awards!

"Put Annie on the phone, so I can tell her she's a good girl." I held the phone to Annie's ear, and Mark started talking and telling her she was a good sugar bug. Annie recognized his voice and licked the phone. What an exciting morning we had together!

Mark arrived home shortly after 3 p.m. Living less than one mile from work had its great advantages. We packed up supplies for the three of us and went on a journey to LaGrange, Kentucky. The directions I had been given were perfect. Parking was at the bottom of the hill inside the fairgrounds. A man was there with a tractor-drawn hayride.

"Want a ride up to Wild West Day Festival?"

"Sure! That would be great."

Then, with a funny look on his face, he asked, "Is that a puppy?"

"Her name is Annie Frances."

When we got out at the top of the hill, we handed the man $2.00 for the ride. He looked at us quizzically.

"Don't you charge for the ride?" We asked in unison.

"Well, I could put it in the collection plate for church." We already made a stir. Mark and I walked up, found our friends Crystal and David and settled in to watch a gun fight. The reenactment was ready to begin. We sat down to watch. Annie and I jumped when the guns went off!

"Don't worry! There's only blanks in those cartridges, ma'am."

"Thank goodness!"

The next entertainment was a man with a very large horse that did tricks. Annie sat in Mark's lap at first. The man rode over and got the horse to rear up.

Annie's eyes got real big, and she took off like a shot towards the big mare! Barking, she headed straight for the horse with Mark in close pursuit.

"Annie! Annie! Stop! Stop!" Mark caught her just in the nick of time! Whew!

Annie was fearless and out-numbered one to one. Everyone applauded and laughed as if it were a part of the show. My heart pounded.

After the show, we walked over for a free concert. They had a singing cowboy. It was the first time we met Pastor Chris Powell. Our group sat to listen to the old and new Christian songs. Mark went and got us waters to drink. I opened mine and poured some into the cap. Chris stopped singing and said to me, "You are going to feed your puppy out of a cap?"

"No," I replied as I got out her dropper to fill it up to give her a drink.

Chris laughed and smiled as he went on with his songs. I continued to feed Annie her dinnertime meal.

After a while, Crystal said to me, "There is the lady I wanted you to meet. Joy Son and her husband, Parson Zeb."

I turned to see a lady with long, dark auburn curls. She was dressed in 1880's gear. Joy had donned a long black skirt with a vest and long sleeved white shirt.

Behind her glasses were eyes that would soon peer into my very soul. But at the time, she was taking care of business. Still barking orders, she smiled as we approached with Crystal and David.

"Joy, this is Debbie and Mark Peyron."

Joy looked all around us as if she was watching the air move. She then tilted her head as if to hear an unheard voice speak. Then, she smiled.

"Hello."

"Hello. It is very nice to meet you. I hear you have been ill. I hope you get better soon. Your reenactment is very nice."

"Thanks."

Joy said she would see us later as things winded down. I watched her run off to help with another project. Crystal asked if we would like to see the inside of the church.

"Yes, of course."

We walked inside to a view of an old Western town. The walls had been painted with pictures of wood-frame buildings. In the front was a stage set up like a barn. There was musical equipment all around us. The only thing that remotely resembled a church were the pews that sat left to right, facing the stage.

Crystal and David introduced us to several congregants. We were told services were on Friday evenings. Crystal suggested we wait for Joy in the first pew. She knew Joy would come and sit with us. Crystal was being led by the Holy Spirit. True to her knowledge, Joy showed up a short time later.

Rabbona Joy Son is a Woman of God — a God talker. She is a seer with Holy Spirit knowledge. Her own mother was a seer as well, and her father a prophet.

Joy walked in all the gifts. She came and sat next to me. I spoke of our three sons, named them and who we were. I also told her that I had heard that she and I had a lot in common. I stopped and smiled.

Joy cocked her head to one side, paused, and then spoke things no one but I knew.

"I see Benjamin. He is of the tribe of Benjamin. I see a wolf."

I visibly jumped in my seat! I told her that both Ben and I, at different times in his life, had heard over him "wolf or werewolf." She shook her head no.

"You heard wolf! Wolf is the animal sign of the tribe of Benjamin. Wolf means protective; he protects, and he is very family-oriented. Wisdom travels with him, and God answers his prayers."

I was stunned. It was as if Joy had known Ben all of his life. She could not have been more accurate.

"I see David. I see his feet. He is walking away. He has on sandals. (It's practically all he ever wears!) He is wounded, but God will bring him back healed."

All I could think to say was, "Wow!"

Joy asked to see my hands. She looked at them and said, "There is healing in your palms. I see heat." I thought to myself, just like in the dream I had!

"There is more power than you know." I believed her.

Then Joy addressed Mark, who was holding Annie.

"Mark is both Greek and Hebrew. He is the best of both worlds." I agreed wholeheartedly.

I told Joy of a dream I'd had. There was a man sitting on our health and prosperity. I asked her to interpret it for me. Joy asked me what he looked like and I told her. Her reply stunned me to silence.

"He is a general in satan's army. He only oversees important and powerful people. When did you have this dream?"

"Two years ago."

"Have you done something to get his attention in the last two years?"

I sat and thought for a moment, then it hit me!

"Two years ago, I wrote *"Miraculous Interventions."* I write about miracles, and we've had real healings."

Joy stared right through me and saw into my future.

I asked timidly, "What I am doing is that important?"

"You…..are that important."

INTROSPECTIVE
(June 24th)

There was so much to think about! A woman I had known for all of 18 hours had read me like a book! And every time I had looked at Crystal, it was as if she had known it would all happen that way. What had I gotten myself into?

My head, heart and spirit reeled! I could hardly wait to tell Ben and the other boys!

What had happened?!

Was my destiny being fulfilled as events unfolded in front of me?

Was there really a war going on in the unseen world?

Did I really have a mission on this Earth?

I had learned so much from Lee and Anne Schwarz, the ones who had prayed for God to heal my back, and Pastor Ivie Dennis and Pastor Fred.

Were there now new teachers on my horizon to move me forward?

Had I run smack into my own future?

I felt part two of my life was just beginning...

"So be it, Lord. So be it."

OUR MAIN SOURCE
(June 26th)

For any of you who have read the first book, *"Miraculous Interventions,"* remember how I said our plans can get in the way of God's plans for us?

Or, He uses our plans as a stepping stool to get us to where we are really supposed to be—which is always better for us than if we would have been left to our own ideas.

Got that?

If not, here is a prime example of how that can happen....

I thought I had everything covered. Despite Ivie's objections and asking us to wait on a private investor to build our home, I forged ahead with my own plans. I thought this was it. The bank was the way to go.

All our paperwork was in order. We were pre-approved and in the middle of the full approval process with no stoppers—we thought.

Our builder had signed his part of the paperwork, all our estimates had been turned in, and we were sure we would be building by the middle of July, 2012.

Our answer was due any day....

Remember, we were counting on my knowledge of the situation!

To be continued.....

NEVER A LOST CAUSE
(June 28th)

The day started out well enough. I had a nice visit with my momma, and I delivered books to Tonini's Church Supply in Louisville, Kentucky. Mark and I even got to go to St. Mary's prayer group that evening.

While at prayer group, Mary, my editor and publisher, told me about a contest for a $250,000.00 prize for a new business. The only problem was that we only had 36 hours to enter!

Mary came back to our house after the meeting, and we got started around 9:30 p.m. We opened the site Mary had written down, and there were pages and pages to fill out.

"Mark! Put on a pot of coffee. It looks like we are going to need it!"

Well, the good Lord gave us wonderful words to put on paper, and we worked until 3 a.m.

At the very end of the site, we found out you had to have 250 like hits. Other people had at least a month to gather them, and we had 26 hours! Time was definitely against us, and unfortunately, since we didn't get enough likes, all our hard work wasn't even considered.

But what we did get was a clearer understanding of what we were doing and our real mission — what was really at stake.

Souls. Salvation. Get it right.

WOMAN OF GOD, *Part II*
(June 29th)

It was the last Friday of the month. Normally that wouldn't mean anything to us, but that Friday was different. Mark and I had just been introduced to Cowboy Church! The church was having their monthly concert night. A local pastor, Chris Powell, was headlining. We had heard him sing at Cowboy Days and dubbed him "The Singing Cowboy." We enjoyed his music and wanted to go and see him for a full concert. Since Mark couldn't go, my good friend, Debbie Grimes, agreed to go with me. Deb thought I should not travel the long distance alone so late at night. She is a very thoughtful and sweet person.

We also agreed to pick up Crystal Murray along the way. I took one copy of my books and our house plans with us for Rabbi Joy to pray over and see if she saw good fruit rising from them. I was on the need-to-know list. I was still seeking direction for my heart's desires. I knew what I wanted, and I had to know if God still wanted it too. I needed to know if I had gotten all the signs right, just like "the Three Wise Men."

Mark and I finished dinner when Deb pulled up. I had agreed to drive. I was armed with a bottle of water, pen and paper, three books and a set of house plans. Mark wished us well.

"Remember, Honey, Crystal says it will be a late night."

"Call me when you are heading home."

"Sure thing!"

We said our goodbyes and set out for an adventure. Deb had also told her husband she would be home late. What wonderful, understanding husbands we had.

The next stop was Crystal's house in Louisville. Deb and I talked all the way there about our expectations for the night. I called Crystal when we got close to her home. She stood waiting at the end of her sidewalk. We were all happy about going together.

On the way to LaGrange, Kentucky, Crystal clued us in on the agenda for the evening. Deb and I listened with rapt attention. Crystal explained a little about the church and their teachings. We were fascinated.

"Ooohhhh..."

Crystal explained what Shalom really meant. It meant peace that passes understanding. We were for it. She went on.

"They will open with a couple of songs. Then the guys from the house band will go back and change while Joy talks to the audience. She will see if there are any birthdays or anniversaries to celebrate. Then "Cuzin Gus and the Boys from Sasquatch Hollar" come out and give their rendition of "Hee Haw."

"A show and a concert?"

"Yes. They will take our donations before the concert to help with expenses."

"Wow!"

"Then, after the concert, we will all talk while dinner is ordered."

"Dinner too!" Oh, this all sounded like so much in one evening!

Crystal nodded as she went on talking, "By 11:00 p.m. the pizza will arrive. We'll all go downstairs to talk and eat. It's not until after midnight when they talk of the deep things of God. "

The three of us were greeted right inside the hall with genuine warmth and kindness.

"Hello! Come on in!"

"Glad you could make it!"

The seats filled up quickly as we all got ready for the night's entertainment.

Up the aisle marched men clad in cowboy gear. From hats to boots with spurs, they were in high fashion! You could tell they took the evening seriously!

They joined Joy on the stage for several songs. If I could show or tell you on this page how beautiful their voices were, it would have to be a design seen in Heaven. The group encouraged others to sing along. All I could do was sit with my mouth open in awe of it all. I wondered then, as I still wonder now, why aren't they a famous group out of Tennessee?

After a few songs, the men of the group excused themselves to change. Joy addressed the crowd and caught everyone up on the events planned for the upcoming month. When enough time had passed, Joy grinned and asked the audience a question.

"Ready to holler for the boys?"

Everyone clapped and cheered.

"Hey, boys! Yeee hawwww!"

The door in back of the stage burst open. Out came the men of Sasquatch Holler. Clothed in patched up bib-overalls, straw hats, long-john shirts or torn ill-fitting tee shirts, and no shoes! Boy, were they a sight! The crowd roared its approval.

I have bad news here, folks. Their jokes were as

bad as their costumes! The audience laughed all the more with us included. Corn was flying high!

The boys sang anniversary and birthday songs to the crowd along with a few more ditties made up on the spot.

All too soon, the first half of the evening was over. They took up donations and gave away prizes for the evening. The main concert soon began.

I had already heard the *singing cowboy* at Wild West Day Festival. Pastor Chris Powell had been with Zeb and Joy for over 12 years. They figured it was about time he headlined one of their concert nights. And they were right!

We sat and listened as Pastor Chris sang a beautiful song of his love for the Lord God and Jesus, our Savior. He moved us to tears time and again. I went to the back of the hall, got on my knees and cried. I felt myself at Heaven's gate listening to an angel sing and speak. A profound love walked with that young man. You could feel it translate right through you. It was a Christian concert by a mighty man of God. I felt privileged to be a witness to it.

After the concert was over, we got to shake hands and introduce ourselves to the band.

Crystal had known them all for years. She introduced us as "Deb and Deb." Chuckles went up.

"And they are both from Corydon, Indiana."

Chuckles turned into laughter.

Crystal went on, "This Debbie is one of our authors from LCW. She writes about miracles."

"I'm privileged to meet you, Pastor Chris. I've never met a singer and a songwriter before," I said with a smile and a handshake.

"I'm privileged to meet you. I've never met a real author before!" Chris smiled back. The mutual admiration society had just convened.

A call for pizza went up. Several members of the band stayed; Zeb, Joy, Chris and Kevin, as well as Crystal, Deb and me. We had a wonderful time. All of us added to the stimulating conversation. Since Deb and I were new, we asked the most questions — and were asked about ourselves.

It was well after midnight when I asked to speak with Joy for a moment. We excused ourselves to the other side of the room, and she waited quietly for me to speak. But I tell you, she already knew what was coming!

I showed her the books I had at the time, and our house plans. Then I waited for wisdom to give me direction.

The first thing out of her mouth was this, "You are meant to write books!"

And without opening up the plans, she saw the land perfectly.

"I see rolling hills with trees in back. Thanks for making the trip and sharing with us. It meant a lot to have you here. We'll talk again."

I gave her my cellular and home phone numbers.

The drive on the way home went back and forth from excitement to quiet. What a night! We were all encouraged from our meeting. We dropped Crystal off at 2:30 a.m. and headed for home.

At 3:45 a.m., we pulled up to my home and Deb left to go home herself. We were all very tired.

Mark and Annie were fast asleep. As I bent down to kiss them, my phone text message signal went off. I went into the kitchen to see the message. It read, "Are you home yet? Call me in the morning. The Holy Spirit has given me a word for you. Joy"

Was she crazy?!
Morning?!
Who could sleep now?
There was no way I could wait until daylight.
I lit her phone up immediately.

4 a.m.

Joy answered with the first ring.

"Thanks for making the trip out and sharing with us. It meant a lot to have you there. Do you have time for revelation?"

"You bet! You talk, and I'll write." The meeting was called to order.

"The Lord showed me Andy, your youngest son. He has the faith of Abraham. It was prominent tonight. God put faith in Abraham. He put faith in Andy too. Not only that, God has faith in him! He is driving him on. Andy has a supernatural gift of faith in his belly. God is cheering him on!"

I was already in tears hearing what I had known all his days.

"Thank you so much for telling me this. I can hardly wait to tell him!"

"The Holy Spirit showed me Mark too. Mark sees differently. He is like a man staring up at a dark sky looking for stars in the city. But he is seeing unclearly. The stars are clearer in the country."

Joy paused for a moment, then went on.

"Mark is created to see God. But he talks himself out of seeing. He sees best when he can't argue himself out of it. Then he knows it's right. "Joy paused as if she was listening for more instruction.

"I am interceding for your home. I saw your hill. I saw angels dancing on your land. They are delighting and dancing between battles before things happen. It is a place of refuge."

"Wonderful!" I cried.

Joy went on, "There is a song in Mark's heart, and God will remind him of it."

Joy paused again and said, "Now about you."

I held my breath.

"Oh! It's all good stuff! There are angels around you. How precious you are to Him. He calls you daughter. Your heart is His heart! God's desire is to give you your desires of your heart. The things you have waited for will come in due season."

A sigh swept through my frame.

"We will have the opportunity to sit down and pour out over each other. We will share and glean off of each other. We will help and encourage each other."

I was silently crying as I spoke to this gentle soul, "I'm so glad. Ever since Lee and Anne left, then Pastor Schuppert died, I have wondered where my next teacher would come from."

"The Lord says you have been at this place long enough. He will be moving you soon and drawing you closer to Him—soon and very soon. He is going to show you more of who you are. You will know it's Him and feel His presence. Glory to glory He comes! You will see yourself as He sees you. You have grown in the valleys. God is looking forward to when He brings you to a new place of glory. He will delight over you."

I spoke a prayer, "Lord, help me to see through Your eyes. What does the Holy Spirit think I will receive?"

"New understanding to old things. The home is in your heart."

Joy paused again.

"The home is not solidified in Mark's heart. It won't come until it is solidified in his heart. When he is ready in his heart, the house will go up. He needs to see light and dark. Then he will decide what he wants in his heart."

"When does Mark turn 54?"

"He is already 54."

Joy changed the conversation.

"The Lord told me years ago I wear the vest of many colors. Gifts. Jesus functioned in all the gifts all the time. In me, they are not there all the time—just when I need them; when I need understanding. In the ministry, gifts are given to all of us. To a few, He gives all the gifts at different times. It has been a hard time finding these people. It is to fill whatever need is there."

Joy stopped to take a breath and continued, "Oh, lots of individuals have one gift. There are only a handful that flow in all the gifts. I have met several. They have been mentors to me. They would explain what I would hear or see in the Holy Spirit. They have helped me to grow and walk. I also could understand more who they were and in how God created them to be who they were. There are not a lot of them out there. I enjoy the opportunity when I get to meet one."

The conversation stopped. A heaviness hung in the air. My heart pounded in my chest! The question waited until I had the courage to ask it.

"Am I one of these?" It would answer so many questions that had formed throughout my life.

"Yes! Yes!" Joy cried out. "The Holy Spirit is in, on and all around you! Become familiar with it. Move in it as you have been created in it. Power and might are coming. God is incomparably great! Your next season is to flow with Him in it."

It was as much as I could contain at the time. My head was swimming.

Now, Messianic Minister, Joy Son became my Rabbi- Rabbona- my teacher to help me see my eternal Rabbi Jesus, Yeshua, Yeshi.

The last conversation of the dawning morning went like this.

Joy spoke softly, "We may all go home during a fall festival."

I offered, "The Hebrews believe it will be between 2014 and 2016."

Joy spoke, "It will be in the fall at the feast of the Marriage of the Lamb."

"When is that?" I asked.

"The seventh month, by the Hebrew calendar; from the middle of September on."

Then Joy prophesied, "There will be a marriage honeymoon; He will rule and reign. A rapture, when we are called up; a Great Tribulation; then we will return with Christ mounted on horses to come back."

How this will all come about? Only God knows.

It was almost dawn when I laid my head on my pillow to sleep.

PRAISE REPORT FROM ENGLAND!
(July 1st)

Long, long ago, in another lifetime, or so it seemed, when Ben was six years old, while at Walt Disney World, our family met a lovely little family from Hazlemere, Bucks, England. The boys, theirs and ours, rode rides together. It was decided by the mothers, Dianna Gething and I, that her youngest son and my oldest son, Richard and Benjamin respectively, should write to each other — which they did for a while.

As they slacked off, Dianna and I decided to write and keep up with each other's family. We grew quite fond of each other very quickly.

David and Dianna Gething have made several trips to the United States to see us. Over the 22 year friendship, we have seen each other through ups and downs, good times and bad, sickness and health, poor and middle class — we haven't made it up to rich yet as of 2012.

Dianna has watched my faith grow as I have watched her faith wane. The last straw came for her when an evil man blew up a schoolhouse full of children in England. She decided then and there that if God would not stop that, then maybe He had never really been there at all.

As a witness to her, I would occasionally ask her about the things I would see and experience. Dianna's reply was, "Debbie, you're a psychic."

Her words sent me straight to Pastor Ivie, who laughed and said I was a prophet. This world calls those who can see beyond the veil, psychics.

It was at that time, I got the word from above to

start writing, with verification from many people along the way. I sent the Getting's a copy of my first book and they bought my second book off Amazon.com.

Over the past several months, Dianna had told me one of her dear friends of 38 years, had an illness that could probably take her life. I asked Dianna if I could pray for her, and she replied it would be okay. So I did.

It was our usual custom to Skype every first Sunday of the month from noon until 1 p.m. EST. July 1st happened to fall on a Sunday, and we Skyped as usual. Dianna was all smiles. She had something to tell me.

Dianna's friend we had been praying for was much better, and the doctors said she was going to live! I was very happy for both ladies. To me it meant, God said, "Yes." Then Dianna said something else to me I will never forget.

"Debbie, between your first book and this, you have given me much to think about!"

The door of faith cracked open a bit once more. Oh, happy day!

TAKING CARE OF BUSINESS
(July 2nd)

Some days are more fruitful than others. Some days are busier than others. Fruitful and busy are not always the same. On this day, it was a little of both.

My second book, *"Miraculous Interventions II Modern Day Priests, Prophets, Pastors & Everyday Visionaries"* was hot off the press. I had book deliveries to finish. The press release was already out, and my book-signing was just days away and I had to work that night.

I took Mr. Tonini from Tonini's Church Supply in Louisville, Kentucky, a book to read for approval to be put in his store. They already had the first book, *"Miraculous Interventions"* and *"Christmas Chaos."* Mr. Bill Tonini himself called me the "Miracle Lady." Tonini's, and Arlston's in Corydon, Indiana, held a special place in my heart. They were the first two bookstores to believe in me!

The library in New Albany, Indiana had also requested a copy of all three of my books. I took them over as well.

After a 106 mile round trip, I was just in time for work, and I got off just in time for bed.

Long days, fruitful days.
Tired days, good days.
Good night!

MISSING FRED
(July 3rd)

In our county, the Methodist hold a *hymn-sing* once a month. Fred Schuppert's band, *Victory*, used to lead the music.

Pastor Fred had been gone from us, but present with the Lord, for two months. Fred's base player and best friend, Bill Mauck, decided it was time to get back on the horse and go play once again. He invited Mark and I to go too. After all, we were the band's roadies for several years.

At the end of the evening, Bill invited Mark and I up on stage to sing a melody rendition that Fred was known for. We smiled through tears and sang with all our hearts! We packed up our dear Brother Bill just like old times.

The ride home was quiet as Mark and I held hands and wiped away tears. Some pages are hard to turn over and let go.

By 10 p.m. that evening, we sat down wearily on our bed and noticed we had a message.

It was our good friend Larry Crosier. He had called about his wife Marilynn. She was very ill, and he had taken her to the hospital. Marilynn was admitted with heart and lung problems due to illness! The doctors said she would be in the hospital at least four days. Could we please pray for her?

It looked as if our marching orders were in for the next day. At the time, we had no idea how busy that next day was really going to be.

CALLED UP FOR SERVICE
(July 4th)

A part of your day of service can be the cleaning of your own house—which is exactly how Mark and I started the day. In three days, we were having people over following an afternoon book-signing, and our home did not look like a willing participant! Cleaning was the first order of the day. Our youngest son, Andy dropped by for lunch. We always enjoyed catching up with his life.

We had our whole day planned out. From the closest to the house to the farthest away, errands were lined up from one end of the day to the other. We started in Corydon, Indiana, and ended up in Charlestown, Indiana.

On the way to the hospital to see Marilynn, we stopped at Mom Peyron's to pick up some chairs for the weekend's upcoming event.

The next stop was the hospital to see Marilynn. It was decided Mark would not go in because he had been sick the week before and didn't want to do any "sick swapping." It was probably for the best. Mark and Annie waited in the truck for me.

I went up the stairs to Marilynn's room, Bible and anointing oil in hand. We greeted each other, and I asked her a few questions. Then I asked the Lord how He wanted me to pray, and the word came down.

I anointed my dear friend with miraculous oil from Fr. Mike, and I went into battle! The Lord had told me in my spirit to pray for a quick recovery. I went into my spirit language and cried out for a fast healing! I looked for the good report. Marilynn said she felt something enter into her situation. I did too.

On the way back out to the truck, I received a phone call. It was from Mary. She was asking for a prayer covering. Strong prayer.

"Sure. What for?" I thought I had asked a simple question. I was not prepared for her reply. By that time, I was just entering the truck.

"A poltergeist."

"What?! A poltergeist?!" Mark sat beside me with wide eyes!

Mary explained, "I have been asked to come over and exorcise a poltergeist out of a house."

"Oh my goodness!"

Mark and I went straight into battle! We prayed angels to surround Mary and drive out the unseen and unwelcome from that house. And to put a Holy Spirit in place of that evil one.

"You call us as soon as you get back home and tell us you are safe!"

"I will," promised Mary.

Our last stop of the day was to one of our favorite places—BJ and Tim McCoy's. That was Mark's youngest sister's home. We were headed over for dinner. With four children, expect loud and wild when you get there, and you won't be disappointed. They are also a loving and God-fearing family. The Bible is no stranger in that home. BJ and Tim own a nursery and landscape company.

One of their favorite hired hands was Kyle, who was getting married to the lovely Miss Ashlie. They stopped by for dinner too. It was a nice crowd.

Most of the food came from the McCoy's ample garden. Fresh homemade salsa, corn, mashed cauliflower with garlic, and a meat headlined the meal. Boy were we at the right place!

The meal was over all too soon. The dishwasher was full, and so were our bellies. People sat in various rooms holding conversations or watching television. BJ and the soon-to-be newlywed couple sat in the dining room talking.

Now, anyone who tells you that getting married and the days that lead up to it are easy, a cakewalk, are not living in this reality! It is hard! It is a lifetime decision. And, your wedding is the biggest event you will ever plan together! And when I mean together, I mean six or eight other well-meaning people that want to help! Parents, step-parents, grandparents, and the two of you. It is not for the faint-hearted.

I remember with my first wedding, I got so upset toward the end of the planning, my Dad had to knock on my bedroom door and slip me a valium through the doorway. Truth!

Well, this little couple's nerves weren't much better than mine were at that time. Mark and I sat down with them and smiled. They related their hurting hearts and how much there was to do. They both poured their hearts out!

We listened with love and guided them with Scripture. Over the course of a couple of hours, hearts and feelings mended. Tears were shed from all of us around the table. And in the middle of it all, we had church! When you are called up for service, it can be from dawn to dusk. And it usually is! That day it was.

GOING HOME!
(July 5th)

Good news! The Toninis approved the second *"Miraculous"* book and ordered copies for the store. Mr. Chris expressed interest to see all in the series as they would come out.

By that afternoon, I heard from Marilynn. In less than 24 hours of being prayed over, she was 98% better. Instead of a pacemaker surgery, she was going home! Praise God for His mercy. That's how our God works!

At prayer group that evening, I gave a praise report. It went right along with the theme the Holy Spirit had given Phil Wermuth to speak on; "Understanding and working in gifts God gives us."

Phil's talk was so insightful. He spoke about how we are all called to have an understanding of this topic. Phil and Melanie Wermuth at the height of the charismatic movement, had been called to start a prayer group at St. Mary's of Lanesville, Indiana; almost 30 years ago as of this writing,. I, myself, had been involved with the group since 1992 — the same year I met Mary there.

A BIG DEAL AT A LITTLE LIBRARY!
(July 7th)

We had prepared well for this event. There had been three newspaper articles run in three different cities in two states. And there were three radio station interviews.

The book signing was at the Corydon Library in downtown Corydon, Indiana. It was to be from 11-3 p.m. Mary, Mark and I arrived early to set up, and found a crowd already waiting on us. And we still had people waiting in line and couldn't leave until almost 4:30 p.m. Wait! I've gotten ahead of the story!

Mary spent the night before at our home. We wanted to make sure everything was ready to go on time the next morning. We all woke up early and got ready for the long day ahead of us.

Mary, Mark and I arrived at the library by 10:30 a.m. to set up. The ladies that worked at the library were so helpful! The library had had a few book signings held there with the usual turn out of about 10 people or less. The three of us prayed, and I asked to sell 26 books. That way I would know God was with us.

We were set up in the front, off to the side, so as to be out of the way in case we had a crowd. I have to admit, I laughed.

"Crowd? What crowd?"

Well, that was exactly what happened! People started arriving well before 11 a.m. with large groups of family and friends. I got up and exchanged hugs. Pictures were taken by several people at once. By mid-day, with so many people that showed up, it looked like "paparazzi!" I was overwhelmed!

"Mary, Mark, take over and help!"

"Yes Ma'am!"

"Stand here, please! Smile! Thank you! Next?"

"Debbie, sign these books please."

Good friends, and people who had seen the articles, came from two states. Mary was also approached by an author who liked my work so well, she asked to come on board with Mary's publishing company, Home Crafted Artistry & Printing. It was an exciting day for us all!

One of the stories I had written about was a gentleman from Kentucky. I had never personally met him until that day.

"Next, please."

"Hi. We've never met but I drove all the way over here to meet you." He stood and smiled in front of me. I knew immediately who he was.

"George! It's you!"

George laughed and nodded his head. I jumped up and ran around the table. We hugged and I felt the Spirit of God in him. Cameras flashed all around us.

Finally, at 4:30 p.m., we packed up to go home for a cookout. The ladies at the front desk came over and smiled at us. They had never seen such a successful book-signing at their library! When we added up how many books sold that day, the total came to 26, just like we had prayed for!

When we arrived, our house was full of people. Mark was already barbequing, and people were eating. Ben, Amanda, and Andy were set to stay the night with us. Wonderful! Annie was handed off to person after

296

person to play with. She was fed off several plates.

Later on, the boys asked Mark to go to a friend's home and watch the fights with them. Mark cleaned up after cooking out on the grill, kissed me and Annie goodbye, and went off with his sons.

As the night grew late, most of the people left, but a few stayed and the conversation grew deep. We talked of God. Mary Smith, Crystal and David Murray and myself sat and spoke of the mystical and powerful aspects of our God — Father, Son and Holy Spirit.

Before midnight, Mary left. She had church the next morning. I thanked her for all her help and conveyed that I couldn't have done it without her. We dreamed of where God was taking us.

The Murrays and I stayed up well past 1 a.m. speaking of our past, present and future and what God had in store for mankind.

Annie had fallen asleep in my lap long before the last two left.

When the kids and Mark arrived back at the house at 1:15 a.m., they were surprised to see someone still there and me up and talking.

It was the wee hours before everyone settled down and the house got quiet enough for sleep to come. Annie was very happy when we finally got in bed together. The little two-pound puppy could finally stop worrying about her family. We were her people! And we thought she belonged to us.

BIGGER FISH
(July 12th)

As I was getting letters ready for other pastors, and several communications and publishing companies, to request to go forward with this series of books, I had a beloved sister who was also in a battle she needed to win. Ivie's battle made my battle seem small. Mine was just for books, and hers was to save her mortal life.

Once again, for the fourth time in Ivie's life, cancer had come back. I have to tell you, she and I were very tired of holding that same conversation.

Mark and I prayed once again together, in force for Ivie's life. As weary as we were for her, we couldn't begin to understand the feeling she was going through.

"Have mercy on her, oh Lord, have mercy."

A GOOD TURN
(July 13th)

The letters were finished from the day before, and my husband felt well enough to go to work. Missions were being accomplished one by one.

I worked early that day and was given $20.00 for a couple of books sold. In turn, I took Mark, and another friend, Karen out for ice-cream. We sat on the porch of the old fashioned ice-cream parlor in our home town and ate. Conversations drifted around town activities, all our children, and how the books were coming. It was a very pleasant evening.

When we arrived back home, Mark paid me back my $20.00.

"Why, Honey?"

"You have it for a reason."

There was a message on our recorder. There seemed to be a problem, a hold up going forward with our approval for our construction loan. I had not been at my job for six months.

I cried to my shift manager. She thought about it for a minute and said to me, "But Deb, you've already been here four months. It's only two more months to go."

Like a light bulb switch, I found my bright side.

"That's only two more months! By my 54th birthday, we could finally have our awaited answer!

Who couldn't hold on for two more months?

I WAS MADE FOR THIS PURPOSE!
(July 14th)

Andy came by to check on Mark's recovery.

"I told you he'd be fine, Momma!"

"Thanks, Son!" Having an advanced care EMT for a son sure came in handy.

That evening, Mary and I went to an LCW meeting. Mark and Annie stayed home and held down the fort.

There was a very nice published author named Steve Flarity who gave the talk that evening. We had something in common, him and me. He wrote about extraordinary people and what they do, and I wrote about an extraordinary God and what He does.

At the meeting, we were all asked to write about each other. We put our names in a hat, and then each of us drew a name out. While I was waiting my turn, I prayed in my head.

"Lord, I want to pick my new friend Crystal's name out! I want to write about her. Please do this for me."

When it got to my turn, the first person's name I pulled out was my own! Ha! I put it back in and held my breath. Out popped Crystal's name in my hand. I jumped up and yelled "Yippee! I prayed for this! Crystal, it's you!"

Crystal laughed and motioned me over. She told me her story, and I told her mine. We both took notes. Then I went back to my chair and began to write, as did all the others in the room.

The words came freely with heartfelt emotions ringing from one sentence to the next. It was the first time I had been there for that kind of exercise. It was the first time the other authors would get to hear my work — and a published author would hear it too.

When it came time to read our papers, I decided it was best for me to go first and get it over with.

I started with an introduction — which I am known for in my writing. To me, it's setting up a story's background. Just like in a painting when you paint a back drop first, the rest will go smoothly.

By the time I finished my first paragraph, to my surprise, Steve hollered, "That's the best segue I have ever heard! Great story!"

"Great story" echoed several times by the time I was finished reading.

People clapped and cheered. I blushed. No one clapped louder or laughed more than my Mary, who was seated next to me. She patted me on the back.

Mary smiled and said, "I knew you could do it!"

I thanked the group members for their kindness. Crystal smiled across the room and nodded her head. It was as if she had known it all along.

By the end of the evening, I knew I was intended for this — to write; to be a scribe for God's activities here on this Earth. Just as I was shown almost five years earlier, I was intended for *"Miraculous Interventions."*

MY SISTER CRYSTAL
By Deborah Aubrey-Peyron

For someone I have not known a great length of time, I am very pleased the God of all creation made the decision to drop her into my life. After all, I had always wanted a little sister. Miss Crystal Murray sure fit the bill. So, when at this writing class, we all had to put our names in a hat for a partner, I started doing what I do best... praying." Crystal, Crystal, Crystal! Lord, I want Crystal for a partner!" And sure enough, I turned the card over, and there was her name.

The questions were given to us on what to ask. Oh boy! I got to learn more than I did before I got to class. What I didn't know was how fast and deep the conversation would quickly go.

Crystal's home life as a "valley girl" in Southern California was not as glamorous as one would first imagine. She used writing as an expression to speak of things beyond her young understanding. Her first writing was a song at seven years old, entitled, "If I Were a Pretty Bird." The song went through birds and butterflies, and by the end of the song, she had decided "I think, I'll just be me." Quite a jump in thinking for a little girl that had been chronically abused by life in general. This little one was destined to be a writer.

By 7th grade, Crystal took a poetry class and fell in love for the first time. Even her teacher knew she was a poet in process. He called her "the poet who knew it."

By high school, Crystal found herself in a girl's home called Hamburger Home. Yes, Hamburger Home on Hollywood Boulevard. During this time, she wrote for therapy of all she had been through.

It wasn't until she met David, at 26 years old, and got married that Crystal was able to sign up for the Institute of Children's Literature for her first actual writing course. Her journey had now begun. Being president of LCW is icing on her amazing cake.

Crystal's most memorable writing is a devotion she wrote as an example for a compilation project. She wanted to make a difference in people's lives. Crystal truly feels if you can make a positive change in someone's life, then your life is not a waste.

What would she most like to achieve in her writing quest? Simply, to be used of God. And if you knew my little sister, you would know every day she wakes up she says, "Good morning, Lord!" And she is already achieving her quest of working for the Lord.

Much love, little sister.

BIRTH OF A SCRIBE
By Crystal Murray

How often are we encouraged by the stories we read in our studies of God's word? And, as we are reading them, do we ever stop to think about the fact that the disciples were called "uneducated men" and therefore only scribbled their stories? Someone, somewhere, was probably called as a scribe to communicate their events to the world.

Deborah may not have known when she first began scribbling stories as a four-year-old, but God knew He was calling her to become a scribe for Him even back then. When her stories became loosely gathered slips of paper bound into kid-size books, she did not know it was a type and shadow of the full-size, perfect-bound books she would publish in the future.

Because God knew this certain future to which He was calling this modern-day scribe, He sowed encouragements into her younger years. Whether it was the laughter of a teacher who read her high school stories, or the placement in the top two of those with whom she wrote in college, she can look back now and see the Hand of God confirming her calling.

In a time of her life filled with some of her greatest adversity, God pulled all of it together to remind her to "count her blessings" on paper. He also asked her to count the blessings of others. After two years of recording her own stories, He began to send people her way to let her know it was time for her book to be birthed. The project that began her journey as a

304

published writer is now the expanded project that fuels her writer's dream as a God-called scribe...to actively record the acts and miracles of God's modern day apostles.

DAVID, THIS IS ANNIE
(July 15th)

Finally!

It was all arranged. It can be hard to get everyone in our growing family together for a family photo. We all have busy lives with school or work. As the mother, I was the one in charge of setting it all up.

Our formal pictures were always taken at Christmas. We all dress in like colors in our Christmas best to send out to family and friends. It's a tradition with us that has been handed down to our children.

"But this is July, Momma." Our oldest son responded to the request. "Why July?"

"I know, Son, but I got this great coupon in the mail for a new studio, and you get your pictures on the same day! How cool is that?"

"Hey! We've heard of them. Make it so, Momma!"

"There is only one problem. They won't let Annie be in the pictures."

"I'm sorry."

"I know. Well, maybe at Christmas we can have her picture taken with Santa. We will bring her with us anyway. You know she does not like to be alone. Besides, David hasn't met Annie Frances yet. I hope he likes her!"

"He will, Momma! Who wouldn't like Annie?"

"Dress code?" Ben asked.

"Nah. It's summer. Be comfortable."

"I'll spread the word."

The day came and the boys showed up right on time. And that was the last thing they did to cooperate!

306

Mischief was in their eyes and we knew there was goofiness afoot! But it was still good to see them. Ben and Andy were dressed casually, like us, as requested. It seemed David didn't get the "casual" memo. He came dressed in a nice suit.

David's first words to all of us were, "What the heck?"

"Sorry, Son! But you look really nice in your gray suit." I responded.

He took off his jacket and rolled up his sleeves to blend in with the rest of us.

Annie was off to the side in her carrier. I walked over to her and opened the door.

"David, I want you to meet Annie Frances."

I picked up our little, solid black two-pound puppy to introduce them.

"David, this is Annie." I smiled.

David looked at her, and she at him.

"She's cute, Momma! But she's so small. Is she okay? Are you feeding her?" There was real concern in his voice for the wee puppy.

"When have you ever known me to not feed something? Yes, Son; I feed her. Annie travels with dry food and water, even milk in a dropper. We are very good to Annie Frances. Would you like to hold her?" I held her out smiling.

"She's so small, I'm afraid I'd hurt her. Maybe when she gets a little bigger."

"Well, she's not going to get much bigger. Maybe a pound more her doctor said."

"Okay."

Ben brought his girlfriend, Amanda. She agreed to hold Annie for us while the five of us had our pictures taken.

The first picture taken was a group shot. Then one of our three boys together, one of Mark and me, and one of each individual boy.

I guess I should have warned the young lady about our boys. Never once have they given a photographer an easy time! The glint in each of their eyes should have warned all of us! They will usually be good for two, maybe three shots and then all bets are off. I keep hoping year after year that they will be better, cooperate, and grow up. Anything! Not so much.

One after another, they blew pictures on purpose. At the last minute, one of them would pull a stunt! But they had us all in stitches, including the photographer.

David did his "smolder" look.

Andy did his "crazy face" look that he perfected while we were on vacation at Walt Disney World. "Thanks, Son."

Ben, not to be outdone by his little brothers, just got silly!

Laughter rolled through the halls until Amanda and I were embarrassed.

The picture that is still on all their face book pages, is the one when the photographer went to take a picture of the three boys together on a background of a brick wall. At the last second, they all turned around, backs forward, hands up against the wall with feet spread apart. Big smiles were planted on all their faces.

I laughed so hard, I thought I'd split my pants! I finally managed to speak.

"Boys! One, Two,..."

It's a crying shame when a mother of three,

twenty-something year olds, has to revert to counting to three to make them behave!

"Shape up, and I mean now!" They weren't so big I couldn't grab an ear!

I wonder from time to time, if any of them will have hearing loss from this form of crowd control. So far, the only one they still have trouble hearing is me. Nothing has changed. I looked to Mark for help to defend my cause. As usual, the testosterone group fell in line together. Mark's eyebrows went up with a look of surprise on his face; he shrugged his shoulders and pleaded the fifth.

Finally, it was over. We all sat down together to look at proofs to see if any were usable. A few made the cut Our orders were taken and paid for. Mark, Annie and I stayed and waited for the pictures to be developed.

Ben, David, Andy and Amanda took off for the pizza parlor across the street. After a few minutes, we received a call. It was from David.

"Hey! We're ordering appetizers and pizza. Get over here!"

We were on our way. They didn't have to tell us twice!

We arrived to smiles and hugs as if we hadn't just been together. While we waited for our appetizers, I got out Annie's food and drink, fed her and took her potty. No one asked us to take her outside or leave. No matter where we took her, no one ever asked us to leave.

It was wonderful watching our sons interact together. Silliness followed them from the photography studio over to the pizzeria. Laughter erupted throughout the meal. Even these hooligans stopped for a moment of prayer and thanksgiving to God.

In the middle of our meal, Mark received a call that the pictures were done and to come and pick them up. While Mark went and got them, we cleared the table so we could spread out the pictures. Mark got back, and in just a minute, people called dibs on which ones they wanted copies of. With everyone satisfied, the afternoon festivities came to an end. We all promised to get together soon.

It is times such as these, I am the most thankful for.

Aren't you too?

LOST, FOUND, LOST, FOUND
(July 16th)

Some days are just set apart for us to be helpers. No matter where you are, or the circumstances around you, you are meant to be part of a solution for somebody. Just like me on this day...

My morning was busy. I had a Skype call with Pastor Ivie Dennis. It was great to see her smiling face and hear her words of knowledge and wisdom fall over matters of the heart.

My next appointment was with a client. This was a wonderful person, and my task was to get them to see what I saw in them. I wanted them to see even a little of what God sees in them. Over the course of several hours, success was achieved. How did I know? The smile on her face as they left told me, at least for a while, things would be better.

I was overdue to get ready to go to work for the afternoon/evening shift. As usual, I ran out the door.

"Come on, Annie! It's time to go to Daddy's work."

Oh, how Annie loved to go to Albin's to be with Mark! At Daddy's work, Annie could shine.

So far, during the day, I had helped a lost soul see and found words of encouragement for myself. I did not know when I pulled up to work that day, I would be having church inside.

I settled into my routine for the afternoon. Like most days, I broke into hymn songs as I walked down the aisles and put unwanted merchandise back on the shelves. When customers would head to the checkout counter, I would be right behind them. Sometimes a line would form right in front of me — which happened late that afternoon, about dinnertime.

Two sets of ladies came up to my register. The two in back of the line quietly waited their turn. The two in front were not! They weren't mad, they were just as silly as geese.

They asked each other questions over and again.
"Did you get the coupons?"
"Did you get this or that on our list?"
"Oh, oh!"

I smiled and patiently waited to check them out. After all had been totaled up, they were short money. I determined from the way they were dressed, it was all the money they had. It did not surprise me. I bent down in back of the counter to my purse, pulled out my change purse and set all the money that I had with me down on the counter. I counted it out to see if we were even close. We were close but no cigar. Hmmm.... They were quite a bit short. Dollars short, and I had none left to give.

At that moment, the two ladies in back of them dove into our conversation — and their pocketbooks. Their money rolled onto the counter and joined ours.

"Is this enough?" They asked.

The two ladies of meager means stood there with their jaws dropped open as three strangers came to their rescue. You could tell from the look on their faces, they were not used to being treated so graciously.

"We're good!" I cried as the needed total was counted.

With grateful hearts, they thanked everyone for their help. One would have thought, as they clutched the bags so tightly as they left, that their bags held

Solomon's gold.

Then again, maybe to them, it did.

The three of us watched them make their way through the parking lot. Another one that had been lost, had been found. We smiled at each other. I asked.

"Christians, are ya?" I offered.

"Yes, yes!" They cried in unison.

"Amen, sisters. Me too!"

Joy spread through us like melted butter on hot toast! There was no condemnation in any of us for the souls that had just left the building. We spoke scripture to each other. We were excited that the Holy Spirit had just used us to show Jesus and acts of kindness to another fellow traveler here on this Earth. At the mention of the Holy Spirit's name, we all three felt His presence among us! Glory to God!

Lost, found, lost, found.

I helped, with merciful words, a lost soul that morning to see clearer.

I found strength through a dedicated pastor who encouraged me to go on doing good.

I helped two lost souls who had not seen the kindness of Jesus shown to them in a very long time.

And at the end of my day, I found two sisters in Christ Jesus doing the same good as I.

What a day! What a perspective.

Being a Christian isn't about being better than thee or thou, but being humble in spirit and rejoicing in it!

I bet you already knew that, didn't you?

TO SLEEP PERCHANCE TO DREAM
(July 17th)

It was 5 a.m., and it started out as a play. Yet in me, I knew it was real, and I was indeed watching it happen before me.

As the play unfolded, I saw the little boy grow into a man. I went from a spectator to a participant. I saw a coliseum arena with an open ceiling. Then I saw the man, Jesus, teaching a crowd. I saw some people go forward and some draw back. He was teaching me too.

Then I saw people in dark colors standing in the background plotting against Jesus. I saw them go after Jesus to kill him! In my head, I thought, "Quick! Take him to a hospital!" But before I could get to Jesus, he got up healed and whole.

This time Jesus was teaching anew! He was tall, and big like a carpenter would be. Strong! Masculine! His long hair was woven with the color of copper embedded throughout. He looked like the Lion of the Tribe of Judah as Jesus' eyes were on fire with a purpose! You knew they saw everything!

By now, Jesus was giving gifts to the young and old alike. I knew in the Spirit, He had on the Coat of Many Nations with colors I did not recognize in the natural. I was close up in the line when I quietly stepped to the side and went and hid in the back, on my knees. I was sure I wasn't worthy of any such gifts. I had let Jesus down so many times in my life, and I still wasn't where I was supposed to be—or had accomplished my mission yet.

When I stepped out of line to hide, Jesus stopped what he was doing and came to find me. Jesus bent down and smiled at me. He smiled at me! I smiled back! Relief spread throughout my body. He was not mad at me! And Jesus had two whole handfuls of gifts he gave me! Then Jesus stood before me and spoke power and prophesy over me.

"Your work has just begun!"

Interpretation came instantly upon arising....

"Stand up! Don't be afraid! You are capable of more than you think! Gifts have been imparted to you. Don't give in to tricks, or snares or doubt. Don't let the unbelievers in your mission get in your way. Set the standard straight. Be on a mission! Have great expectations! God makes great expectations that are from Him come true."

How about your gifts?
What you are capable of?
Be on a mission too!

FIRST HOUSEWARMING PRESENT
(July 24th)

Our new friends, and to-be-owners of our home, came over for brunch and dinner. It was to be a ladies day. Crystal and her sister, Candie, and I got to know each other better. And Crystal had been thinking!

"Deb, where is your dining room table and chairs?"

"We sold them in a yard sale."

"Why?"

"We were trying to raise money for our home construction loan. Besides, someone needed them more than we did."

I could already see the wheels turning in her head. After more conversation, the subject was brought up again.

"Deb?" Crystal began.

"Yes?" I replied.

"We have a dining room table with six chairs in our basement. It is not even being used. It would be like moving in one piece of furniture at a time. You could get good use out of it until we get here. What do you think?" Crystal paused.

I did not want to take advantage of my new found friend. Yet, I could not think of any reason it couldn't work.

"I'll call Mark. When would you like us to pick it up?" I asked innocently.

"Tonight!" Crystal smiled in triumph.

It was settled! Our brunch time turned into dinnertime with stimulating conversation. My, what a good time we all had!

316

All too soon, the evening was over and Mark and I followed Crystal back to her house in our truck. David, Crystal's husband, was waiting at their Louisville house when we arrived. Crystal had called ahead and told him of the situation.

The two men pushed and pulled all seven pieces into our truck. We said our goodbyes well after 11 p.m.

The next day, we brought the table and chairs into our home/their home in six months. That was when we noticed it.

I said, "Honey. Their table completely matches our dining room China Cabinet."

We stared at the pieces of furniture with wonder in our eyes.

"What are you thinking?" Mark ventured.

I eyed the situation.

"I don't think that's our China Cabinet anymore."

"It's a $400.00 dollar piece of furniture! Are you sure you want to do this?"

A peace settled over me. I was already smiling.

"I think I'll call Crystal and tell her we've picked out her house warming present!" I made the call while Mark nodded his approval.

I opened the conversation with, "Crystal! You won't believe it! Your table and our China Cabinet are a perfect match."

"Really?"

"Yes! Do you have a China Cabinet?"

"No. I have never had a China Cabinet in my whole life."

"Well you do now."

"Wait! I don't even know what to put in one."

"Uh, china and good glassware? You got any?" I

was in new territory. I had four sets of china and crystal.

"I have some Cape Cod glassware. Do you mean things like that?"

"Yes! Now you are getting the idea."

"Oh boy! David, did you hear that? They just gave us our first housewarming present."

It was the first of many to come.

I KNOW! I KNOW!
(July 28th)

God is a good God. He is very patient with me. He shows me things over and over with confirmation, so I know I am on the right track. Perhaps He does this for you too.

Pastor Ivie Dennis held our twice regular Skype meeting. It was a great way to spend a morning and catch up with each other's lives. For two-and-a-half hours we talked, taught, preached and prophesied over one another.

Ivie preached strength into me. She reminded, me that I, too, was called to be a general in God's army.

Then an epiphany moment happened....

Ivie saw what God had been showing me for five years in the Spirit. All the gifted people the Lord had led to me were going to come under one roof to meet. They would all come together to speak of the deep things of God.

I started to holler, "I know! I know! He has been showing me this for five years!"

ANYTHING!
(July 29th)

"Oh, you're right! That flag pole has to go. Mark can help you put up a new one."

There I went again. I volunteered my husband for something without asking him. But that time, I was pretty sure I was safe with that request. After all, Mark loved my little brother, Ron. He always said he would do anything to help him. I just beat Mark to the punch! At least that's what I told him when I got home.

Mark, Annie and I arrived early that Sunday afternoon at Ron and Devin's. Devin and I helped the guys any way we could be of benefit. We were having a flag-pole raising. Ron was retired Navy, and his son, Joshua, was in the Marines. Ron was not about to sit in his house and stare out his front window without seeing two flags atop a pole –the United States flag and the United States Marine Corps flags respectively. We all pitched in to help.

Annie pranced back and forth between Momma and Daddy to see what we were doing. I took pictures of the guys digging, and Devin took pictures of Annie watching them.

Mark did all the grunt work as Ron gave direction. Ron had been laid off from the post office with a back injury and could not assist with the physical work. While the men were doing the last of the work, I went inside and read Ben's story in Ron's upcoming book on our five generations of military service. The story was heartfelt and brought many tears to my eyes as Ron described how Ben almost gave his life for our country.

It is still something I can hardly talk about.

After we finished up at Ron's, we all went over to Momma's for dinner.

"Hi, Momma!" we said as we came through her door.

"Hello, children!" She greeted us back.

Then Momma paused and said, "Hello, Annie."

Annie blinked up at Grammy Fran as if to say "hello" back. We all had dinner together including Annie. She had a mix of what she could digest off my plate and her regular soft puppy food. (Only organic and the best!)

After dinner, the kitchen was cleaned, and we went outside to the backyard so Annie could play.

It was during this time, Mark felt a bad headache come on quick—a nine out of ten in pain range. We treated it with medication and prayer. Needless to say, we came home early.

Mark and Annie went to bed before I did. After a bit of housecleaning, I slipped into bed myself. That was when Mark told me he smelled cigarette smoke in our bedroom—strong—just like three nights before when I had smelled it! We wondered at the time what that could mean.

Mark and I were awakened late that night by Andy and Samantha. They had made it to Walt Disney World just fine and were having a great time!

We wondered what that would mean, too.

PRESSING IN
(Aug. 1st)

"Happy birthday, David!" We texted and left messages for our middle son. We sent David a card with his usual birthday amount in it. It was not in his heart to have a big celebration that year.

"Maybe next year, Momma."

"Alright, Son."

I worked on the computer that morning and made calls to the bank. We thought we were getting a home construction loan through them. Even though this was disobedient to the prophesy given to me that a private lender would come forward to finance us. Some lessons are hard-learned.

During the afternoon, I cleaned house and made a nice meal for Mark and I. It was to be family movie night for us and Annie. We would have dessert, and Annie would have some of her puppy snack crackers.

With dinner and the dishes over, we all curled up together to watch a movie. Annie had her own blanket, and I had mine. Mark happily sat in the middle of us.

About halfway through the movie, I began to feel uncomfortable, or should I say a lack of feeling. Numbness started down my left arm. I wiggled out from under my husband's side and thought I had cut off my own circulation. I tried to move it around to bring it back, but to no avail.

Then the feeling of numbness crept down my left leg. I tried to move it too. My heart rate was climbing as fear started its attack. I tried to stay calm.

"Mark, turn off the movie."

"Why?" The tone in my voice sent chills up his spine.

"I'm going numb on the left side of my body — my arm and leg."

I had Mark's full attention! Mark was ready for orders and to do battle for his wife's life. Warrior shields were up!

"Get your Bible and the anointing oil out. Pray over me from my head down. Please hurry!" I felt time was of the essence.

With calm quickness, Mark assembled everything requested. He laid me down and read from Scripture. In my head, over and over, again I cried out, "I believe God! I believe God!"

Mark opened the flask of miraculous oil, which had in the past been very temperamental. I had no control over it. There had been times when we had tried to pray over people with it and couldn't coax any oil out of it at all. It all depended on God's timing. This time, immediately as Mark took the top off, before he could turn the flask over, oil overflowed onto his hands! We both knew what that meant! With a big smile, Mark anointed my head, neck and all down my left side. As the oil touched me, all feeling came back to normal, and I was healed.

The attack on my life was stopped. Fear and suffering were cast out of my body and spirit. Victory overflowed the situation.

When Annie saw Mommy and Daddy smiling so

big, she jumped up and kissed us both! Even she knew something huge had happened.

We all felt perfect peace when we went to sleep that night. The perfect peace of Jesus!

The Prophesy

Rev 1:1-3 "The Revelation from Jesus Christ, which God gave him to show his servants what must soon take place. He made it known by sending his angel to his servant John, who testifies to everything he saw – that is, the word of God and the testimony of Jesus Christ. Blessed is the one who reads aloud the words of this prophesy, and blessed are those who hear it and take to heart what is written in it, because the time is near."

ANCIENT OF DAYS

If you felt God had saved your life on a particular evening, what would you do the next day?

Well, I basked in His mercy. I took it easy. I smiled from one end of the day to the other. I took phone calls but did not make any. I felt born again all over again.

I didn't even need to make dinner. God had already supplied that need. Our good friends, the Horne's, had asked us over for the evening meal. They had been remodeling their home and land for as long as they had been on it. Lisa wanted us to see what they had accomplished next.

They have a busy household with four young'ins

scattered about helping Mom or Dad. Mark and I "oohhed and aahhed" as we went from room to room. Annie kept the children busy at play — that was the job she did the best.

We gathered all nine of us around their kitchen table and ate together.

Conversation was sprinkled with the days accomplishments and anything the children thought important to inform us of. The whole evening had a nice homey feeling.

After the meal, each person had chores to do. The men went to sit and held more conversation. Soon, Lisa and I were off on our own to discuss things that were on our hearts too. As usual, and in short order, our conversation turned to God.

Lisa started the query.

"There are some letters in our family, left by an old aunt who had great prophetic ability. I would like you to see them."

"I would love to. Do you know what they are about?" It was an innocent enough question.

"Yes." Lisa paused.

I waited.

"She saw the fall of 2016."

In my spirit I knew what was coming.

"She saw the Ancient of Days and the fall of 2016."

Stunned, I sat and processed what she had just told me.

"Do you think this is important?" It was Lisa's turn to ask an innocent question.

I smiled and said, "Important enough to be put in a book."

** This set of 8 stories took place over three years. It came together during 12 months, starting in 2012 and on into 2013. Due to this story's content, it will all be covered under, *2012, the Miraculous Year*, (book III in the series).

** Lisa's husband wished to remain anonymous throughout this story. I will comply with his wishes. Their last name has been changed.

THE STORY BEFORE THE STORY

Sometimes the story behind the story is as important or amazing as the story itself. The same with this one.

The thread travels back between 50-60 years to another generation in another time. How the information fell into my hands took the reorganizing of two families and their trek to a whole new region of the United States.

In other words, God moved Heaven and Earth to get this information into print, to you, the reader.

I sat in a borrowed room, in a broken down chair to write and bring this to you.

Scripture teaches us, when a prophesy is shared among the brethren, they must discern what to do with it.

I am telling the whole story, here and now.
The ball is in your court.

CONFIRMATION

Another month went by before Lisa and I could talk again. I asked Lisa to call her sister-in-law to make sure of the whole story. It was the week before the fourth of July when Lisa called with more information. That was when it all started to come together with all its history.

FIFTY YEARS IN THE MAKING

1st Corinthians 14:29 "Let the prophets speak two or three and let the others judge."

Lenora was a visionary from her youth. I myself have understanding of the personal cost paid for this type of gift. Lenora's brother, Wilfred, 75 years old in 2013, walked with Holy Ghost fire and anointing. You could feel the air change around him when he walked into a room.

When Lenora was young, she had a vision concerning the United States of America. She wrote it down and put it away inside of a book where it stayed for almost 60 years until its time.

It is time.

A LOVE STORY

There once was a bright, young man who worked with a beautiful, sweet, young lady. They were both in unhappy marriages for one reason or another, and they found solace in each other's company. Their hearts fell. Marriages were dissolved, and families were rearranged. In the meantime, the new young bride sought peace! Her husband, trying to please his new wife, agreed to move them to another area. They left behind loving family members.

Down they traveled through the states until they came to Indiana. First one area, then another, until they settled in southern Indiana. The husband went from one job to another. The first baby came, then quickly, a second one!

It was about that time he met my cousin at a business meeting in the community. He asked Gail for any contacts she might have, and she gave him our name and number.

HAPPENSTANCE

Mark and I were living on Mathis Road at that time. We had all our boys at home and were getting ready for our second annual Christmas Open House. Mark brought home a name and number of a new family in our area.

"Do you think we should invite them to our open house?"

"Sure, why not?" I said. I had no idea at the time, nor did I for many years, how that simple answer would change so many lives.

The little family arrived the day of the party, along with 80 or so other family and friends. Their smiles were sweet and timid, after all, they knew not one single person in the house! We took their coats, and told them to make themselves at home.

"Feel free to eat when you're ready. We've already blessed the meal."

I busied myself between so many of our guests, set out more servings and plates, cooked a second ham and even got to mingle a little. Every once in a while, I would go over to the new family that occupied our couch in the living room and would ask them if there was anything else I could get them. I hoped they had a nice evening.

Over the course of a couple of years, we saw them again at the yearly parties. We assumed the family wasn't quite comfortable with us, not having heard from them in between times.

Until. ...

One day, out of the blue, the husband called and asked to talk to me.

"My wife, Lisa, just had our third baby, and all our family is back in Wisconsin. There is no one to show our newest baby to. You seem so nice, would you mind going to see her at the hospital?"

"Why sure! I'd love to see your new baby and wife. When?"

"Well, now."

"Oh my!"

He told me which hospital Lisa was in, and off I went on another good deed. I stopped to pick up diapers and a card along the way. Having something beat going empty handed.

I walked into Lisa's hospital room, and quietly wondered to myself if she would even remember me. There was this beautiful, young lady with long auburn curls surrounding her face, holding her precious newborn son. The Madonna surely was as lovely as this.

We greeted each other and talked for a minute. I handed her the diapers and the card, and she handed me her baby! I felt a part of something very special that day. I found out how lonely Lisa was for a friend. It was then that I promised I would be her friend. She would not have to be alone anymore.

Her husband found another job over in Kentucky. A move was planned. They bought another home and had another baby. By that time, we were seeing much more of their family. And at least, they always needed help moving.

The Horne's watched us go through all our trying times as well. They watched us struggle through the recession of 2008, the selling of our "home sweet home," the buying of the land in back of it in hope of better times, and regular family times together as well. We invited them to join us in a little home church we found in Corydon, Indiana. We spent several happy years there together.

Every once in a while, Lisa would give a word of knowledge to me, like the time she said, "The devil has been trying to kill you since before you were born." Don't think that didn't send revelation chills down my spine! It explained a lot of happenings in my life and why I needed more than one guardian angel. She also prophesied to me, "Your home will be up and finished before mine is completed."

Finally, one last time we moved the Horne's back to southern Indiana to stay. The little block house's basement needed to be redone — put back together. What were friends for? For almost two years, we went over a couple of times a month to clean, and re-cement their block basement walls back together.

The Horne's had many projects going along the way. We would occasionally go over to see their new room addition; changing of walls, windows, whatever the case was. Mark and I were invited for dinners and Bible studies. Lisa told amazing stories of her husband's family members and of the generation before us. I was called, on several occasions to interpret dreams.

In 2010, Lisa had been to see her family up north. She also had seen her husband's family. Lisa called to ask me a question.

"Debbie, my sister-in-law has seen a vision. Diane has had an open vision while sitting on her couch. Can you help us interpret?"

"I will try." I wasn't used to hearing that come out of anyone's mouth but mine!

"Diane had a vision about the year 2016. The year just popped into her head and flew up in front of her eyes! Then it crumbled to the ground! She knew the president would serve a second term. Then she saw the statue of Liberty with a huge rope around the middle of it. The rope pulled to the east and broke the statue in half. The statue fell, head first into the ocean toward the east. The other half fell toward the west. Then Diane saw a missile come from the east and hit America right above Florida. She knew in her spirit where the missile was sent from. The last part of Diane's vision was the date June 6th, which hung in the air as a silent warning."

I knew in my heart, there was something about that date. What was it?

That was all Lisa told me at the time. I told her it meant real trouble was coming! We would need confirmation on this vision. Look for it!

The rest of the story took almost three years to unfold.

Almost three years later, again while Lisa was on vacation in Wisconsin, she called me with the rest of the story. By that time, we had sold our home to the

Murray's and were living with Mom in an upstairs bedroom waiting for our builder's health to come back so he could start our home. Time was running out on that project, and we were fighting the weather to start- - over four months late.

Mom hollered upstairs to me, "Debbie, the phone is for you!"

"Thanks, Mom!" I ran down the stairs and took the phone back upstairs with me and sat in my comfortable old, very old, corner chair.

"Hey! How's vacation going? You and the kids okay?"

"Yes, we made it here just fine. The weather is nice, and it is good to see family."

I could already hear it in her voice. I could feel it inside me. My stomach churned.

"Something's been found. It's a letter from Aunt Lenora who died two years ago. Her daughter found a letter in a book that *just happened* to fall off a shelf while she was cleaning in a room. The book fell open to a page that had a slip of paper in it. Lenora's daughter read it and called Diane right away."

"And now, you're there. Tell me the note."

"The 60-year-old note reads as follows: I saw the statue of Liberty sticking out of the water, drowning. America is being weakened. We are losing our liberty. ----------- will attack America on the east coast with missiles."

It was the same attacker that Diane had seen.

I told Lisa to call me when she got home from vacation. I would pray for her safety on the road. There were several people I knew who would want to hear her family's stories. In the meantime, I felt I had to get to my editor, Mary, and let her know we were on to something far bigger than miracles! Mary and I agreed to meet four days later.

Confirmation.

I received another call that day. It was from a job I had done to step in and help someone. They would send me a check but would no longer need me. They were going to hire someone else less expensive. Even though the Lord showed me that this was for the best — best for the patient and best for me, eventually my heart was sad over it.

I held a conversation with God.

"Lord, if I am not worth $40.00 a week to man, how can I be worth anything to you?"

I cried for myself and for my husband.

An hour later, I received a reply from God through Lisa. She called me back on the fourth of July, Freedom day. I had all the notes lined out and made sure with her the stories were straight. Lisa also gave me Diane's phone number. I would still have to contact her. After going over it all, I realized the magnitude of what I was being given to write.

In the world's eyes, I was not worth $40.00 a week. But in God's eyes, I was good enough to be a scribe for the King's prophets. I was the one to sound the warning bell!

I had to talk to Diane before I saw Mary and Mitch.

I had four days.....four days.

DIANE

For the next two days I called and left several messages for Diane. Lisa had taken her my first book, *Miraculous Interventions*, so she could see that we had much in common. Diane was my first-hand link to the whole story. I knew I needed information that only she could confirm. Once confirmed, I knew I had to take it to Mary.

On Friday afternoon, I received a text from Diane. She would be able to call me in an hour. One hour before we had to leave to go to church, Diane contacted me. It was good to hear and meet the lady whose shoulders this important prophesy lay on.

I called Diane back to save her phone bill. She was friendly from our first greeting. The first thing she wanted to do was thank me for writing my book.

"Well, thank you. Why?" I was always curious to know what people thought.

"I'm not alone anymore. I'm not the only one out there," she replied.

Tears formed in my eyes for that unknown sister. She was one of us! A seer from her youth. Diane gave her history. She was raised Catholic but not instructed on how to read her Bible in the 1970s. Diane had her first vision at the age of 17. She saw a woman's face in front of her, and she knew the lady had passed away.

At 21, Diane had a very specific dream. She was in a white space. (I imagined it was much like what Andy saw when he had his out-of-body experience.) Diane saw seven angels, seven trumpets, seven bowls, and seven lamp posts. Then she heard a male voice speak with authority!

"What you fear is true. Read Revelations, it's true!"

Diane got up and read, for the first time, Revelations. It was 1981.

Over the years she, saw darkness or light around people. It let her see people's hearts or motives. Since 2010, and the open visions she has received, Diane feels things are accelerating. There is a hurry over life here. Diane was told in 2011, in a prophetic dream by Jesus,

"When your lamp is low, ask and it shall be given unto you. Light is love from me. You will be a light in the coming darkness."

Darkness is coming. We are to warn the believers. We have been selected and called to warn the believers.

Consider yourself warned.

Sunday was still two days away.

SIVAN 28

Sunday was a good day. It started with all kinds of errands to run. The storage shed we had rented, Mark's truck, and my car all needed our attention. After we cleaned all three places and vehicles up, we headed for our homeland to see if any digging had been done yet. I called our neighbor and told her we were on our way over for dinner. She informed us that someone was on our property, and there was smoke! He was burning something on our property. Was it going up in smoke?

My prompt reply was, "We can be there in ten minutes. Mark, step on it!"

When we arrived and walked over to where the smoke came from, we recognized our other good neighbor. He had taken the time to burn away the molded hay from all the rain we had. We had a nice long talk with him and looked forward to one day, soon, living there.

Mark and I walked back to the truck and took our picture on our homeland. Another neighbor, Jeremy Ward, drove by and pulled up beside us in his truck. We, again, had a nice long conversation that ended with, "I look forward to being your neighbor!"

We were now officially late for dinner. She was still there to greet us but her husband was off on another errand. Dinner was almost ready for us. She had prepared a wonderful meal of grilled chicken and side dishes. We visited and prayed together. She, too, could hardly wait for our next home to go up!

I called Mary's home, our next destination. We were going to be 45 minutes late for our clandestine meeting. Her husband-once-removed said we were not late. Mary had to work over and would meet us right about that same time. I call that God's time! Mary pulled up to her house ten seconds after us. We walked each other inside.

Since Mark and I had just eaten dinner, we sat in their living room while Mary, Mitch and their family had dinner together in the kitchen. We settled our spirits in prayer as we waited for them to join us in a life-changing conversation.

After the meal was over, Mary and Mitch came to sit on the couch and chair next to us. I told the story, beginning to end. It needed no explanation as to how important the message was. At the end, I asked what she, as my editor, wanted to do. After all, this was a game-changer, maybe for the rest of our lives. The couple needed no words between them.

Mary spoke first, "Scripture states, when there is a prophesy, you are to send it out to the Church and let them discern the message. This is from first Corinthians 14:29 "Let the prophets speak two or three and let the others judge.""

Something was still bothering me.

"June 6th" I murmured.

Mary said quietly, "D-Day."

"I know that, but I feel there is something more."

Mitch suggested we go to the computer and look it up under "Today in History." The men went to one room, and we went to the other. Mary and I sat at her computer and looked up the date. The dates started around the year 1200 and worked their way to the current date.

"No," I said. "It's going in the wrong direction.

Try Hebrew BC."

Mary plugged it in, and the computer told us the Hebrew calendar did not recognize the term BC. We had a good laugh over it and asked for guidance from the Lord. In our flesh, we were stuck.

We thought to try the Hebrew calendar again. We looked for June 6th. Up popped a calendar for conversion purposes. June 6th registered to the Hebrew date of Sivan 28.

"Okay."

Mary and I went back into the Hebrew calendar to history and put in Sivan 28.

Sivan 28 — Friday, June 13th in 929 (BC) (June 6th on our calendar) "Israel is divided into the northern and southern kingdoms with the Death of Solomon."

Division. Just like in Diane's prophesy — east to west.

The side note sent chills through our bodies as we cried out for our husbands! The men came running down the stairs!

We all read it together:

"It is interesting to note that this same date in 30 AD, is the date of the **Ascension of Jesus."** (June 6th **our calendar).**

No one spoke a word. Now, we were more than miraculous scribes, but keepers of a prophesy to send out to warn the brethren!

Before we left their home, we all prayed softly over each other for protection. We knew from then on, we would all have to be very careful.

All I am saying here is, we are told in sacred Scripture to notice the signs and the seasons we are living in…. and to prepare.

341

CONFIRMATION FROM AN UNNAMED SOURCE

The attacks on us started two weeks later. The private lender pulled our home construction loan. We would have to sell our land before the end of the year. Our promised home was now a "dream impossible." I knew it was a casualty of the war we had just entered.

During this time, I felt a great push in my spirit to tell this prophetic journey to several people. The first couple listened intently and agreed to help my books get out to the general public.

The next push I felt was to tell a certain one of my church friends.

"Why?" I received no answer but obeyed the call I felt.

After church, I requested a little of this person's time. I related I had a story to tell. As before, I told the story, beginning to end, just like I told Mary and Mitch. At the end, I paused to wait for the reaction. Quiet settled over us in contemplation of what to say next.

Then this person had a story to tell me:

"I have a good friend who is a successful financial adviser. He is not a Christian but does know this world well. We were having lunch one day together when a lady of low financial means approached him and asked what to do with a small windfall she had received. She asked if she should invest it. He quickly said *no*. The advisor told her to take her money and put it away and save it. Do not put it in a bank.

I am sure I looked puzzled and asked him why he

had said that to the woman. He told me he fears there is going to be a stock market crash in 2016. If so, it would destabilize the whole world. It could be a world crash. There could be rioting in the streets, and the government would have to call out the National Guard. It could be two months we'd be under martial law. All the banks and stores would close, grocers—all of it.

Now, this man is not a Christian, and he knows nothing about Revelations or Jesus. I have waited for the confirmation of these events."

We sat in the quiet church as our hushed, whispered conversation came to a close. My next orders were to tell Mark as soon as I got home. An eerie calm spread through me. I knew the next day, I would tell Mary and Mitch the rest of the ongoing story.

October 19th, 2013
Out of time.
We were running out of time.

A MID-SUMMER'S DAY DREAM
(August 3rd)

I started the morning looking for a better job.
"Nothing until October, thanks."

I ran errands and came back home for lunch. I knew we had a busy day ahead of us. Mark and I were to pick up friends and take them to a concert at Christian Country Cowboy Church.

As I drove up to our home in Corydon, I noticed storm clouds on the horizon. I came in and made lunch for Annie and myself. Afterwards, I urged Annie to go outside quickly. Storms were approaching! We came back inside after she finished and I cleaned up the kitchen.

The house grew dark and quiet. Quiet enough to put a puppy, and her owner, to sleep. I felt so drowsy. Annie and I drifted off to sleep. It was during this time, the Lord led me in a dream. How did I know it was from the Lord?

If you saw the hand of God come out of the clouds on Judgment Day, you would know it was Him too!

The Hand of God

I dreamed I was in a fast food restaurant getting ready to be served. I looked over to the seating area and saw clouds forming in one corner. Even in a dream, I thought this occurrence was unusual.

Then I saw a huge hand come out of the clouds, like in the DaVinci painting. People wearing royal purple robes were running up to it to be picked up and

345

taken away. I ran to the counter help, and yelled, "Do you see that? The hand of God is taking His saints away!" The ones behind the counter were quiet.

I went to sit at a table by myself and started to pray. All the people in the restaurant started to mock God and threw heaps of verbal abuse my way for praying. With my eyes closed, I went into my spirit language, the gift of tongues. I heard people around me gasping in wonderment. I opened my eyes. We had all been translated into a courtroom. The judge's bench was a beautiful blue color, and it had a white sash covering it. I knew the courtroom awaited the King of Judges to enter and start the judgment. But He was not there yet. I felt sorry for those that had been in the restaurant that day. I knew there had not been enough time to save them.

Then I awoke. Sorrow filled my being.

I spent the rest of the afternoon making dinner for Mark and myself. He came home after work and we ate quickly. Kelly, our friend showed up right on time. She was to go with us to church and spend the night with us. We were also to pick up Crystal Murray on the way to church –which we did.

COWBOY CHURCH

Our group arrived at the church parking lot with a few minutes to spare. All the regulars greeted us, and we sat down to wait for the festivities to begin. It was our first concert there together. I had been at the one the month before that had headlined Pastor Chris Powell along with the house band. It had been a wonderful time, and I looked forward to Mark and Kelly's reaction to the show.

The house band sang several songs. Joy spoke to the crowd, while the men of the group went backstage and changed into their costumes. It was almost time to call out for the boys of Sasquatch Hollar! I giggled while I waited for their appearance. Mark and Kelly and Annie had no idea what they were in for. Joy set the stage.

"Are ya ready to holler for the boys?"

The crowd roared "Yes!!"

"Hey, boys!"

Out they came through the back stage doors, a tripping and a jumping over each other. Mark laughed out loud! Kelly smiled. The boys had on baggy overalls, torn tee-shirts and straw hats at odd angles covering their messy hair. When the crowd quieted down, they went into their routine. At least, I think they had a routine. One corny joke after another flew across the stage! They were received with laughter and smiles all around. At one point, they must have startled Annie because she barked at the stage. The crowd roared as someone said, "The next joke must be going to the dogs!"

Once their show was over, the church took up donations for the evening as the main headlining group got ready to come on stage.

The small church in LaGrange, Kentucky, is on the circuit for some of the best Christian Country artists in the nation. The one they had that night was no exception to the rule. The two-man group called "Branded" sang their hearts out! Crystal took pictures while Mark clapped his hands. Annie hid in my blanket. The noise was too much for her little ears.

After the concert, people stayed for a midnight dinner, just like the time before when I had come with Debbie Grimes. By 1:30 a.m., Annie was asleep, Mark and Kelly were tired, and our little group agreed it was time to say goodbye. When we got up to leave, the men who had sung onstage got up too. They approached me while I held Annie.

"Ma'am. I have a little dog like that too, at my home, back in Texas. Would it be okay if I took her picture to show to my family?"

"Why sure!" I replied.

At Cowboy church, even our puppy baby was well appreciated!

We dropped Crystal off at two in the morning and started our long trek back to Corydon, Indiana. The car was quiet as passengers drifted in and out of sleep. Thankfully our faithful driver, Mark, stayed wide awake and alert on his mission and got us all home safe and sound.

$40.00 AGAIN.

(Aug. 5th)

For some people, money can be hard to come by. It seems to elude them, no matter the good they do or the work they've done. I can't explain it, but I have walked that path many a day on my journey.

So, when I myself had saved up enough money to get Mark an anniversary present, I was thrilled! One hundred and thirty dollars is what I figured it would take to buy him a really good weed-eater. He could retire the old one and use it for parts. My plan was set—until I ran into God's plan.

I held onto my money so tightly. I kept it in my purse next to me. I was fixed on "money for Mark, money for Mark." A few days before we were to go out shopping, it hit! I came across a family who was in dire need of $30.00. They would be stuck without it. I felt a tug in my heart.

"Sigh."

"Yes, Lord."

A cheerful giver I was not! But what I was, was obedient to the call. At the time, I hoped I still had enough to get my husband a new weed-eater of any kind.

We arrived at the store on Sunday afternoon. I was not feeling very well. Annie kept me company as Mark looked up and down the aisle for a particular kind of weed-eater that he wanted. Of course it had to be a nice one! Nope. One hundred dollars would not do. I finally had to confess what I did.

"Mark, Honey, I only have $100.00 on me. You see, there was this family that needed $30.00 real bad! I'm so sorry, Dear."

I sighed and prayed a silent prayer for help.

Almost immediately, a young man came around the corner. He was a sales associate and ready to help the next customer along his path.

"Hi! I'm Matthew! Can I help you folks?"

Mark chimed in, "I'm looking at your weed-eaters. This one looks nice."

Including tax, it was $140.00. The two men looked it over until they were satisfied that this was the one for Mark. I felt worse by the minute. Both men looked toward me and saw my demeanor.

"What's wrong?" Matthew asked.

"Well, you see, it's our anniversary. And I tried really hard to save $130.00 of my own money for Mark's present! I had all of it until this week when a couple was in desperate need of $30.00. Now I only have $100.00. I don't have enough to buy Mark his present anymore." My words hung in the air for just a few seconds. Matthew brightened up with a smile!

"I can sell this to you for $100.00. That will be a savings of $40.00 including tax." He was still smiling.

I dropped my jaw. Suddenly, I felt physically better. God had indeed heard my silent prayer for help. He had read my heart's desire. And delivered it right on time!

We left the store jumping for joy! Our next stop was to Mom Peyron's for dinner. Several family members were there as well. Sandy and Danielle got to meet Annie. We made plans to go visit BJ and Tim later that week to pray for healing in Tim's arms.

After we left Mom's, on the way home, David called and we got to talk to our middle son. Right after that, I heard a beep beside us from a truck. It was our youngest son, Andy, who motioned for us to let him in front of us. Then he stuck his arm out of the truck window for us to follow him. Mark and I looked at each other and shrugged our shoulders and took off after him.

Andy wound around several back streets until he came to a small house in a neighborhood next to a school. He hopped out of the truck and smiled at us.

"Hi, Momma! Hi, Mark! Good to see you!"

"Good to see you too! Where are we?" Hugs were exchanged.

"There's someone I want you to meet."

As if on cue, out of the house came a petite, pretty blond in a nurse's uniform. She met Andy with a hug and then turned her attention to us. Introductions were in order.

Andy said, "Momma, Mark, this is Samantha. Sammie, these are my parents, Debbie and Mark."

In the front window of her home, two little heads peaked out at us.

We all smiled and said our hellos. Mark and I smiled at each other with approval. "It's very nice to meet you."

A few short minutes later, two small figures bolted out the front door at a dead run headed straight for us! I braced for impact!

"Momma! Momma!" And they weren't talking to me!

"I told you kids to stay in the house." Samantha

sounded like a real momma!

Zoom! Zoom! Around the mother they went.

"Matthew won't stop..." whatever it was that he was doing at the time. The little girl stopped in front of us and smiled. At barely six years old, she was already a beauty queen. She had long blond hair and the biggest blue eyes that I had ever seen. Mark and I couldn't help but smile back at her. Then she cried out, "Thomas! Thomas!" and ran into our son's arms.

"Hello, Lily pad! Lily, these are my parents, Mark and Debbie."

The little princess had a name!

"Hello! You sure are pretty, just like your momma."

Both blonds smiled their approval.

In the meantime, the boy "whoosh" kept running around and around his mother, oblivious to all around him.

"Matthew!" Andy and Samantha shouted in unison. As if awakened from a running sleep, he looked up and said, "Momma! Thomas!" He jumped from one set of arms to the other.

"Hi, Buddy! Did you have a good day?" Andy asked.

The squirmy roly-poly nodded.

"Matthew, these are my parents, Mark and Debbie."

Out came a shy "Hi."

The four-year-old was finally still long enough for us to get a good look at him. He was of small stature, even for a four year old. He was petite, like his mother. His short, sandy blond hair stood straight up on his head. His eyes looked from thing to thing in the yard, never quite settling in on us. Mark and I looked at each other. Then I looked at Samantha and waited for an explanation.

"That's my Matthew!" Samantha said.

Samantha took the boy child in her arms and communicated in a strange language all their own.

"Mee, meee meee. Mee, mee meee mee?" His mother cooed at him gently.

The boy mimicked her back. It was communication on a level only they understood. I smiled as long-ago memories flooded my brain of my three little boys and our conversations when words weren't necessary.

Then Matthew joined our conversation with words. Why, he really could talk! Shortly, we said our goodbyes and looked forward to seeing them all again.

On the way home, Mark and I wondered if this was the nurse, our friend, Kelly, had prophesied about; the woman that would heal Andy's heart.

A GOD INCIDENT

My job at the time was pretty menial. I got my satisfaction from the customers that came through my checkout line. It could feel like church.

I worked the long shift on that Monday. That meant from two in the afternoon to 9:30 that night. I stocked shelves and waited on customers. As the afternoon waned into evening, I waited on three sets of customers that let me know I was at the right place at the right time.

It started with a lady and her daughter in my checkout line. Her daughter was quite ill, I could tell right away. With my usual flair for being discrete about such matters, I jumped in with both feet!

"Oh, dear. Aren't you feeling well?" I inquired.

"No, not at all." The young mother replied.

"Do you believe in the power of prayer?" I asked.

"Yes! Yes we do!"

"May I pray over your daughter?" My heart was sincere.

"Please!" And so was her mother's heart.

I asked God to bless the intentions of a mother's heart and restore her child. I asked for the little girl's name and said I would remember her in our nightly prayers. The lady thanked me as they left the building.

The next lady in line came up to be checked out. She looked me in the eyes with such intensity, I knew immediately something was wrong!

"What is it? Tell me! Tell me!" I cried out.

"My sister just died! Today!" I could feel her

354

sorrow all around me.

For that one, I stopped what I was doing, walked around the counter, and hugged her. Rocking her, I prayed God would soothe her torn heart and that her sister be joined with the Lord in Heaven. When I finished, she said to me, "I knew, when I walked into this store, I was supposed to meet you. That is why I am here."

I took her name too. I agreed with her as she paid her bill and walked her to the door.

The last lady in line, who had observed all the goings on, walked up to my counter. I smiled at her. She stared at me for a full minute. As with the other two, I knew something was coming. I had to ask.

"Are you okay?"

She finally said, "No! Actually, I just got a bad diagnosis from my doctor today! I had an MRI, and they found a mass!"

I prayed a prayer over her for her healing. I took her name to pray over that night with my husband. When she left the building, she was already feeling better.

I arrived home shortly before 10 p.m. I got ready for bed and sat down with the prayer requests I had accumulated throughout the day. As I prayed for each intention, I felt heat fall into my hands as if healing were spreading out and being delivered to each person. I thanked God, with tears in my eyes, for being a useful vessel.

HAPPY ANNIVERSARY!
(Aug. 7th)

Some people take celebrations to the maximum! We are such as those. It was our 13th anniversary and we decided to celebrate for 24 hours!

Shortly after midnight, Mark and I gave each other our anniversary cards and scratch-off cards. I won $21.00.! God and I gave Mark a weed-eater (at 30% off), and God and Mark gave me a new outdoor table and six chairs for our deck-to-be (at 60% off). We had been at the right place at the right time for these things to occur. We cuddled and fell asleep with Annie beside us. We were one small, happy family.

Mark and I slept in until late that morning. Together, we made steak and potatoes for breakfast. Cut up very fine, even Annie received a taste of what had obviously smelled so good!

That afternoon, we went by to see Mom Peyron. Betty wished us a *Happy Anniversary* too. We asked her to babysit Annie while we went out to dinner. Mom was very happy to oblige us. She and Annie were good friends!

Annie was known for running around Maw maw's house and would jump up in her chair to kiss her hello. I'll never forget the time we arrived, and Annie ran up to mom's chair, and she wasn't there! Annie turned and looked at me with panic in her eyes! I could just hear her saying, "Where's my Maw maw?"

I laughed and said, "Come on, Annie! Let's go find Mawmaw." We found Betty in the kitchen. Annie jumped for joy! Her Mawmaw was not lost anymore.

Mark and I went out for a nice meal to a restaurant that we had never visited before. The view along the river was beautiful and the meal was scrumptious. We decided to forgo dessert there. Our plans had been to go to an old-fashioned ice-creamery to top off the meal. We watched the sun go down along the Indiana riverside.

Mark and I picked Annie up from Mom and headed back to Corydon. The three of us stayed up until midnight to finish our celebration.

At the time, we figured by our next anniversary, we would be in our new home. How odd we thought it would be, moving in August. All the other times in our life together, big events always happened in, or around, December.

BROTHER TIM

(Aug. 8th)

It was a challenging day. There was a lot to be done in a 14-hour period. Mark worked his usual day at Albin's, and I worked the morning shift until 3:30 that afternoon. As soon as I got home, I had two wellness clients lined up to meet with. It was imperative that I be right on time.

By 5:45 p.m., I had changed clothes when Mark stepped in the house. At 6 p.m., we were all out the door again. We had a dinner date to keep with BJ and Tim and their family. There was a meal, a Bible study and a prayer request lined up for that evening.

You see, Timothy had worked so hard all his life that he had very painful arthritis in both wrists. As the owner and head workman of *McCoy's Nursery and Landscape*, this was not an acceptable condition to be in. It would not do!

I had prayed and sang praise songs all day at work to gather strength for the battle ahead, and for Tim's faith level. I was sure Mark did too.

We pulled up to the McCoy Charlestown home and were met by their four children in the driveway.

"Did you bring Annie with you?"

"Yes, of course we did!" Annie Frances was always welcome wherever we went. Annie jumped out of the car and went potty in an acceptable grassy area. Then she went off to play with the other children.

What an aroma that met our noses as we walked into their house! It looked like BJ and Tim had been cooking most of the afternoon. Five fresh vegetables from their garden; steaks and hamburgers were hot off the grill. Drinks and desserts were ready to be served. We felt like modern day apostles being greeted by the faithful!

BJ called the children to dinner. Hands were washed, and they sat down quietly. We all bowed our heads to give thanks to God Almighty for the day and evening to come.

"Amen."

Annie was seated with me. It was what she was accustomed to. I fed her small bites of any vegetable she liked; green beans, carrots and peas, along with her favorite dog food for meat. We brought her water container with her special water that was made with vitamins and glucose that her veterinarian suggested due to Annie's small stature. We cheered when she reached two pounds at the vet office!

After dinner, the four adults walked the grounds and looked at the new and improved patio area. It was so beautiful! Timothy had designed it himself. It arched around from side to back with large pots of herbs that decorated the edges. It had a feel of peace about it. Annie sniffed everything she came across. We talked, caught up with each other's lives, and laughed with the children until time to go in for the evening.

Tim settled the kids in the office with a movie and closed the door. Mark and I brought out our Bibles. We all four sat in the dining room for the real reason we had come over, to pray for Tim's healing.

Mark and I both read healing Scriptures to shore up Tim's faith for a miracle that very night. Then, we took turns and prayed over him with the laying on of hands and anointed him with miraculous oil. For twenty minutes, we evoked God Almighty, Jesus and the Holy Spirit for mercy and healing.

Tim reported he felt warmth over both his wrists.

BJ reported the next day, Tim felt so good that he worked outside for seven hours straight!

In fairness, I must report Tim's pain did come back, and he had to take medication for it.

CHURCH AFTER CHURCH
(Aug. 10th)

Mark and I were both off from our day jobs; we had planned it that way. That day was to be dedicated to our side job of landscaping. We worked until 3 p.m., and all was accomplished. Annie was with us. Half of our conversations started and ended with, "Annie, stay away from the road!"

We arrived home shortly after 3 p.m. We showered—including Annie, who was not a fan of water. The three of us curled up together and took a two-hour nap. Dinner was a quick meal. Afterwards, we grabbed Annie, her bag and blankie, her travel kennel, and took off for church.

I guess Mark and I were still tired because we got into a big fight on the way there! It is very unusual for us to fight in that magnitude. Then, God spoke to my heart.

"Do not come into My house with a grudge against your brother! Clean it up!"

I was convicted in my spirit and heart then and there! I told Mark what I had just heard from the Lord and what we needed to do. I started the conversation.

"Who goes first?"

Mark responded, "On three..."

Together, we said, "One, two, three, I'm sorry!"

Laughter and smiles returned to us. We were best friends once again.

When we pulled up to church, I knew I was to be there for the blessing with Rabbona Joy. True to the word I had been given, Joy came up to me with a smile and asked me to give the blessing with her. I felt honored to do it.

Afterwards, I joined Mark and Annie in the pew. Songs were sung, and announcements were made. Then Parson Zeb got up to speak. It was time for his sermon. And the title of his sermon was "Phones." Parson Zeb is a big cowboy who speaks softly.

Phones
(A sermon)

"Did you ever wish you had a phone line direct to God? Not like a human phone that drops calls in the middle of your conversation. One that would be open and on all the time—an open line to Him."

Parson Zeb chuckled, "You ever butt dial God?"

The congregation laughed and blushed as Zeb's question hit very close to home for many of us.

Zeb went on, "With God, we have something better. Most of the time, we pray for others' needs. What we don't do often enough is pray for ourselves— especially our spiritual selves; pray for ourselves to be right with God."

Parson Zeb allowed a minute to go by for the message to sink in before he went on.

"We need to become what we are supposed to be. Keep moving forward."

Then the good parson quoted Jeremiah 29:11 "For I know the plans I have for you, declares the Lord, plans to prosper you and not to harm you. Plans to give you hope and a future."

Not only were those words right out of the Bible, but right off the front of my first book! He was talking to me! I knew his words were for me too.

"When you see God's plan, go do it. There are six

362

phrases that help me—they will help you too."

1) Search me, Oh God!—Show us where we lack. Know my heart, not my actions.
2) Break me, Oh Lord!—Send me in the right direction.
3) Stretch me, Oh Lord!—Help me to do things I think I can't do.
4) Teach me, Oh Lord!—Teach me and show me new things; how to be a new person in You.
5) Lead me, Oh Lord!—Be pliable and moveable, like a child.
6) Use me, Oh Lord!—He has something for each of us to do.

"Say *yes* to His opportunities. Whether it be His plan for you right now, or for a season, say *yes*. You may be learning something you will use later. "

In my spirit, I cried out, "Yes!" I knew all my life, things like this had happened to me. I was elated!

"Preach on!" I cried.

With fervor, Zeb cried out to the listeners, "Look for what God wants you to do! Don't neglect yourself in prayer. You are commissioned to go higher up. Have a desire to serve God. Don't you realize you are knights? Drop to your knees before the King! You are at His mercy."

Zeb stopped for emphasis. He looked out at eager faces with tears in their eyes and continued on.

"We are knights! Warriors! Do what you thought impossible!"

Parson quoted Philippians 2:13 "For it is God which worketh in you both to will and to do of His good pleasure."

Zeb pleaded with his congregation, "Don't just be saved! Yes, fully enjoy the assurance of our salvation. God wants more for you! He wants there to be an impact from your walk. With kindness and a smile, you can save a life. Live in front of others like Christ. Represent the King well."

Parson quoted John 14:20, that we are one with Christ; Romans 8:10 that our spirit is alive because of Jesus' righteousness! Zeb ended with, "Go and live what you believe! Have a healing touch."

Some people stayed for fellowship and others left. Even though it was a late hour and we were tired from the early start to the day, we stayed too.

Mark talked with Parson Zeb and Pastor Chris. Joy came over to where I was seated. We sat in two pews and talked of family, our lives and the sermon given. I did not realize until a little later in the conversation, the Holy Spirit was in attendance too.

I could see Joy listening to two conversations at once. It was as if it were natural for her to bounce our conversation past the Holy Spirit before responding. I told her what I saw. I told her about my books and how whole families were counting on me. I asked her, "Am I to continue?"

Joy became animate, "Oh, yes! Never give up the books! You are called! You will see even more. You will go further. You and your books are not just for this region. God is going to stretch you like in Zeb's sermon."

I knew it! When Zeb had said those points in his sermon, I leaned over to Mark and said, "Traveling, I see traveling." Yes indeed! I knew this confirmed to me that this was a big call from God.

Rabbona Joy knew, the first time we met, the Holy Spirit was going to send me and her on a journey. When He called the time right, we would spend a night at a hotel and glean from each other.

"I'm for it! Let me know and I'll drop everything." I replied to the invitation.

I offered to pay for it all. Joy shook her head *no* and said the Holy Spirit would pay for it all.

As we wound down our conversation, we talked of my new little sister Crystal and her sister. By that time, it was well after midnight, and we were past the 17th hour of our hard-pressed day. Home seemed the best place to be to soak in all the new revelations.

THREE AMIGOS
(Aug. 11th)

A phone call interrupted my housecleaning. How could I ever thank them?

It was Buster and Debbie Richmer. They called to inform us they were coming over the next day to help us with the patio we were refurbishing.

"Thanks!"

Buster and Debbie are good people with good hearts, and evidently had free time on their hands. We agreed that if they would help us, I would cook!

I gave Mark the happy news as he arrived home from work. We had just enough time for a quick meal before going to Mary's.

Mary and I had been asked to speak about publishing books, at The Louisville Christian Writers' meeting that night. We packed up books and supplies and put them in her car. After we made room for ourselves and Annie, we took off over the river and through the suburbs to LCW.

We arrived nearly on time. Mark helped us carry boxes and bags down into the lower level of the hospital where the meeting was held. Eager faces greeted us at the door.

As president of LCW, Crystal Murray was all smiles and all business. As we set up our display, Crystal went over the agenda for the evening, Mary asked to speak first.

"Fine by me!" I said. I was more than happy to do the cleanup work. Mary had asked to go first because she was nervous and wanted to get her part out of the way. We prayed together before we got started. Mark positioned himself as photographer for the evenings' events.

Crystal called the meeting to order. Her husband, David, said the opening prayer and then gave a short homily on the Scripture verses he used. Then David introduced Mary Dow Bibb Smith, owner and Chief Editor of HCA&P – Home Crafted Artistry & Printing. Polite applause erupted as Mary walked to the podium. It was her first official speech on the subject of publishing. I smiled and nodded at her from the other side of the room. I knew she was better at this sort of thing than she gave herself credit for. I wanted the room full of people to know the Mary I had known for over 20 years. I wanted them to see her strength, her boundless energy, her enthusiasm for God's work, her intelligence, and her perseverance.

Mary started out slowly, much like a steam engine that gathers speed as it moves forward. She spoke of how it all started with her love of snowflakes, and a book 12 years in the making. She told how her family encouraged her to publish it herself and about her first book-signing. From the beginning, God showed her this would be the first of many books to come!

Mary spoke of how God dropped me into her lap with a manuscript as raw as they come! Our first book together, "*Miraculous Interventions*" (Originally titled "*Walking in the Supernatural*" 2011, changed for trademark purposes) was a guinea pig for everything else we would do later on.

As Mary's story unfolded into the technical side of publishing, hands went up all across the room. Intelligent questions were asked that needed intelligent answers!

That was when Mary Dow Bibb Smith took off and flew on her own! Her eyes danced with intellect as she led people step-by-step from problems to solutions. I don't believe she realized before that moment how much she knew and how invaluable she really was to people in her new field of study. God had made her a warrior with great strength. Mary spoke with enthusiasm for an hour-and-a-half before we all took a break. The crowd applauded with approval and smiles. I, myself, stood and applauded her success. Mary greeted Mark and I with hugs as she came back to her seat.

"Bravo!"

"Well done!"

After a ten-minute recess, David introduced me to speak as an author. I spoke for 20 minutes on being pliable when God calls you to do something that you have no idea about or where to get started. I spoke about how integral Mary is in the development of everything I work on; and how grateful I was that the Lord led us to Crystal and David and LCW. I received polite applause at the end. Mary gave out cards to prospective new authors.

By 9 p.m., the room was packed up, and Annie had had her bathroom break. The Murray's, Mary and ourselves were ready for a second meeting. The five of us, along with Annie, went out for a meal. As usual, we had Annie's food and water with us. We also had her carry bag and blanket.

Our men and Annie sat on one side of the table while Mary, Crystal and I, and Crystal's laptop, occupied the other two-thirds of the table. This was where Mrs. Crystal Murray got to shine and show her intelligence! Crystal walked us through the other part of publishing that Mary and I didn't have an understanding of — the promotional side.

Crystal knew all the sites and setups and where we should go, step by step. She was also an excellent editor! She was just what a fledgling startup printing company with several, new interested authors desiring to come on board would need! We sure could use Crystal's expertise and contacts in the field to move forward.

Crystal and David had already agreed to buy our home in Corydon and become Hoosiers. It looked like that was only the beginning of our foundation together.

"Would you consider working with us when you move to Corydon?" I asked with anticipation.

"Why sure!"

Crystal had found what she had been searching for her entire life in her heart — a big sister, which was my honor. A new home and a position were in the making.

We knew God's work with us was just beginning. I felt in my heart, all the players were now at the table.

Where would we go from here?

THE LITTLEST ANGEL
(Aug. 12th)

Mark and I slept in due to the late bedtime the night before. I made breakfast, as Mark got things ready outside to finish the patio. It was a day of helping on both sides of the fence. Ben, our oldest son, was also due to come by that afternoon. He was going to help me with computer work and a *YouTube* project. I was going to help him set up paperwork for his new business in the physical fitness field.

Buster and Deb Richmer arrived early that afternoon. The men went to work while Deb and I started dinner preparations. When Ben arrived, Deb and Annie went outside to help the men. Ben and I went to work on the computer. We had a lot of ground to cover in just one afternoon.

Ben set up my account and put a video on for me. By the time that portion of our work was finished, the group outside was also finished with their project. Everyone cleaned up and got ready for dinner. Annie received a tablespoon of vegetables with her meal.

Mark, Debbie and Buster had an early church service to go to, and Ben, Annie and I stayed home to work on Ben's projects. By 5 p.m., half of our group was out the door. Ben, Annie and I settled down to launch Ben's fitness business. We went through all my papers to see which ones would incorporate well into his client data sheets. Three hours later, our mission was mostly accomplished. But Ben still felt frustrated about the progress. Things had not moved along at the pace he had hoped for. I prayed for Ben as he felt overwhelmed by all his projects.

As Ben walked out my front door, he realized there was something else he had forgotten to work on. He screamed in frustration, and I cried. Ben paced on the porch between me and his car. I prayed God would please send an angel to lift his burden quick!

Annie watched from my arms as her big brother cried tears in frustration! All of a sudden she jumped from my arms to his! Ben caught her, and she climbed up his shirt and licked the tears off his face. She gave Ben kisses over and over! God had sent the littlest angel to calm Ben down and comfort him.

Ben finally managed a smile and said, "How can anyone stay upset when given puppy kisses?" He thanked Annie for being a good little sister, and he left peacefully.

It wasn't much later when Mark and the Richmer's arrived back home from St. Columba. I had dessert waiting for them. Everyone helped themselves in the kitchen with plates, and we all went back into the living room. We enjoyed fellowship, and I got to catch up with the sermon of the evening. My part of the conversation lasted a few minutes and ended with my answered prayer for Ben. Their part of the conversation took much longer. Amazing stories were being carried from church to our house.

I cried out, "Wait a minute! I can see this will need pen and paper." I ran and got a notebook and pen, settled back into my chair, and said simply, "Okay, go!"

It was Deb and Buster Richmer's first time to Fr. Mike's church, St. Columba of Iona. Buster was thrilled! It was the first time he had been given communion in years—since he had been a deacon in the Catholic

Church while in the military. Fr. Mike had officiated in shorts and a tee-shirt with no shoes! There were 12 people at mass.

Praise went on for half an hour, then Father started the mass. Scripture was read, and the sermon was given. Father Mike started with Psalm 68:13. It talked of God's gold. He read from Proverbs and Revelations. Fr. Mike talked about silver and gold. God wants us to have His gold, not the world's gold.

"There is excitement in Heaven! Time is so close for Jesus' return. God's gold is like dust falling from Heaven, being released on believers. God wants to cover His children with gold!" Father Mike sang out.

The congregation went into more praise. After communion, Fr. Mike felt he was to anoint everyone with oil. They all lined up to receive more of what God wanted in their lives.

Patti, Mike's wife, also prayed over people. She prophesied over Mark and Deb Richmer. She prayed over Deb. Patti saw Deb as a strong prayer intercessor. It was confirmation of a word given earlier in the day from me.

Then Patti turned to Mark and laid hands on his head. She had a word for him, too. Patti saw how far Mark had come. He had defeated big enemies that had come against him. All that was left were little, knaggy doubts. Patti assured Mark he would get victory over them too. They were not a constant trial anymore; only occasionally. He was getting victory day by day.

Fr. Mike prayed over all three for a double-portion of what God had for them.

First, he prayed over Buster.

"I see you working with angels. I see you and your

372

wife clearing away cobwebs in your minds that have been holding you back. I see oneness with the Lord. Clarity."

Then Deb, Buster's wife, for the third time that day, was declared a prayer intercessor. Fr. Mike told her to go with it and let the Lord lead.

Finally, Fr. Mike came to Mark and said, "I also see the clearing away of cobwebs in your mind that have been holding you back. You will receive greater understanding of things of the Lord. Again, I see oneness with the Lord. Clarity as well."

As Fr. Mike was ready to close the mass, he was shown a picture of me in the Spirit.

"The Lord just showed me a picture of Debbie Peyron with two suitcases in her hands. She is skipping along happily. Mark is with her. Suitcases are symbols of travel. I see her doing speaking engagements and book-signings."

Mark confirmed his words and said, "Wonderful!"

After mass, Buster told Fr. Mike what a wonderful time he had. Buster told Fr. Mike that he had been a deacon in the Air Force. He hadn't had communion since he got out. Buster had been seeking out other things besides the Catholic Church. He and Deb were still searching at the time.

Of course, they were told to come back anytime.

"Wow!" I said. So much had gone on in one short evening. We were all so very glad to have been in two houses for the Lord!

TROUBLED WATERS
(Aug. 14th)

Attacks were coming in on my family. I had worked most of the day and got home after 4 p.m. I called my mother, and she was very sick with a stomach flu. My younger brother, Ron, was suffering with his back as well. It was decided the doctor would do an ultrasound on Momma.

I called Mark for prayer on all the situations. He led us in prayer right away! Crystal, my new little sister in Christ and in my heart, called. She and her husband had been arguing all day long. Crystal needed prayer too! She asked to come over and we said, "Come on!"

Crystal showed up an hour later. We listened over dinner and prayed for their marriage. After dinner, she talked of their 22 years together. I could tell there was love on both sides. The Lord gave me a word to give to her for her husband. Satisfied, Crystal left for home at 11:30 that night.

Troubled waters stilled for the night; we went to sleep ourselves.

RADIO
(Aug. 15th)

As an author and promoter, I was always looking for ways to get the word out about my books. There was a local minister who had a wife with her own talk show. Every once in a while, she would dedicate her show to local authors. I and four other authors had been chosen to meet for an interview for the hour-long program.

We were shown around the studio and encouraged each other as our names were called. I was the last one left to go. Those in front of me had run long, so she only had seven minutes left for me.

"Okay. I'm ready."

We waited for the commercial break to be over. She gave me a countdown and then started the conversation. She introduced me, named all my books, and then asked me what put me in this field of work.

I told her of my love of writing since my youth, the loss of my job in 2008, and God's redirection of my life.

She thanked me for being on her show, and it was over. There was no time left to tell about the books themselves. Slightly crest-fallen, I thanked her for her time.

A little later that afternoon, I received a call from a family member about my mother. Momma was very ill. Her gallbladder needed to come out. The surgeon would operate that Friday. I told them I would be there.

That evening, I was invited to Mary's for dinner in honor of the Assumption of Mary. It was the highlight of my day! Mary and I caught up with each other on our days as her girls and Mitch prepared the food and set the table.

We all bowed our heads, made the sign of the cross and listened as Mitch and Mary said prayers together. As they went through the saints, we responded, "Pray for us." Their grandchildren added their own "saints."...

"St. Mitch — pray for us"

"St. Mary — pray for us"

"St. Katie — pray for us"

"St. Deborah — pray for us"

"St. Gail — pray for us"

It was everyone seated at the table!

You see, it was a reminder at the end of each and every day that we are all called to be saints, ready to serve the Lord in any capacity He sees fit.

FRIENDS
(Aug. 16th)

Friends fill your life with fellowship, in good times and bad, in sickness and in health, rich or poor, why even in ordinary days!

The day started early. My friend, Deb came over. Now, I know several Debbies. Let's see. There's Debbie Richmer, Debbie Grimes, Debbie Kinberger, and last but not least, there's me.

I try to keep them straight this way: Debbie Grimes is Deb, Debbie Richmer is Debbie, Debbie Kinberger is Cowboy Debbie and me, whether it be in an office or work or some I have known, I am usually singled out as Deborah.

Back to the story.

Deb came over to spend the day with me. Deb very much loves the Lord, and we usually go into deep conversations together. Deb hears from the Lord frequently, has had healing come from her hands, and prays and listens for the Lord's utterance. She is a staunch Catholic but tolerates me well. I count myself blessed to be in her company. While she was over and we were in conversation, another friend, Buster came by. Buster belongs to Debbie Richmer. That day, he was doing a good deed of which we were a part. He needed to borrow our three folding tables to take them to another friend who was having a large yard sale.

Buster came in for a little while to catch up with our families. We could tell he had something on his mind and asked him as much.

Buster had trouble with a friend. He had been friends with this person for a long time. Anymore, it was difficult for them to have a conversation together. Their good times were getting less and less frequent.

After listening to Buster's cares and concerns, we chimed in on the subject. Deb and I had both experienced that kind of relationship in our lives. We explained to Buster that not all friendships were based on good, solid relationships. I had myself experienced a couple of friendships that I had to walk away from, for a while or permanently, due to the stress it had put on my heart and feelings.

Deb had experienced the same. She and Dave, her husband, had moved all over the United States, and met lots of people. Some became friends; others did not.

We both told Buster not to be sad, whatever he decided. God would provide even better friends for him; friends who would care about him and not abuse his kind nature.

By the time Buster left, he was feeling much better. Deb and I knew it was a God setup. We had been God's ears and heart for another brother in Christ Jesus.

Deb left around dinnertime to cook for her family. Mark came home, and I was filling him in on the day's events when the phone rang. It was a family member who needed consoling over an issue on their heart. We took time for them as well.

Mark and I had hardly hung up from that conversation when the phone rang again! This time it was other friends. It looked like bad weather was coming, and we might want to ride it out at their house. I was all for it!

Mark, Annie and I left to go over. Thankfully, the weather split and went around Harrison County. It didn't stop us from having a nice time visiting with our good friends in our old home.

At 10:30 that evening, we found ourselves back home and in bed, curled up and reflecting on the day's events. We marveled at how God worked all to His perfection. We were thankful God used us from morning to evening, and counted it as a very good day with friends.

WORD OF KNOWLEDGE
(Aug. 17th)

Some days, we as believers in Christ Jesus are just on it! Words come down from the Lord as if flowing water. On this day, it didn't seem to stop.

I had been over to see my mother, and she didn't look well. I checked her heart rate and it was low — below 40 beats per minute. I was very concerned and told her so. She promised she would go see the doctor early the next week. I was sure her medicine was too strong for her.

Later that morning, my best friend of 38 years called. She had gone walking with her son, Gary, and had come back rather breathless. Vicki wondered if I could advise her over the phone. A word of knowledge came down immediately. Her medicine was too strong! She should call her doctor right then. She did!

Vicki called me back a few minutes later. She could not get in to see her cardiologist until October! I told her to call her family physician and get in to see him. Her family practice doctor could write prescriptions for tachycardia too. A phone call later, she was able to get in to see him that Monday. We both felt a little better.

Later that afternoon I received another call from a friend, Marilynn Crosier. She was having trouble. Marilynn had a rash and trouble breathing. She had tried to call her doctor but no answer. Immediately, a word came down for her.

"Call your doctor again and go straight to the hospital! Have Larry take you to the hospital right away!"

Marilynn did exactly as I suggested. I knew in the spirit, she needed an epinephrine shot.

Mark came home from work and packed us up, including Annie, and off to a friend's house we went. Jim and Ann Carter had asked us out to dinner.

The Carters had been in the miracle ministry for a long time. Their shared stories and experiences always shored us up to go on with ours. And they loved Annie! Many times in their life, they had small dog-family members themselves. We knew exactly how they felt. Annie herself did not know she was a breed, but knew she was loved as our daughter.

After dinner, we went back to their house for card games and fellowship. Evenings with the Carters always ended in prayer and words of knowledge. That evening was no different.

Ann for me: "It's okay to trust Mark."

Jim for Mark: "Everything is going to be all right."

Later that evening, a phone message awaited us. It was from Larry, Marilynn's husband. They had gone to the emergency room, and Marilynn was treated. It seemed she had an allergic reaction to her blood thinner. The doctors had stopped her reaction just in time! We gave God the glory.

A good day, all in all.

LIVING ON THE EDGE
(Aug. 19th)

We went with friends to a church that we liked to frequent. It was headed by double pastors Tom and Bridgette McCullum. They are a Holy Spirit-filled family. They had all girls and we had all boys. The McCollum's were working on spoiling their grandchildren, and we told them we were not through spoiling our children!

Tom and Bridgette had special speakers that came to preach occasionally. Five of us, including Annie, arrived and settled into our chairs as praise music sounded through the old movie theater renovated into a church. We looked forward to the experience.

Songs wrung out for almost an hour, when Pastor Tom took over with announcements and introductions. For almost three hours, preaching from a visiting minister and prayers were heard in the halls. It went something like this...

"God has set us free and sought us out as His people. He fills us up! This does not happen just once! God helps and saves us numerous times. He will save you even before you are saved!

Easter is a *divine reversal* with the fall of Adam. God loves to surprise us and do what we are not expecting! God is so unique in what He does. He can choose the least-likely object to show His awesomeness.

Look at the lengths of what God has done to bring us to this moment. A one-in-a-million shot. He marks our destination. He will do something for us we can't do for ourselves. God is working overtime for us to meet our destiny. It is our appointed time! Get this in your minds and hearts!"

This touched my heart so, that I cried great tears while taking down notes. Mark had to hold Annie.

The speaker went on:

"We can get all messed up with the cloak of religion, secret sins and wannabes. You serve a greater purpose than your paycheck! Rise up! There is a purpose for your life. You are the intervention for a nation! You will impact people's lives. You are going to make people want to be a member of God's family. Find God's secrets—ask God to tell you! Paul, in Corinthians, called it hidden treasure. There are keys that unlock people's hearts, and then lives are changed."

I thought of the time I had met with a lady for help with her prescriptions. During the course of the conversation, she told how upset she was with doctors who had damaged her child. She hated them. It dismayed me, so I responded with this comment, "Oh please, you must forgive them! Jesus himself said no man can enter the Kingdom of Heaven with hate in his heart! You must forgive, so you can be forgiven. Don't let another person's actions rob you of your Heavenly home."

The next day, she came back to my office to pick up her paperwork. She looked like a new woman! She came in and smiled at me, and could hardly wait to tell me what had occurred the night before.

"I did it!" She cried. "I prayed and I forgave everybody! I feel like a burden that I had carried for years has been lifted off my shoulders!"

"You're free." I smiled.

"I'm free!" She smiled in return.

We cried together. I slowly came back to reality and listened again to the man preaching.

"There is a shift taking place now. God is on the move! You have a destiny. You were created for a purpose that you have been moving toward all along. You may have been detained, delayed, deterred, diverted, but not undone! We have been knocked down but not out. Second Samuel 5:1-2 speaks about people who had to remind David of his prophetic destiny. Just like David, God will fulfill our destiny. We have made a covenant with the Lord. King David reigned for 40 years. We are here to send the enemy notice! There isn't a battle that we go into where God isn't there before us. We want Godly strongholds. Righteousness! We need to look more like God than the world. Then, God will restore us and raise us up!"

He went on, "Psalm 23 states that the Lord will prepare a table for us before our enemies."

I thought of an enemy, *lack*.

"Where you fight the enemy is always where something is important to you; vitally important to you." On this I thought of our land and the home we desired.

"The enemy will fight you in the place of your greatest blessing." I thought of the books the Lord had me write, and how I knew in my heart they were to be shared with many others.

"The devil wants you to stop dreaming of the things of God. Don't give in!"

Then he spoke Amos 9:15, the same word I was given over five years ago. "I will plant them upon their own ground, never again shall they be plucked from the land I have given them, say I the Lord, your God."

I couldn't believe he was preaching such an obscure verse; the very Scripture the Lord had given me to hold onto.

"Talk of the words and works of God! God will deliver you! God will break through! Are you ready for your breakthrough? In everything? Finances? Healing? Is America ready for a breakthrough? This is what God is asking us. God wants to bring you up! Do you know what it takes? Egypt and Israel needed a breakthrough. David needed a breakthrough. Worship God like David did. There was no one like David. Learn how to speak to all situations." Then this Heavenly pastor went from preaching to teaching.

"There are three main reasons the devil hates you."
1) Anointing — He can't have it! We do! It's trouble for him. The yoke was broken.
2) Position — He can't have it! It's only ours! God has raised us up. God positions us for His glory. It's from the Heavens.
3) Authority — Different than power.

"Are you tired of the enemy winning battles? Not for long. There is a third great awakening coming."
There are five elements:
1) Genuine communion — with the Lord.
2) Encourage yourself — energize yourself.
3) Revolutionaries — prayer life and worship.
4) Corporate worship — all of us together.
5) Individual — person.

Then, that insightful man went into prophesy.

385

"When the Heavens open and the angels go on their missions that is when we will move into a new dimension. God will give us victory! Release the supernatural over the natural! This is your moment."

At the end, another prophesy came. He cried out with a vengeance!

"It is okay to dream again!"

It hit me hard and I cried hot tears.

He prayed over Mark for his skin rash. Then he prayed for me. He said I have a gift of creative artistry. He knew this by the Holy Spirit. Then the good pastor prayed over me for favor and prosperity to add to our house. Tom prayed for our friend, David.

Do these words hit home for you too? Is God preparing you for battle for your own ground?

ENGAGED!
(Aug. 20th)

Shortly before 1:30 that morning, Annie woke up with a start and did something she rarely did. She jumped off the bed and started barking at the front door! All two-and-a-half pounds of her.

"Mark! Mark! Something's wrong! Annie's at the door barking!"

By that time, we had gotten out of bed and almost to the front door ourselves. We heard keys rattling on the other side of the door. The next second, Ben started through the door with a big smile on his face. Before he could get all the way through, an arm thrust past him with a hand extended out. There was a ring on that finger! An engagement ring!

I started squealing as the rest of Amanda Wilder rushed past Ben and into the house. We jumped up and down, while father and son hugged. Annie was barking and jumping up and down too! Finally, Ben picked Annie up, and they sat on the couch. Mark and I sat in our chairs. We knew they would tell us the whole story. We were not disappointed. After all, Ben is as good a storyteller as his momma!

With eyes that danced, Ben told their story…

"We met on the 20th. The number 20 has been special to us on many occasions. Amanda has made me aware that October 20th was the only Saturday 20th left in the year for a wedding date. So, I knew this summer, we had to get engaged. I had already picked up the engagement ring from Mark in secret. I took Amanda to the Merk Farm for an all-day picnic. We had a great

387

time. Well, after a while she wanted to go home. In my head, I'm thinking, 'No, we can't! I can't propose to her until after midnight, to make it to the 20ᵗʰ.' So I said, 'Oh, honey, I would like to see the stars come out. Can't we wait a little longer?' Of course, my sweetie said *yes*. By 11:00, she was again ready to leave. Then, I told her I was too tired to drive, and I needed to take a little nap."

Ben and Amanda were both on the couch, giggling and smiling as they relived the moment by moment replay.

"Amanda finally agreed to a nap. I set my watch for one hour. When it was finally just after midnight, I opened my door and got out of the car to walk over to her side of the car to propose."

At that point, Amanda interjected, "I didn't know where he was going or what he was doing. I didn't want him to leave me by myself in the car in the dark."

Ben picked up the story from there. "I opened her car door and got down on one knee. Then, I asked Amanda Sue Wilder to marry me!"

Mark smiled and I cried happy tears. We took pictures, and the kids agreed to spend the night due to the late hour.

Later that morning, at a reasonable time, they went to pick out Ben's ring at Albin's.

While they were out, I was busy taking my mother to all her pre-operation testing at the hospital. At almost 84 years old, Momma was headed straight for gallbladder surgery.

MISSIONARY CLOSE TO HOME
(Aug. 22nd)

It was still dark out when the alarm sounded at 5 a.m. I was to meet my family at the hospital by 6 a.m.

I rolled out of bed, brushed my teeth, put on jeans, a tee-shirt and shoes. I was out the door before I could see.! I prayed on the way there for it all to go smoothly. I knew it would not be an easy operation for a frail little woman days away from her 84th birthday.

I arrived at the appointed time. The nurses were just taking Momma back to get her ready for surgery. I sat with my family members in the waiting room until the nurse would bring us back to see her before the surgery.

It was agreed I would stay all day — and all night if need be. My nephew would come and sit with us later that afternoon. The other family members had to leave by noon to go to their respective jobs.

When they brought Momma out of recovery and to her room, I was there waiting for her. She was still very groggy and slept most of the afternoon. The nurses came in and checked on her every couple of hours. The day crew was wonderful to her. They checked her breathing, her heart rate, fluffed up her pillows, brought food, checked her comfort levels, etc...

When my nephew arrived, Momma was sleeping in her bed. I was sleeping in a reclining chair in the room. I woke up to find him quietly working on his laptop. We got Momma ice chips and water, and called the nurse when requested. I bought dinner for my nephew and me. I thought if we had a meal together in her room, Momma would feel more like eating.

As Momma's anesthesia wore off, the nurses stayed on top of her pain medications. After dinner, Momma could sit up and hold small amounts of conversation. She could give orders, and we even watched a little television.

Shortly after 8 p.m., the nurse came in to give Mom something to help her sleep through the night. Momma told us we could leave because she was doing all right. The nurses had taken excellent care of her, and she would probably be leaving the next morning.

At that point it had been a 15-hour day for me, and I was glad to be going off duty. We kissed her goodbye and left together. I called Mark on the way home. He was in the middle of a Bible study at our house. Everyone would be glad to see me when I arrived. They were all happy to hear that my Mom was doing well when I left.

I arrived to a house of believers: Miss Evette, Brother Bill, and our good friends Deb and Buster, Mark and Annie. They were in full worship and study as I walked through the front door. Of course, Annie was the first one I kissed!

The group brought me up on praise reports and answered prayers. I was just in time to hear the last of the teaching. Then I, myself, was privileged to write down each person's prayer requests.

We had many prayer requests from outside our group that were offered up first. Then for family members' health or salvation. Finally, for our own intentions. My requests were for the same thing they had been for almost three years—for our home to be built on Nicholas Drive, and for the selling of my books.

Several of the ladies had brought dessert. Mark made coffee while food was given out. We fellowshipped until I could stay awake no longer. My 18-hour day was done. As I put my head to the pillow, I could still hear the voices of our prayer group until almost midnight.

SUFFICIENT FOR THE DAY
(Aug. 24th)

I was sufficiently rested by that morning to once again tackle a full day's obligations. Mark, Annie and I started the day after a breakfast for the three of us. We were headed for my mother's neighbor Kathleen's home to do needed yard work and house repairs.

While Mark got all the equipment out of the truck, I set out all of Annie's items; her water bowl with her special syrup water, her special dog food for premature puppies, her carrier with her blanket, and of course Gumby and skinny bear who she carried everywhere she went.

We set her items in the fenced backyard in the shade. We left the gate open, so she could follow us around to the front of the house.

We worked all morning and afternoon. With all the inside and outside work accomplished, Kathleen made us a wonderful meal of chicken and dumplings. Kathleen enjoyed Annie and told stories, while Mark made out a very fair bill. Kathleen allowed us to get cleaned up and ready for church that evening.

We said our goodbyes and arrived with time to spare for fellowship at Cowboy Church. We were looking forward to Pastor Chris Powell's sermon.

Greetings were called out to us when we entered the building.

"Hi, Mark! So glad you could make it!"

"Hi, Deb! It's nice to see you again!"

"Hello, Annie! How's that baby doing tonight?"

Annie had long since gotten used to Christian Country Cowboy Church. By the time the preaching would start, she would be in her carrier fast asleep. As we went from worship into the opening prayer, Annie had indeed gone to sleep. I got out my notebook, and Mark opened his Bible. We settled down to listen to the word of God.

Pastor Christopher Powell's Sermon
(Aug. 24th)

The young man stood at the podium with a serious look on his face. The Lord had given him a message that was bigger than the small congregation gathered before him. Pastor Chris adjusted his glasses, his microphone and dove right in.

"The news is full of negative images. How can we deal with such discouragement, and anxiety, and overcome fear? What can we do? Anxiety and worry can grip you. Thoughts come into our head uncontrollably.

There is good anxiety or destructive anxiety. We see a world of unbelievers that bank on power and gold. But for us, the Lord provides for us today! He brings just enough for us each day.

Where your treasure is, your heart is also. What is an example of man's treasure? Time, finances, and energy. I tell you, don't chase after these things! God said seek first the kingdom of Heaven, and all will be added to you. Christ is faithful to finish what He has started in us."

Pastor Chris paused to watch his words settle into our hearts. It was important we got this message. It was important that I got it!

"Doctors, today, have many ways to help us control our thoughts or depression. It's called Cognitive Behavioral Therapy. They use medications, hypnosis, and herbal therapy. When anxiety attacks, you can't breathe. The Bible says in the last days many men will die of fear. Fear fuels anxiety. Jesus dealt with it, too, in this fallen world."

Pastor Chris paused for a moment to let his words sink in, then he went on. "This is not our home. We are aliens passing through. How do we get back to our real home? Do what God tells you to do."

The good pastor preached on Matthew 6:25-34. It was on how no man can serve two masters. You can't serve God and mammon — which is the love of money. Chris told of lilies of the field and how God takes care of them and how it related to man — to us.

Chris went on to say, "Take no thought of what you need. Your Heavenly Father will take care of you. You can't add to your life one minute, with worry. Worry will pull you apart! It can bring on illness! This is what is meant by torn asunder. It is a devil's tool! The devil is trying to teach you not to trust God. The ministry of the Lord is faith. The ministry of the devil is fear."

"Proverbs 12:25 states that worry will weigh a man down. Worry is waste. Who we are is important. It's important to God! Look at God's work in our life as an example of how He is working for you!

We question whether we are valuable to God. God cares about all of our needs and cares. Don't think we are a bother to God Almighty!"

Then Pastor Chris smiled, "Charlie Brown was a

394

worrier. He stated, 'Even my anxieties have anxieties!'"

"The root cause of worry is no control over your life. You feel you have no control in your own little world. Give control over to God! Worry clutters up our tomorrows. Have you noticed people will worry about anything? They'll give themselves a mini panic attack! Man makes things to worry about such as with the CDC and pandemic bird flu, or 1999 and Y2K digits. So many things we worry about never come. "

40% never happen.
30% of our worry is in the past.
12% are about our health.
10% are petty issues.
Only 8% are legitimate concerns.

"92% of our worry-time is wasted energy. And, it's all outside of our control. Our energy is wasted on worry; worry that God can't or won't take care of us. Did you know satan only goes where he is welcome? Don't put out a welcome mat for him! Are our problems bigger than God's promises? Think about that one! Don't fill your mind up with stuff that takes you away from God."

"Luke 21:34 states to be careful or your heart can become weighed down. Worry is a wasted expenditure. It is self-indulgent and a distraction. It is a battle of unbelief! It is sinful to have an unbelieving heart. Seek out where the Lord may use us. There are tasks at hand. Let the Lord lead us and guide us! Go to God! He will help you make good, practical decisions for daily living."

Pastor Chris wound down his sermon, "When

you worry you assume responsibility for the day around you. Take God's yoke for it is light. Stop fighting, and He will make things work out well for you. Anxiety is atheism in action. You can have peace when you focus on God.

Peace and quiet, where do I find it? In the crickets and stars on a country evening. God's family is who you want to be with. That will bring you peace, too. But the greatest peace you will achieve is by having a desire to worship and know God, and be about the *Great Commission.*"

The altar-call was given as the church band played. No one was eager to leave. Fellowship went on for several hours.

After all, we had found peace in this place.

GETTING IT RIGHT
(Aug. 27th)

Waiting was the order of the day—and phone calls. I knew I had been given a sign, at the very start of all this miraculous ministry, to tell all I had been shown of the Lord's mercy. Why was it not moving forward?

So, I went to the Lord in prayer in my quiet place. I asked, "Why Lord?"

The Lord God's answer came quick to me, "***Get it right!***"

There was something in the books that needed to be corrected and, Crystal held the answer. In some of my paragraphs, I had some words that ended in "ed" and others in "ing" in the same story. Crystal said, in a verbal story, it is fine but not in a written story.

I did not want to believe I would have to tackle two books all over again. "Sigh."

The Lord's message only confirmed what I already knew. I poured back over the books. It seemed there were more errors in book one than in book two. I was once again on a mission.

While I took a break with lunch, I decided to make a few phone calls to dig up publicity. I called several people in the Charismatic community—from local to national.

The first one I got in touch with was Pat with the Charismatic Connection. She knew who I was, and I asked for a moment of her time. It ended up being almost an hour! I knew they reviewed new books, and I asked for *Miraculous Interventions* to be put on their list.

After listening to me for a while, Pat took an interest in how it all began. What was the spark that had turned our interest?

"I wasn't aware you and Mary we're working on book projects. How did you get started?" Pat asked.

I told her of the twenty-year trek we had been on, and how God had orchestrated our whole lives for this moment in time and for this purpose. Pat loved the idea of the books, but she thought the real story was of the faith-walk of the last twenty years. She likened our story to the story of Abraham. Pat wanted our story to print. Could I make that happen?

I called Mary and told her the good news! I asked her to come and help me write our story together. Mary loved the idea, and said she would be over right after work.

During the afternoon, I went through my first book and made corrections as Crystal had suggested. I also managed to have dinner ready when Mary and Mark arrived from work.

Over dinner, we caught each other up on our day's events. By the end of the meal, Mary and I knew we had a job to do. Mark, once again, agreed to be our backup support team!

Mary and I wrote long into the night about our journey apart and together. We decided to give the piece a title of *In the Beginning*.

As we wrote, we realized there had been no such thing as coincidence in our lives, but orchestration from our Heavenly Father to keep us or put us back on the track of the way we should go. His inspiration and angelic guidance would take us farther than we ever imagined.

Mary downloaded our story from my computer and sent it to Pat early that morning. Now satisfied with the work of our hands, we awaited her reply.

Surely, with all that effort, we were getting it right.

IN THE BEGINNING

By Deborah Aubrey-Peyron and Mary Dow Bibb Smith

In the beginning, there was always God. His plans are perfect and far exceed our plans and dreams! Though I have always been a Christian and sought the Lord, it is still wonderful to look back and see how my efforts were always part of His plan all along! As Gandalf said in *The Hobbit**, "You don't really suppose, do you, that all your adventures and escapes were managed by mere luck, just for your sole benefit? You are a very fine person, Mr. Baggins, but you are only quite a little fellow in a wide world after all! (Thank Goodness!)"

You see, I am a publisher, by God's grace. A beginner in the field for sure, but a publisher none the less. But, I am getting ahead of the story. And since my primary author is such a wonderful storyteller, I will let her tell our story. - *Mary Smith*

"In the beginning." Such a simple way to start a story. God saw fit to start His Holy Bible with it. The meaning of the phrase showed God in the mix from the very start. The same goes for the story of Mary and me.

All we have ever done, all our gifts and talents, all that we have seen is now being employed for God's Holy purpose. Together, we are writing the continuing "Acts of the Apostles" to encourage the brethren and inspire the secular world. How did such a daunting task occur in our lives? Why, at our beginning of course!

*The Hobbit was written by J.R.R.Tolkien.

Every good story has foreshadowing, and so does ours. Fifteen years before Mary and I met, she met my younger brother, Ron at a retreat at Mt. St. Frances. I, too, was supposed to have been there, but I allowed my boyfriend at the time to talk me out of going. Like Mary, I was in love with Jesus — as my Savior, Brother and example of how to be a loving and forgiving human being. There was much need for that in my short life at the time. Having been hurt by man and his escapades, I knew Jesus would never hurt nor fail me. I am not going to go into great detail here. My story is already recorded in the book, *Miraculous Interventions,* but I will give a bit of it here.

Mary and I grew up not far from one-another, but on opposite sides of the Ohio River; Mary in Southern Indiana, and I in Louisville, Kentucky. We have much in common. We are both charismatic Catholics, artists, mothers of three children, divorced, and "remarried" – I to my current and forever husband, Mark; and Mary has a chaste but close relationship with her former husband, Mitch.

We met in 1992 at Covenant Prayer Group at St. Mary's Catholic Church in Lanesville, Indiana where we still attend. Mary was just a little ahead of me in a newly-single walk. I followed three years later down that same path.

Fear not, readers! God's hand was on us even then. Happy beginnings were well on their way.

About the time Mark and I met, in 1997, God also inspired Mary to write an arts and crafts book called *Fantastic Snowflakes!* It took 12 years to complete, but it was a lifetime of love. When Mary was little, her mother would have to call her in from playing outside in the snow. She loved to catch snowflakes and marveled at their structure and minute detail!

In 1st grade, a memorable art project was the cutting of a paper snowflake from folded paper. Instead of becoming a beautiful snowflake, the paper fell apart, and she cried in disappointment! She never forgot it.

Years late, Mitch, a US Army soldier, was stationed in Germany. Mary and their twins [another miraculous story covered in *Miraculous Interventions II*] were allowed to live there with him in Army-supplied quarters. Another child was born to them while living there as well. A U.S. friend there, knowing her love of snow, taught her how to fold the paper correctly to cut a six-sided snowflake, since all real snowflakes are six-sided – as all snowflakeologists know!

Many years later at a new job, with the Christmas season rapidly approaching, Mary pulled out of her bag of talents, the paper snowflake. She cut so many paper snowflakes to decorate the company Christmas tree, some truly amazing ones that people started asking her how to do it. The idea of making an instruction book was born. Then after twelve years of writing and illustrating, *Fantastic Snowflakes!* was finally ready to be published.

As good as this book was, she could not get a publisher to even look at it. She set it aside.

Out of adversity, the hand of God moved. Even though much had occurred in Mary's life while writing the book—her mother passed in 2002, she bought her mother's house, her ex-husband came to live with her (renting an upstairs room in her home) and she took an extra job at Office Depot in order to make ends meet—

she felt that God really wanted her to proceed with the book. A brother suggested that Mary publish it herself. This was confirmed multiple times. And, since God had placed Mary at Office Depot, one of her new talents was printing and binding. Imagine that!

We were all very excited to hear of Mary's first book-signing during the Christmas holidays.

Meanwhile, back at the ranch...my new husband, Mark, and I were busy living life and raising three boys. Not a small task in and of itself. Occasionally in my lifetime, I had been asked or assigned to write articles or stories for various schools or organizations on many topics. Writing was easy for me, so I never gave it much thought more than a nice hobby. Mary and I saw each other each week during prayer group at St. Mary's. Having similar backgrounds and interests, we were naturally drawn to each other.

Mary watched as we built our first home together. She and her girls helped us move in! The preparation for our first Christmas Open House was made into a whole weekend together. My boys stayed at their father's home while the Smith's came and cooked and cleaned, hung up decorations and had a blast! For two evenings, after cooking all day, Mark would bring in dinner, and we would all sit afterwards and talk of our days activities, read books, braid hair and listen to a tape of *The Twelve Days of Christmas*. What we did not realize at the time was that God was setting in place the foundation for our destinies.

A few years after building our home in 2002, I suffered a fracture in a vertebra. It changed the direction of our lives. We had no insurance to pay for the hospital and medical bills. Mary, my friend now of 10 years, came to help take care of me while I recuperated from a procedure. Again, she prepared meals in my kitchen and cleaned up after our family. We prayed and cried together at the prospect of my being an invalid, without divine intervention. Four days later, through the hands of a retired minister, I was miraculously healed! I still thank God for His mercy.

The year 2008 was pivotal, not only for Mary as a start of her God-given career change, but in my life as well. As she ascended to her new goal, my life's goal, at the time, was being plunged into disaster. The business I had fought so hard to build, to help save lives and homes, was tumultuously taken over and lost; our own home being a casualty of the battle. I had now been broken twice.

I wondered, "What can God do with me now?"

"When I am weak, He is strong." I had been in battles ever since I was three days old. But I serve a God who is a rescuer of my body and my soul. He came through and spoke to my very essence. I said, "I am all washed up. I want to die. How will my family survive this?"

God said to me, "You will live and not die! Write down everything I have ever done for you! Every miracle you have ever seen me do in your life and those around you –all the stories that have filled your life. This will help you to go on."

At the time, I thought it was to save my life and for my children's sake. I wrote for two years without telling a soul; not even my husband knew. God brought back to my remembrance events from my youth when I first heard His voice as a command to save a house from catching fire, all the way up to the present day.

As with Mary, God sent people to tell me it was "time to write the book." Wonderful! I didn't know I was writing a book. But God did. It would be a book on miracles, on God taking adversity and turning it around into blessings. I found healing and hope in its pages even as I wrote with the help of the Holy Spirit. I wondered at the time, could this book help anyone else?

As soon as I finished my manuscript, Mary was also asking God, "Okay, I did this snowflake book because I thought you wanted me to. Now what?"

At the next Thursday prayer group meeting, I walked in, manuscript in hand. I said to my group, "Well, I have written a book, and I don't know what to do with it."

Mary quickly replied, "Well, I do! I can turn it into a book for you!"

Our destinies had just joined together forever. Now, we were where God wanted us to be all along.

As the book was almost ready to go to print, I was also given the gift of a beautiful little poem that just dropped into my head. It was about three unruly boys with a less-than-fortunate run-in with St. Nicholas. It was told with humor, verse, and Christ, of course! Mary was able to put it in at the end of my first book, but said it would make a good children's book all on its own if we could find a good illustrator. That very week, another friend of mine who just happened to be a book illustrator, Kelly Riddle, came by for a visit.

The rest became history as we soon published a second book together called "Christmas Chaos!"

I thought surely after that, we were done with all this. I must have exceeded expectations by now! Ha! As we both found out, being guided by the Holy Spirit, we were just getting started. Amazing people started dropping into my path. Stories abounded from everywhere. The next book was not so much about me and my path, but about theirs. From ministers and priests, to everyday visionaries, they all came forward to boldly tell their stories, so I could write their miraculous walks of faith.

We have come to realize and believe that our story is meant for more than just us, and even our area. With Pope Benedict XVI calling for 2012-2013 the church year to be the "Year of Faith and Sharing," God's plans for Mary and I are certainly more than just for our "sole benefit," even though we are only "small fellow[s] in a wide world after all." As we said before, God's plans are perfect and far exceed our plans and dreams! If he can do this with us, what are His plans for you?

"For I know the plans I have for you, declares the Lord. Plans to prosper you and not to harm you, plans to give you hope and a future." (Jeremiah 29:11 NIV)

THREE CENTS
(Aug. 30th)

In the five months I had worked at the store, I had never been told in my spirit that I needed to buy someone, or a family, groceries — until that morning.

I was minding my own business, putting away stock, when I went past a certain aisle. I felt a *stop* in my spirit and a push toward a family with a cart of groceries. Information dropped into my head like water. I was on a mission in an instant!

I walked up and made small talk with the young lady. I asked a few questions, gave out information about another store she should also go to, and asked her to wait a minute before going up to the checkout counter. She agreed with a look of question on her face.

First, I had to ask permission from my boss.

"You want to do what?" My boss asked as she looked up from her paperwork.

"I know! But I don't think it's up to me. I am being told strongly in the Spirit to buy this lady's groceries."

"Are you using your debit card and not cash?"

"Yes, Ma'am."

The okay was given. Then I had to call and ask the other half of my equation.

"You want to do what?" The question in my husband's voice told me I had some explaining to do.

"Sweetheart! How much money do we have in our bank account? It's a God thing!"

He groaned a reply, "Not much. $15.00. How much do you need?"

I told him all that had gone on and promised not

to go over that amount. Surely, the Lord was not asking me to overdraw our account. The second agreement was given.

Motion carried.

I called out to the young lady with her three small children.

"Over here, Miss. I am ready for you! Do you have everything you need?"

"I'm afraid I don't have enough money..." she stammered.

"Do you have everything you need?!" I waited patiently for her reply.

"Well, we could use some crayons for my little ones to color with."

I ran back to the crayon aisle and picked up the ones I felt were best for the situation and ran back up to the front counter. Her total climbed past the amount she had in her pocket. The young lady started to protest with tears in her eyes. I ignored her pleas with a smile on my face. I knew God was working it all out for His glory and her benefit!

Her total came to $14.97... of course. I bent down and pulled my wallet out of my purse. I walked around to the front of the register and ran my own numbers. Her balance owed was zero.

I turned to look at her; I told her of the love of Jesus and now, just like the woman in the Bible who needed a blessing, her money too, would go twice as far that day.

It did not occur to me to be sorrowful when God required us to spend our last stipend in the bank, only leaving us with three cents. I was happy to be of use. I was happy I had obeyed.

Even though we were happy to be of use, we never said it was an easy path to be on. Over and over again, we have been asked to give—at times, what felt like everything, for the sake of others. As generous as we are, even we grow weary at times. A dear friend once consoled me with, "Deb, don't grow weary in doing good." I keep Dr. Annette's words in the front of my Complete Jewish Bible.

It's Scripture, you know.

"I'm trying, Lord."

Later that evening, Mark and I had a dinner date with friends Meredith and Peter Snyder. Meredith set a beautiful table and served a scrumptious meal! Yes, we brought Annie with us. We all talked of our children, our lives and jobs.

After dinner, with coffee or tea in hand, I started the story of how God once again sold a home right out from under us! What could the Lord have in store for us now?

By the time I finished my rendition, a television program started we had wanted to see together. We all had a glass of wine after dinner.

At first all went well. After fifteen minutes or so, my nose started to stop up. Mucous thickened. It became hard to speak.

"Mark, I am having an allergic reaction to the wine!" I croaked.

My throat had started to swell. With no Benadryl in their home, we had to leave quickly! I took a half of another pill in the same drug class, which brought me a little relief. I took the other half.

Nothing.

Rats.

We started in prayer.

Right about that time Crystal called. I still couldn't talk. Mark advised her of the whole situation quickly. Crystal told Mark to get out our anointing oil, and she and David would join in our prayer! Well, those mighty sons and daughter of God called down healing from the throne room!

Crystal felt me heal while on the phone with us! I tell you readers, she is empathic from her head to her toes.

I was finally able to sigh a deep sigh. I could breathe once again.

REASONABLE
(Aug. 31ˢᵗ)

I slept-in that day with Annie Frances due to the medication I had taken for the allergic reaction to the wine. I was in a vulnerable state. My immortal enemy knew it, and he went on the attack!

How you ask?

In a dream...

I saw myself sitting in a chair in a poorly lit room. There was a well-dressed man with dark hair and a pocket watch standing close to me. He bent down to talk to me.

"Be reasonable." He cooed. "If God was going to help you, He would have already done it."

I fell to the floor crying. This man was trying to reason me out of believing in God's promises for me. In between sniffles, I whimpered, "I believe God! I believe God!"

I woke up greatly disturbed and wrote down every detail I could remember. I felt in my spirit this was a very important dream. I took it with me that night to church to ask for interpretation.

Our friends Larry and Marilynn Crosier were coming over that evening to go with us to Cowboy Church. As usual, we would leave one vehicle at Mom's in Clarksville and go with each other from there for fellowship before and after. There was always so much to talk about in the Lord!

We arrived on time for concert night. There was a one-woman band that sang that evening. And boy could she sing! After a few songs from the house band, a visit from the "Cuzins of Sasquatch Hollar," it was time for Nannette Vaughan to be on stage.

Love for God and His creation radiated from Nannette as she sang song after song. Tears and laughter abounded from the stage to the audience. Before we all knew it, the concert was over, fellowship began, and dinner was ordered.

Those of us who decided to stay went downstairs for a meal and conversation. I am not sure how it started, but before I knew it, I was involved in telling a story that everyone ended up listening to. Our guest artist asked me to pray over a request she had. I was honored to do so. At the end, we both cried. We hugged as sisters in Christ Jesus.

Then I asked Rabbona Joy for a little of her time, for an interpretation of a dream I had earlier that day. Our little group went back upstairs and sat in a pew to be more comfortable. I told Joy the whole thing. By her first question and my answer, Joy knew who the being was in my dream.

"Deb! That was the Spirit of the anti-Christ! He is higher than the general in your dream from last year!"

My mind started clicking.

"You mean with my first book, they sent a general. And with my second book, they sent an anti-Christ?! Higher with each book?"

"Yes! You are being investigated. Your name was on his list."

My skin crawled, and my heart sank at the prospect of evil lurking nearby.

I felt vulnerable in the flesh.

Joy cried out, "Don't worry! You are protected

and covered! He had to have permission to be there from both God and you. But he only knows what you tell him. That is true with all enemies. They only know what you tell them. What they don't know is if their plan against you is working; unless you show them! Stand on what you know to be true."

Joy paused for a moment to allow her words to sink into my spirit. Then she began again, "The devil's angels are limited by number. When they approach you, send them, by the Holy Spirit, to the dry place, so they cannot return to harass you."

I asked her how many were working for satan. Less than one-third than there were before. For those that were sent to the dry and barren place are gone.

Joy also said, "The enemy doesn't create, he perverts. When you remove the platform he stands on, he has to leave. We have a choice to keep it or make it gone. We are here to be encouragers to each other.

Forgiveness is for our health. Claim the blood covenant! Tell the evil one he has to bring back seven times what he has stolen from you!"

At the end of the evening, I told Joy I had been praying for her sleep. She recalled she had been sleeping better lately. I told her I felt the prayer had come from the Lord. She told me to keep listening for the Lord.

"Sure, and amen!" I countered.

I tell you, keep listening for the Lord in your lives, too.

GOOD DEED DAY
(Sept. 7th)

A few short days ago, I had asked the Lord to order my steps. That usually meant there was someone who needed our help somewhere or somehow. This day was no exception to that rule. Mark and I were off together. When we're off together, it does not matter what we are doing, we had fun.

The first order of the day was to take Momma to the doctor for a checkup. I was more than happy to be part of her support system. Lunch was at a fast-food restaurant.

By early afternoon, we were headed to Mark's Mother's, back across the river. On the way, there we took Annie to a pet supply store to look for sweaters for the fall and a dress for her to wear to Ben and Amanda's wedding. Annie wore the smallest size they made. When we got there, all the outfits were half off! Annie's doctor had told us, with her being so small, she would need to keep warm over the fall and winter months to keep down illness.

We arrived at Mom Peyron's and helped her around the house. Mark did yard work. Annie was very glad to see her! She went running through the door and up to Mom's chair. Mom wasn't there! Annie turned and looked at me as if to say, "What did you do with Grandma?"

Mom was in the kitchen cooking dinner for us. While she watched Annie, we busied ourselves inside and outside. Fall was soon to come, and we wanted her yard to be ready. My own mother's yard was due for a trim two days later.

Mark and I got everything done just in time for dinner. Our day had been full, back to back. We hardly finished dinner, when it was time to go to the park and meet Ben and Andy for an exercise class Ben had developed. Annie played while we trained. We all had a lot of fun as a family and got in shape together. As the workout wound to its end, we noticed dark clouds on the horizon.

On the way home, we checked various radio stations to see what was up. Bad storms and tornadic activity were west of us and headed our way. When we got home, we called our friends Kevin and Doris and asked to spend the night at their house. They said to come on!

We packed our belongings for the night, and our all-weather radio, and took off for their home. We arrived just before the rain started. The Peterson's already had their television on. They gave us an update. We took our things down the stairs and into the bedroom. Annie stayed close by us.

The four of us stayed up a while, and Doris made tea. Finally, it was decided that it was safe for everyone to go to bed; them upstairs and us downstairs. We turned the television on low, put Annie in her bed, and went to bed ourselves.

Ten minutes after our heads had hit the pillows, the all-weather radio alarm went off! The severe weather front was four counties off to our west. Mark and I got out of bed, went to the downstairs living room and looked to see what our local weatherman had to say.

The system that was to march through, west to east, had bow echoes up and down the line. Funnel clouds were forming along the slow-moving system. There was lots of wind energy associated with that front. I knew that wasn't a good thing any time of day or night.

Mark and I watched and prayed for everyone in its path. Our local weathermen were right on top of things! There would be no casualties if they could help it!

By 2:30 a.m., Mark and I were exhausted and took turns with cat naps. That was when the alarm sounded for our area. We had twenty minutes to take cover. I went upstairs and knocked on Doris and Kevin's door.

"We're under a tornado warning! Let's go!" Marching orders were given.

"We'll be down in a few minutes."

We trudged back downstairs together and all four of us prayed for our area. At 3:30 a.m., our warning expired, and the front moved to the east of us. Now we watched as it approached our families. Phone calls were in order. Louisville was directly in its path!

"Momma! Get downstairs to your safe place now!"

"I know! Sirens are going off everywhere!" she responded. Momma went into her basement.

While I was calling my mother, Andy, our youngest son, was calming Samantha, telling her there was no way they were in trouble because I hadn't called them yet.

With the first ring of his phone, Andy shook his head and said softly, "Dammit." Samantha answered the phone and I heard Andy yell in the background, "I'm on it, Momma! Come on kids, in the bathroom!"

Samantha asked in a rising panic, "Have we got time to run?"

I looked at Mark, who was watching the radar. He said soberly, "It's right on top of them."

I repeated Mark, and yelled into the phone, "It's right on top of you! Get down!"

The phone line went dead.

Twenty minutes later Andy called. Everyone was safe, thank God! The funnel cloud had not come down in their area. We could finally put our weary selves to bed. Our last conscious prayers were of thanksgiving.

TRUE COLORS
(Sept. 9th)

I had been seeing colors around people and things for a week! The night before, my dreams had been riddled with color. As I awoke, various colors surrounded my area of sight. While I was in this Heavenly realm, the phone rang. It just happened to be a friend who would know what it all meant. She could interpret!

"Please! I've had visions and dreams all night! Tell me about these colors I've seen."

She got out her prophetic dictionary and began to recite what each one meant.

I had seen pink around two women.

Pink — spirit of femininity — can be rebellious.

I had seen orange around Pastor Mallory.

Orange — Holy Fire! Tried and proven.

I had seen red around our prayer group leaders at St. Mary's.

Red — royalty — a warrior color. It also meant warfare.

I had seen a bright yellow-gold the night before as I sat in the bathroom. It was all around me and my feet.

Yellow Gold — God's color.

I had also seen that same color while reading biblical Scripture a few days before.

In my lifetime, I had also seen a gray cloud at a mass; once at a healing mass, and once in my home.

Grey — wisdom — Shekinah Glory of God.

White — Color of God

I had seen green during my time of healing, years

418

ago and in my dreams.

Green—color of a prophet--divine activity—also linked to prosperity.

I had seen that color at the beginning of 2012 all around our friend, Jeremy.

A nurse I once knew smiled at me and said I had the most beautiful blue aura she had ever seen.

Blue—communication—written and verbal. Celestial and Heavenly.

It also meant powers and ruler ship. Unimpeded growth. Potential. God's appearance.

I thought of the time my dear friend Lee had said I had no stoppers in my faith. I believe this is why, when people see Mary, the mother of Jesus, she is wrapped in blue or a blue hue.

I have seen the color of black only once.

Black—sin and death.

I was told to pray for the person I had seen it over, to call off the attack on their life. I did with all my heart! It was over my husband, Mark.

We were up early that day. Andy needed to borrow our truck to move Samantha's things for her, and we were off on our own little mission trip. It was time to trim bushes and spray trees at my Mother's home. It was a hard day's work for all of us involved. We never were ones to shrink from hard work.

It also meant Momma would fix us a wonderful home-cooked meal. Chicken pot pie with yeast rolls and real butter. Sweet tea and an even sweeter homemade dessert awaited us after our chores. People would do just about anything to get an invite to a meal at Momma's—including us!

After we finished her yard work, we cleaned up and came to the dining room table. The smell greeted us as we came out of the bathroom. We smiled all the way to the table. I poured our drinks, and we sat down for prayers. The traditional standard Catholic meal prayer was said.

"Bless us oh Lord, in these thy gifts that we are about to receive through thy bounty in Christ, our Lord. Amen."

The meal was wonderful, and the conversation was lively! We spoke of our lives and our children, politics and the church, anything that brought up discussion.

I helped with dishes after dinner until all was cleaned up. Then we all went outside to see how the yard looked as we walked off our meal to make room for dessert.

It seemed to me, it had been a hectic week. It was not easy cooking food for our neighbors, family and friends. A person can get low on fuel if they are not careful.

But I know a lovely fount that can fill us up once again. The Living Water that flows from the throne of Heaven, past the cross of Jesus Christ and into our souls, refreshing a life as there ever was!

TALK OF MIRACLES
(Sept. 13th)

After the late night, I was glad I didn't have to be at my best friend's until 11 the next morning. Vicki Sampson was the spryest 80-something-year-old I knew! She had been my best friend since I was 15 years old — 38 years as of this writing.

Annie and I arrived right on time. Vicki had errands to run, and we were her taxi. First was the doctor's office, then the beauty parlor, a department store, and then lunch. That would have been enough to poop out any normal 40-year- old much less an 80-year-old. But not this one!

We chatted non-stop. Vicki and I caught up on family life, friends, life in general and oh yes, miracles! She and I both talked of people we knew who had recently gotten miracle homes. At the time, we were fighting to stay in the running with a bank in New Albany. They kept promising for our home construction loan in the fall.

As we talked of miracles, we made a stop at Vicki's bank. I stayed in the car. I asked God a question from my deepest heart.

"When is our miracle coming, Lord?"

At that instant on the car radio, rang out a song, "I Believe in Miracles." Since I don't believe in coincidence, I felt God was talking back to me. Believe in miracles! Believe in Him! Vicki got back in the car to the sound of sobs. She looked at me. I told her how I thought God answered my prayer just at the right time. He had heard me.

Lunch was wonderful at a nice sit-down

restaurant. By the end of the meal, it was time to take Vicki home. We hugged goodbye and promised to see each other soon. I didn't know how Vicki felt, but she wore me out! I knew I had to take a nap after keeping up with her. And that was exactly what Annie and I did! After all, when Mark came home, we still had St. Mary's prayer group to go to that night.

At Covenant Prayer Group, which had been meeting for almost 29 years as of 2012, we met another spry 80-something-year-old that also didn't look a day over 70. His name was Dennis, and he had come with our good friend, Billie.

Our prayer group started with shouts of praise and worship for an hour. Then for an hour, our leader, Phil Wermuth, or one of our group spoke on the readings, parables or something that had happened during the week either for prayer or a praise report.

That was when Dennis started to speak up. It turned out, he had been clairaudient since he was five years old! I got excited to find another that could hear as I could! Mary, my editor, who also attended St. Mary's prayer group, was there that night. We looked at each other as he spoke. We got in our purses and got out our business cards and handed them over to him. We told Dennis, when he was ready to write, we were ready to print. He couldn't believe there was a publisher in our group.

What really set him apart was when I told him some of my experiences that mimicked his. He got goose bumps and hugged me. Finally! He found someone who had walked the same walk he had. Another person who would really understand! As I spoke to him, I watched him listen for the Holy Spirit to give him utterance. I smiled. I had seen that before.

We looked forward to seeing him again at Covenant Prayer Group. I knew exactly how he felt. I wasn't alone either.

CHRISTIAN COWBOY FAMILY
(Sept. 14th)

While I worked the late morning and early afternoon shift, Mark and Annie went to our good friend, Debbie Grimes', home and took care of some landscaping for her. After work, we all went home and cleaned up for church.

Mark and I ate quickly, packed Annie up, and went to Lapping Park to meet Ben for our weekly workout session. Ben was a great instructor for keeping a body strong and healthy!

By 8 p.m., we were at Cowboy Church. Rabbona Joy was to preach that night. When she preached, it wasn't like being preached at. It was as if we were all having a long talk together. She drew you into the conversation.

Just like this....

"This is the time to provoke people to jealously of what God has done for us. Tell people of the relationship we have with God, Jesus and the Holy Spirit." Joy started her sermon. She gave example after example of what she was speaking about and how it might look in our own lives.

Joy could have talked all night as far as I was concerned. She spoke of God and how He impacts our lives through Jesus Christ.

Afterwards, we stayed for a meal and fellowship. We fed Annie and took her outside for a potty break. When we brought her back into the church, she was ready for bed and crawled into her carrier and fell sound asleep.

Pastor Chris opened up about his life and some of what the Lord had helped him through. I was surprised and sorrowed that we had been through similar experiences.

Then Joy and I had a chance to speak together. She advised me to test all the spirits of helping people to make sure they were from the Lord. They could be imitators. Be careful.

As we were leaving, Pastor Chris told us that we were all family now—and that he loved us. Of course, we loved him and the rest of the church body too.

How grateful we were for that little church in LaGrange.

Are you in a church or a group of people you can rely on?

I hope so.

OPEN YOUR EYES!
(Sept. 16th)

The Lord God has had a tendency to wake me up early to show me things, share a word of wisdom, or just talk with me. This morning was to show me what was really going on in His world!

The command came.
"Open your eyes."
I sat straight up in bed, someone had pushed me. It was very early, still dark outside. I knew God had called me to wakefulness. I knew I would need paper.

I sighed a loud sigh, grabbed my glasses and a pen. I opened my notebook.

"I'm ready."
Revelation came so fast, I could hardly keep up! It came with visual and auditory.

First, I was shown my first book and how it caught the attention of a general from the underworld.

Then, I was shown my second book. The anti-Christ tried to reason me out of doing work for the Lord God.

Then, God spoke:
"Keep going! You are stirring up the atmosphere!"
Wow! Glory to God! Encouragement from on High! How could a body go back to sleep after that? I could've danced on thin air!

We were expecting eight people for dinner that evening. Evidently, I needed an early start. After a hearty breakfast, Mark and I cooked and cleaned all day. Crystal, David, Andy, Samantha and the children were coming that evening for dinner. I had been given words to a beautiful song for Ben and Amanda's

426

upcoming wedding. Andy and Samantha practiced a tune on guitar and violin. They wanted to practice it with Crystal, who would sing. She had a beautiful voice, and we wanted to make use of it.

They all arrived on time, and we had a lovely evening. The children, Lily and Matthew, played with Annie all through the house and in to the backyard. The adults talked of their week and general interests. Then, all were called to the table, and prayers of thanksgiving were said. A resounding "Amen!" was given, and we dug into the meal. There was just enough room for all of us at the table. Annie took turns going from my lap to Daddy's. Annie did not want to miss anything that was going on at the table!

Afterwards, we cleaned up for dessert at everyone's convenience.

Meanwhile, Andy got out his guitar, and Sammie her violin to share with us and go over the tune they had picked out to go with the lyrics.

Crystal listened to them play. You could almost see her mind, where notes and lyrics lined up. By the third time, she sang along with them. After a few times of Crystal's clear notes joining their rhythms, as if right on key, Andy added his soft, almost raspy singing in contrast to Crystal. It was so beautiful I cried. It was icing on a beautiful cake.

"Perfect."

Days before they were to meet for the recording, there was a big fight on the part of the one who was to record it all, and at the last minute they pulled their services.

The song, *Two Hearts*, was never recorded.

GOD SETUP
(Sept. 18th)

All day long, I took calls. People needed to get together for a variety of reasons. The only day they could all make it was Sunday, September 30th. Allow me to do some explaining here. I had decided, with a wedding on the horizon and everything we still had to accomplish, my birthday, September 30, could be overlooked. No problem.

Even one of our pastors called me and said she had a day off, and she was going to be in the area! Could she come over? From out 71 North to Corydon, Joy was going to be in our area! I giggled as I finally realized God Himself was planning a get-together.

Mary and Crystal needed to hold a meeting; friends wanted to come over that day; Joy needed a place to go; the kids wanted to come over, etc., etc.....

Deal.

I guessed we were having a party.

ONE DAY
(Sept. 19th)

Mark and Annie went to Mark's work, and I went to mine all day. I made it home just in time to fix dinner and clean up a little bit before they arrived.

It was setting up for a beautiful sunset. The three of us climbed into Mark's truck, after dinner, for a ride over to our homeland. We always took our Bible with us to pray and speak the word of God over a home there. In the natural, we were hanging on by a thread with an okay so far from a local bank.

Mark pulled up onto our land as if there were a driveway there. Then, he pulled up to where our home would be. Mark turned off the ignition, and we sat and looked at our view.

The sky was a myriad of blues, purples, yellows, and pinks, all coming together in a symphony of color. A quiet peace prevailed over us. Even Annie quietly looked out the front window.

"One day, Lord."
"One day."

We read Amos 9: 15
*"I will plant them on their own soil,
no more to be uprooted from their
land, which I gave them,"
says Adonai your God.*

THE FRAGRANCE OF PRAISE!
(Sept. 20th)

I fielded calls all morning, while I did daily chores and housecleaning. David, our middle son, had been able to get off and would be at my un-birthday party.

As happy as that call was, the next one brought sorrow.

"Hello? Miss Jean? It's nice to hear from you. Oh? I'm so sorry. I can come by on Friday afternoon. I'll bring my anointing oil. Yes, Ma'am. Goodbye, and God bless you."

I hung up the phone. John was very ill and had been diagnosed with cancer. Miss Jean wanted me to come by and anoint her husband and pray for him.

Mark came home and, over dinner, we talked of the good news and the bad news. Since it was Thursday night, we readied ourselves for prayer group at St. Mary's. Soon it would be their 30th anniversary as a group. 2013 would be the big anniversary. I had been around for 22 of those 30 years. I felt very blessed to be a part of it. Yet, in all those years, the Lord had never chosen me for a word of knowledge when everyone spoke in tongues—until that night.

We arrived with Annie in tow. All the regulars were there. We sang as usual, until tongues hit our group—each in their own language. That was when it happened. For the first time in 22 years, I got an interpretation! The Lord God had to repeat it three times before I was brave enough to share it with everyone!

"My children! The beautiful smell of your praise and worship of me has reached me! I love you!"

Everyone clapped. Mary's eyes misted with tears.

After the final prayer of the evening, Mary drew me aside to talk. She wanted me to know that the word I was given was just for her.

"How did you know it was for you?" I asked her.

"My stomach has been bothering me all night with gas. It kept interrupting my praise and worship. But the Lord let me know, through your interpretation, that it was all okay! He heard me anyway." Mary smiled.

ENCOURAGER OF THE FAITH
(Sept. 21st)

It was a wonderful day! It started with my weighing and measuring. I had lost eight pounds and six inches. "Size 8 here I come!" I wanted to look nice for Ben and Amanda's wedding. I had reached my goal with one month to spare. Now, all I had to do was hold on.

That afternoon, I went to the Laundromat. Everyone was so helpful. Mark and I had just bought two new comforters that were so big we couldn't get them in our regular-size washer.

While there, I held a conversation, with a lady, about God. It got deep very quickly as we encouraged each other to go on with our daily ministries. One of the ladies said a nice, young man behind me was also talking to me. I turned around and he repeated himself.

"You are as lovely as the first day I met you. You haven't changed a bit."

He was all smiles. I had worked with his mother at Lifeline Outreach Ministry. The young man was now 30-years-old. His name was Joseph. We talked while my laundry was in the dryer. Joseph was not up to much. I asked a few more questions about his life.

Joseph had been close to a degree but had dropped out. I encouraged him to go back to school and finish his degree in engineering. I told him his Heavenly Father would want him to. As the encouragement took hold, Joseph became excited.

Yes! He would go back to school and make something of himself! I knew Joseph wouldn't let God down!

As I walked back into the Laundromat I knew it was not mere coincidence that I was there doing laundry for the first time ever. I knew it was a divine incident. I was to be God's eyes and ears that day. I had gotten the message right. And with a pure heart, I had delivered it. I was grateful, once again, to be of service to our Lord God.

The rest of the afternoon, I went to the home of Miss Jean and John. God was not through with me doing His work; being His hands and feet. I knocked on their door with several copies of my newest book with me—the one with them in it. And, I had brought the anointing oil as requested. I was led in as they were waiting on customers. I also got to meet their daughter.

We talked for a while, and then, when their store was all clear, we prayed, and I anointed John and asked for God's mercy on their lives. As I was leaving, their daughter pressed money into my hands. It was just enough for what I had needed. My God of just enough had come through once more. We had needed money for that evening.

After dinner, Mark and I met Ben at the park to exercise. I told Ben the good news about my weight and inches that I had lost under his program. Ben was proud of me. I rode with our son to a local ball game that Amanda's brother was in. We had a night out with him and his new family-to-be. Of course, we had Annie with us. Ben and I talked all the way to school. As we pulled up, we could hear the shouts from the parking lot.

Every once in a while we got up to go to the restroom. It was a good time to take Annie out as well. We received more compliments on her when we took her for a walk. Some asked if we were going to allow Annie to have babies. Mark said, "No!" Mark was afraid that as small as Annie was, she might die in birth. To Mark, Annie Frances was our baby, and that was all there was to it. "Thanks for asking."

That night, Daddy slept with Annie a little closer to him. She was just fine with that.

All was right with our world.

As our prayers were said that evening, we both took turns thanking God for using us in His service throughout the day.

CHARLIE BROWN LEAVES
(Sept. 22nd)

We had lots on the agenda for the day. Mark took Annie to work with him, so I could go to Amanda's bridal shower. I even got to help! Shortly after I arrived at their church, I asked Deanna what I could help with.

Up on the stage, where they were putting all of Amanda's gifts on a table, were some plastic fall-colored leaves. Deanna wanted them hung up on the wall to be a decoration in back of where Amanda would be sitting.

As I stood in front of my first project, I wondered what to do with them. I saw a pleasant vision unfold in my head. It was a scene from the *Charlie Brown Special*. I could see the different colored leaves falling to the ground. The pile was becoming larger with each second that passed.

"Wait!" I cried out in my head. I knew that was a great idea. I took all of the leaves out of the bags they were in and mixed them on the wall as if falling from a tree. After a sufficient number of leaves were falling, I started placing a pile on the ground. By the time I had finished, it looked just like a scene from the television show.

Deanna and a few other ladies came by to see it, and they loved it! I was so glad I had come in handy. The party went off without a hitch. The lady who made the cupcakes did a wonderful job. I brought a couple home for Mark — none for Annie.

It was a jam-packed day. When I got back home, I had to get ready for a very nice wedding and reception.

Good friends had gotten married that day, and we went to the reception. Miss Annie stayed with Grandma.

After the reception, we picked up Annie and headed home. Mark changed into jeans and I into pajamas. Mark had another event on his schedule. He was going to Andy's house for Ben's bachelor party. It was a night at the fights on television for the guys!

I consoled myself with talking to Crystal from 11:30 until 1 a.m. I couldn't stay awake any longer! Mark moseyed in well after two that morning. Annie met him at the door! Now, we would all sleep together.

BEAUTY FOR ASHES
(Sept. 23rd)

Mark and I had a nice day planned. Not as busy as the day before, and we could sleep in. Even Annie slept in. We made a nice breakfast for the three of us, showered, it was Mark's turn to bathe Annie, and off for a road trip! We wanted to go see where Ben and Amanda were getting married.

We arrived at the Forestry an hour later, and walked around. Annie played in the leaves as we walked. I had a concern over the parking, and Mark assured me there would be plenty of spaces for all who would be in attendance.

This was also a day for us to shop. We had several good coupons for some stores we liked to frequent. The first store was a Christian store. We had a nice 40% off coupon and went in to buy a wedding present for Ben and Amanda. I also found a beautiful plaque, just like the one I had left behind in our beloved home on Mathis road. "Be Still and Know that I AM God." Mark found a Bible that he had always wanted since I received mine as a birthday present. We would be able to study scripture together!

Our next stop was a pet supply store to get Annie a few more outfits for the fall. They, too, had a 20% off sale going on. Could this be the trend of the day?

The next stop was a major department store. On the way there, we fed Annie some of her snacks and her special corn syrup water, so she wouldn't get weak with all the places we still had to go. Annie had her own doggie purse that she could travel in when we went into stores. With her own blanket, it was very comfortable for her.

We arrived at the store with their brand of cash, and a 30% discount card! I had needed some clothes, and we went in to pick out the needed parcels. Of course, we went to the Christmas aisle while we were there, (I know it was September) but we walked right up to where we felt drawn to go. Just like the Bible Mark wanted, it was the last ornament they had of the kind we collected. It, too, was on a great discount. We ended up paying less than the original cost of one item for the both of them! Everywhere we went that day, our money had gone almost twice as far. Little blessings had appeared all day long before us.

Mark and I stopped and picked up dinner on the way home. When we arrived back at the house, our order was wrong. I told Mark I would go see the fast - food restaurant after church. One last trip to the grocery and I left Mark to unpack while I went to a Spirit-filled church that held a revival that night.

I arrived a little late, and Pastor Bob was already preaching. My friends had saved me a seat toward the front, on the end of their pew. As usual, Pastor Bob was walking and talking on fire with the Holy Spirit.

Pastor Bob is an old-fashioned preacher man. He came complete with a woman who played the organ alongside of him. She gave musical emphasis to his "umph." At one point, while he was preaching, Bob walked through the congregation and listened for the Holy Spirit to give him utterance. As he walked past me, he pointed and said, "God has given you beauty for ashes." The Scripture that came to me immediately was, even our best efforts are as filthy rags before God without Jesus' intervention for us. His is the blood covenant that allows us to go boldly before the throne of God.

I pondered his words as I stopped at the fast-food restaurant to inform them of their error on our meal. The young lady at the counter took the receipt to their manager, who examined it. I thought at best, maybe she would give us the item we had been missing. But, no! Favor was still with me that night! She gave me two ice-cream drinks for our time and inconvenience.

"Thanks!"

Mark was very happy when I arrived home with a free dessert for us to enjoy. I put a small amount of vanilla in a dish for Annie. We all had ice-cream together.

We sat in the living room, and I told Mark of the marvelous word I had received at church. I told him of the revelation I received to go along with it.

We counted every blessing we had received through out that day. It was good to sit back and review God's interaction with us. It helped our perspective for the days ahead.

Does it do the same for you?

ENCOURAGEMENT
(Sept. 24th)

One more time, I met with the gentleman at the bank where we were to go for our home-construction loan. I had now been at my job for six months, and they could process us again.

I had read through my second book, now all finished, any grammar-tense error had been removed. I felt compelled to call my good friend, Deb Grimes. It was good that I had because she had heard from Fr. Bernie. He said when we got his section of book two all right, he would endorse it! What he didn't know was, we had taken all his notes and rewrote what he had asked us to. I sent him a second-edition copy through Deb. Then, he could heartily endorse the book and our work. It was an encouraging word.

When Mark came home that evening, he brought the mail in. He gave out the mail after dinner as was his usual custom. He handed me a letter.

It was from a federal prison. An inmate had seen the article the Corydon Democrat had written about me and my books and how to contact me. He was contacting me! The young man was very courteous and asked permission to correspond with me. He also wanted a copy of my first book. Mark and I prayed together over the matter.

When we awoke the next morning, we felt clearance for me to write Mr. Anthony Wheeler back. After all, Mr. Wheeler wanted to be a Christian author too! Couldn't I be an encouragement to him as well? Well, of course!

MOVING SOON

(Sept. 25th)

It started about midnight. The dreams came, one after another, until 7:30 a.m. They were a continuation of telling dreams.

First I dreamed my momma sold her home. Each of us children got two items to remember our childhood home by. We moved Momma into an apartment that she didn't like; so we had to move her again. This was over two dreams.

The last dream, we moved her into a home. This one she liked. I went around the block to check out the area. There was a really nice house with a stone sign on it. My dad, who had died when I was 21 years old, came out and hugged me. I could feel him hug me. He asked, "Where's Mom?" I told him that I would go get her. She was just around the corner. We could move her in with dad. I knew she would be excited!

As I woke up from those set of dreams, I woke up with a word, *"Moving soon."*

I felt six months in my spirit.

It ended up being seven months.

While at work, I was told our hours were being cut down to 10 per week. When I was given the word we were moving shortly, I knew it to be good news. But in the natural, my work hours were being cut in half!

I asked the Lord, "What do we do? What does all this mean? When will I hear an answer to this cry?"
... Turn the page...

ANGELS UNAWARE

(Sept. 26th)

I awoke the next morning with the question I had asked the night before fresh in my mind. I asked again.

"What are you going to do Lord? I did all I know how to do. And I gave all our finances over to You. Help us find a way."

I took Annie for her checkup that morning. As I came back home and in the doorway, the phone was ringing.

"Hello?"

"Is this Debbie Peyron?"

"Yes, it is."

"We just met your son, Ben. He gave us your number. We are at the hospital, and we need prayer quick!"

The elderly lady told me a story all-too-familiar to me. An elderly couple, both so ill. I had heard it numerous times as a patient care advocate.

"Yes, I would be happy to pray for you."

"We both fell quiet as I searched for words that would stir the very heart of God. Within seconds, I was answered. I spoke what I felt compelled to speak. Betty felt something too! She felt the movement of God in their situation. Betty felt better as the minutes went by. We gave glory to God, our rescuer!

I worked that afternoon and evening. Annie and Mark were at Albin's. There was to be a Bible study at our home that night. I would catch up to everybody after I got off work, but not until a rather peculiar

442

incident happened while I was at work.

It was exactly 8:15 p.m. Two elderly men came into the store. I greeted them as usual. They picked up a couple of items, practically nothing really, and walked right over to me. It didn't take one minute to check them out. This is what occurred during that 60 seconds.

One of the gentlemen asked me, "How are you?"

"Fine, thank you."

"Fine as a millionaire should be."

They looked at each other and smiled at me. As they walked out the door, I followed them.

"What?! What did you say, millionaire? I believe you! I believe you!" They had spoken with authority.

They turned around and spoke again, "That's right, you should."

Angels, I think, bringing with them the favor and blessings of God. There was such an heir about them! There was quiet confidence in their words. I could hardly wait to go home and tell Mark what had happened!

Finally, 9:30 arrived, and I bolted for home! I ran into the house and cried out for my husband.

"Mark! Honey! Oh, hi, Bill. You guys, I think I was visited by angels tonight!"

The men pulled me up a chair, got me a cup of coffee and a dessert, and sat down across from me. I told the story from beginning to end. I told how, when they spoke, I had Spirit bumps all over me, as if the spirit in myself acknowledged their Spirits. The same way Elizabeth acknowledged Mary when she came to visit her, in the Bible. I understood entirely.

Both men agreed, I had been visited in answer to my prayer.

God had sent messengers.

MARVELOUS!
(Sept. 27th)

"*Miraculous Interventions II*" was finished. Mary and I had done what God had asked of us. "Get it right." Fr. Bernie still had to read and okay his revision, but as far as I was concerned, it was put to bed. I was free to work on book III, *Miraculous Interventions, 2012 -The Miraculous Year.*

Mark took Annie to work with him while I saw wellness clients and went to a business meeting. A local group of business women had monthly meetings and an open house to showcase their businesses. The public was invited to "come on by." I set up my simple wares, my books, and offered to take blood pressures for people as part of a wellness check.

The first person to stop by was Janelle's husband. Janelle is a lady that I befriended earlier in the month. The Lord had shown me that she needed encouragement. I accomplished this task through Scripture verses and compassionate words given to me in my spirit at the time. It made such an impact on her that she shared them with her husband. So, that afternoon, when she pointed me out to him, he came over and thanked me for the kindness toward his wife. My simple act of obedience meant all the difference in the world to them. I told him in reply, simply, "God is kind." The young man asked me to continue to pray for them.

"I will."

After that, people lined up for blood pressure checks while others showed interest in my books.

Two ladies came up and sat down with me. They

wanted their blood pressures checked. The first lady watched me closely as I told a few quick stories about the Lord while I took her blood pressure.

She asked me, "Are you Pentecostal?"

I replied with a smile, "Amen!"

Then she said strong words, "You're a prophetess! I'm like you! I know a woman at the hospital like us. I promise I'll call you!"

She took my card.

How excited I was to be in the service of the Lord.

At the end of the evening, prizes were drawn. I won two tickets to our local theater to see their new Christmas Play.

My day was not over as I packed everything up. I still had to go to St. Mary's Covenant Prayer Group meeting. It was their 29th anniversary, and Melanie, the wife of the leader, Phil, had prayed for 29 people to show up. I stopped and picked up a few items for the celebration and took off for church.

When I arrived, I was pleasantly surprised to see so many cars at our church. My husband was already there. Since we were only gone for a few hours from home, Mark left Annie there in her carrier.

Thirty-three people attended the celebration. Phil, Melanie and Mary sang and played praise songs as people came in. Mark saw me enter the building and greeted me with a hug and a kiss. He smiled as he looked around the room at all the people that had been members from years gone by! And, some of our group's brand-new people were there too. A sweet elderly man had come all the way from Louisville to attend the function. He, too, was prophetic and we always enjoyed his company. Several of my friends had come as well.

There was some singing, and some preaching and thanksgiving that went on for the first hour. Then, a meal was served and fellowship began. As word got around that I had been at the women's meeting with books about miracles, several people came up and asked if I had any for sale.

"Yes."

I spent the rest of the evening signing and numbering books for our prayer group and church members.

Our son, Andy, called while we were there, to give a praise report. He said that everything he had prayed for at work had happened! He knew that God's favor had gone before him!

Toward the end of the evening, a friend came up to me with prayers in his hands. Dennis said those prayers were powerful and to say them with my husband in the evenings. At the end of our conversation, this gentle man looked at me, smiled and said, "You're marvelous!"

FAVOR!
(Sept. 28th)

Two nice e-mails came over the computer that morning. For me, it's always nice to receive encouragement.

The first was from a lady named Tracy. She had won my first book in a raffle. She wanted me to know she loved it and recommended it to everyone who visited her website!

"How nice!"

I received a second e-mail from one of the bookstores that carried my series. They ordered six more of each of my books. I prayed, "Lord, let each book bless a life."

I worked from 4 p.m. until 9:30 that evening. Mark and Annie, along with Deb and Buster, went to Cowboy Church.

When I got home from work, I took one last look at both of my book proofs, checked one last time, they were fine, and now, just as the Lord had said, it was up to Him. His favor.

As I reflected over the day's events—even my life to that point—prayer bubbled up from inside me. Tears fell, as I spoke in tongues. I felt fire fall on top of my head!

Surely, God was with me!
After all, this was His journey too!
Just like yours, Dear Reader, just like yours.

PLANS
(Sept. 29th)

It was my birthday weekend and Mark had taken time off work to be with me. It was also a few short weeks until Ben and Amanda's wedding. I had thought I would forgo my own personal birthday party in order to get more tasks accomplished for the upcoming nuptials. At least that was *my* plan.

Mark's sister and brother-in-law always held the September birthdays at their house. Andy was bringing Samantha and her children to the McCoy's for the first time to introduce them to the family.

It was a long day. I had cleaned our whole house while Mark cooked for the birthday party at the McCoy's. We packed Annie up and took off for the day. It was a beautiful fall evening. There was a nice crowd at the family festival. Three birthdays were being remembered, mine, and two nephews. Lots of presents were exchanged, stories were told, and laughter rang out as children chased our two-and-a half-pound puppy through the house and out the door! I knew Annie Frances would be squealing right along with them if she could!

As the party wound down, BJ, Mark's youngest sister, and I spoke of the deep things of God.

Of course, we did.

HAPPY BIRTHDAY!
(Sept. 30th)

The beans were spilled early that morning. I thought people were coming over to practice a song for the wedding. Well, that was part of it, but, it seemed I was going to need a birthday cake for the occasion! Sixteen people were to drop by.

I asked Mark, "Did you know we were having a birthday party for me today?"

With a smile, I knew he had suspected as much. He didn't figure our boys were going to let their momma's birthday go by unnoticed.

I started to pull pots and pans out of the cabinets. I had a cake to bake!

"Can you go to the store for me?" I asked Mark.

He nodded. "Spaghetti okay for your birthday dinner?" Mark wanted to cook his favorite recipe.

"Sure, fine."

I baked a cake and started the side items for the impromptu dinner. I was still cooking when guests started to arrive. Ben and Andy arrived with their families-to-be in tow. Annie greeted them at the door, and they acknowledged her back. It was a half birthday/half pre-wedding party!

Andy and Samantha were the first two in the kitchen to greet me. Sammie spoke first, "Hi, Momma! Is there anything I can help with?"

"Yes! Only everything!"

Samantha laughed as I tied an apron around her tiny waist. Ben and Amanda found Sammie and myself busy in the kitchen while Mark and Andy, along with the children, Lily and Matthew and Annie, were out back playing in the yard.

By early afternoon, we were joined by other dear friends and family. Our middle son, David, showed up with a beautiful violet orchid. The Murray's, the Richmer's, Deb Grimes, Connie and Rabbona Joy all showed up as if on cue with presents. Other friends dropped off gifts but could not stay. I was amazed that so many people knew when my birthday was. I was pretty sure they had a little help from a friend I like to call husband.

By 2 p.m., it was brunch time. The food was ready and so were our hungry tummies!

"Dinner is served! Mark, please open the meal with a prayer." I requested.

Mark said a moving thanksgiving prayer for all the people that were there or had stopped by with a gift. He thanked God for his wife and family and that we would all have a blessed year. As usual, the crowd sang "Happy Birthday" with gusto and as off key as they could make it. I opened gifts with Annie in my lap. She was after the cake!

It was decided in the late afternoon that a group of us would go over to our homeland and pray. Joy, Crystal, Connie, Deb Richmer and myself drove two cars over. Somehow, in my spirit, I felt I had a date with destiny.

When we arrived, Connie, Crystal and Deb sat on our park bench at the front of our land. Joy asked me to take her to where the front porch would be. I knew the other women would pray for us. We walked onto fields of wild flowers and bristles until we stood on top of a hill that overlooked rolling hills and a horse farm located in back of our land.

No sound was heard, but the leaves that rustled in the ever-present wind. It whistled as it rushed past our ears. I felt something stir in the atmosphere. I took a step forward as if walking up onto a porch. Joy watched me with keen interest. She knew what was coming. Joy knew God had His own birthday event planned for me.

Suddenly, the gift of tongues fell on both of us! God was there, and He wanted to communicate with us in His language! It was the most beautiful speaking in tongues I have ever experienced. It took me to my knees!

Joy spoke what she saw and heard.

"Don't fret! Don't fret! Don't fret! You have the favor of God this year. Visions come forth!"

Joy stopped for a moment as if she were adjusting her vision, then she spoke, "I see the front door and the back of the house with all the windows. I see your valley."

Then Rabbona Joy saw two large angels appear over our 10 ¾ acres. One was at the left corner, and the other was at the right corner, as if they were standing guard. For a reason unknown to me in the natural, I asked Joy if I could speak to the angel on the left side. She smiled and said, *yes*. The one I had asked to speak to was a messenger angel.

On my knees, I spoke from my heart. I cried and told this Heavenly visitor of the vision I and many others had seen. I spoke of how I had served the Lord, "go here, go there" as the Lord God had commanded. I spoke of the future ministry from there to serve God.

I asked Him to help us! I begged Him to please help us! I asked the angels to make a way. I asked them to take my message back with them to the Lord. Joy listened and smiled. She saw a second vision. This one, she had to explain to me. Joy spoke.

"I saw barbed wire on the ground. Then I saw God's gold come down, and it all parted. The Shekinah glory came down. Say this, I have the favor of God this year!"

I was instructed to say the line over and over again until I could get it into my heart and mean it.

Joy went on, "Ask what you will and believe it will come to pass!"

With tears that ran down my cheeks, I shouted my request for a home on that land!

As we got up off our knees, I felt in my spirit a word drop into my conscious.

"Deal with Mark about his unbelief."

Mark had said something damaging two days before. It was brought up to my memory, "Everything will be hard if nothing changes! We won't be able to tithe or help anyone! We won't even be able to take our mothers or our kids out to eat!"

I had my orders.

When we came back to the house, I took Mark into the kitchen. This had to be dealt with. As I started to speak to him about what he had said the day before, Mark interrupted me.

"Honey, the Lord has already shown me my unbelief. I was listening to the enemy. I have repented, and I repent now to you. I'm sorry!"

"Oh, honey, thank you! You know we have to be of one mind and accord to get this done."

"Yes, I know." Mark answered. "I won't listen to fear again!"

For the rest of the evening, from 8 p.m. on, our group, all that stayed, talked in the living room over coffee until after one in the morning.

Questions were asked of Joy all night about the deep things of God, people's lives, the world around us, the second coming of Christ, etc. Joy laughed and said that if she had known there was going to be a quiz, she would have been more prepared.

No one wanted to leave that evening. But as they left, they all left a little wiser than they had started the evening, including Mark and I.

»» INTERMISSION ««

"AND THE FATHER LOVES HIS SON"
The Book of Matthew

John 3:16 *"For God so loved the World that
He gave His only begotten Son,
that whosoever believeth in Him,
should not perish, but have everlasting life."*

There once was a little boy with bright blue inquisitive eyes, and strawberry-blonde hair that stood straight up on his head! No amount of coaxing with either water, gel or spit, could tame this young'uns hair — or spirit. His name was Matthew.

Now Matthew came into our lives as part of a part-and-parcel with his sister, Lily. Their mother, Samantha, and our youngest son, Thomas Andrew, had fallen in love.

We met the family in Samantha's front yard. We had been heading back home from Mom Peyron's, and Andy was behind us in a pickup truck. He beeped his horn for us to let him in front of us. Then, Andy motioned for us to follow him. Miss Samantha had just gotten off work from the emergency room, and Andy thought it was as good a time as any for us to say our hellos.

As the four of us introduced ourselves, two small children peeked their heads out the front window. Before we knew it, they came running out of the house. One skipped over to us, Miss Lily, and the other, Matthew, ran like the wind — possibly tornadic, as he did circles around and around everyone!

"Matthew!" Heads turned to follow his progress.

"Matthew!!" Dizziness began to set in.

"Matthew!"

Over the course of the next year, I was occasionally called on to babysit as the two adults became a couple. We have shared many interesting meals together. Both children knew about prayer and Jesus. Samantha's childhood household was half Catholic and half Protestant. When we made the sign of the cross before and after meals and at bedtime, it was somewhat familiar to her children.

Lily asked why we made the sign of the cross, and I shared with her the best understanding I had to give to a six-year-old.

"It's like opening up a conversation. Instead of just diving in to what you plan to say, it's rather like an introduction. For example, 'Hello, Lord, I'm starting my prayer. Lord God, Jesus my Savior, and the Holy Spirit please be in attendance.'

'In the name of the Father, and of the Son, and of the Holy Spirit... in their names, I lift up these prayers.'"

It made good-enough sense to Lily. Pretty soon, she was making the sign of the cross with us at meals, whenever we would hear a siren—as a silent prayer to go out to whoever needed it at the time, or when someone wasn't feeling well. She would plant the sign of the cross with her fingers, squarely on the ill person's forehead.

But Matthew saw and heard these actions differently than we did. After we would all pray at the end and say our closure, Matthew would say it too, or so I thought.

One evening, while I was having dinner with Andy, Sam and the kids, after our prayer, conversation started.

Samantha said, "Momma?"

I replied, "Yes, Dear?"

"Have you ever heard Matthew pray at the end of prayers as you make the sign of the cross?"

"Yes, I think so." I sought my memories to give me a clue.

Samantha turned toward her son and smiled sweetly, "Mattie, what do you say at the end of a prayer?"

Matthew smiled and said something shyly that I didn't quite catch. I looked at Sam with a question. Samantha smiled and repeated Matthew's rendition.

"He said, 'And the Father loves His Son'," as she made the sign of the cross.

Revelation hit me like a solid rock! This precious little tornado had understood far better than many a gray-haired theologian had ever taught!

"And the Father Loves His Son."
This is the word of the Lord.
Thanks be to God.

John 3:17 *"For God sent not His Son into the world to condemn the world; but that the world through Him might be saved."*

Season III

Sorrows and Mysteries
(Oct. 1st)

Jeremiah 31: 25 "For I have satisfied the weary and filled the needs of all in distress."

I still remember the Lord's exact words He spoke to me several years ago: ***"I will bring you back to Myself in the fall of your 54th year."***

From mid-October to November 30th, God did indeed call me back to Himself as events unfolded that took every ounce of prayer, time and strength Mark and I could muster.

At the end of September 2012, my 54th birthday, plans quickly came together for the marriage of our oldest son, Paul Benjamin, and Miss Amanda. And, our builder, Bill, and his wife celebrated the arrival of their first grandbaby.

"It's a girl!" We could hear Bill smile over the phone.

Mark and I thought, at the beginning of October, with the way events shaped up at first, it must be a season of celebrations. At least it started out that way...

SUKKOT! FEAST OF TABERNACLES
(Oct. 4th)

Sukkot — tents or Sukkah equals tent
Feast of Tabernacles — from Leviticus —
Remembrance of crossing the desert with Moses.
Rejoice and celebrate for seven days.
Lulav — blessing of harvest — wave palm up,
down, and in 4 directions to thank God for being
the provider of the harvest.
Some believe this was the actual time of Jesus' birth.
Yeshua was born around 4BC.
Yom Kippur is the highest Holy Day.
The Feast of the In Gathering — Harvest.

The King above all Kings was brought into the world with the harvest of the work of man's hands. Jesus, Yeshua, Messiah, was the harvester and was the work of God's hands. After all, how many times did Jesus say He only did what He saw the Father do, and said what the Father told Him to say?

We met Deb and Buster Richmer and went to the Murray's for a Sukkot celebration. On the way over, we prayed for a lady at our church that was in great peril. We prayed a rosary, and at the end I received a word, "promoted." When we arrived at the Murray's, I told Crystal what I had heard, and she confirmed the beautiful lady would indeed "be promoted to God." (We heard the report of her bodily death two days later).
Buster and Mark helped David with the last of the physical tent preparation. Crystal handed out platters

of food to Deb and I to arrange in the tent. We kept Annie in her carrier until time to start.

Crystal and David explained to our group what symbolic meanings were attached to the Feast of Tabernacles.

"This is done in remembrance of crossing the desert with Moses. We rejoice and celebrate for seven days the goodness of God."

We prayed Sabbath prayers with traditional Jewish prayers. We each waved the lulav, and spoke of miracles that had happened over the past year in each of our lives.

By this time, Annie had settled down to sit with us. She was all wrapped up in her blanket. After a while, Annie was passed from one person to the next as she got wiggly in our laps, just as you would take turns holding a baby.

Crystal explained through timelines about Jesus' birth. She believed that this was the actual birth time of Jesus, between the end of September and the first of October. The culmination, on the eighth day, was celebrated as part of Sukkot, that Jesus was circumcised on Simchat Torah—the Joy of the Word.

John 1:1-5 "In the beginning was the Word, and the Word was with God, and the Word was God. He was with God in the beginning. All things came to be through Him, and without Him nothing made had being. In Him was life, and the life was the Light of mankind. The Light shines in the darkness, and the darkness has not suppressed it."(CJB)

After the celebration, the meal commenced. There was fresh fruit and vegetables that adorned trays depicting the harvest of that day. Crystal had made wraps of meat and cheese to serve as finger food. Water, tea and other various drinks were served.

Fellowship was enjoyed until 11:30 that night. The four of us plus Annie left with hugs and kisses to those we considered family.

On the way home, Buster and Deb thanked us for having invited them to the celebration. It had been our pleasure to have them along with us.

Mark and I hoped it would be the beginning of many more to come.

GOD'S SCRIBE
(Oct. 5th)

It was early in the morning, 6 a.m.-ish, when my telling dream began.

I could see my family was at Mom's for a meal. Mark and I had a baby boy about four months old. He was so beautiful! I was so in love with him! He was a happy baby with many smiles and much laughter. I held this infant and talked to him.

At first he made baby sounds, then he went into rudimentary words, sentences, finally conversation. Mark was next to me speaking to someone else. I told him the baby was talking with words, and Mark looked at me as if I was being very rude for interrupting him. Mark went on with his conversation.

The baby started a conversation with me. He said yes, he could talk, and he was talking to me! This amazing baby confirmed the calling on my life, saying, *"I have called you! You are to write and record miraculous happenings that are all around you! Go forth!"*

By that time I was crying and still trying to get Mark's attention. At the time in the dream, he would have none of it.

As I awoke, I heard *"Remember your prayers of old, Infant Jesus of Prague, provide for us!"*

The interpretation came quickly. Jesus was speaking to both of us.

That night, Mark went to Cowboy Church while I stayed home with a sick puppy. Annie had diarrhea on the hour. A trip to the doctor was in order for her.

IF MY PEOPLE WILL PRAY...
(Oct. 6th)

My dear friend, Deb Grimes, called.

"The Catholic Church is asking for prayer at 3 p.m. for our nation. Five decades of the rosary are to be said during this hour. The first one is for our nation and the others are for your personal intentions. Can we count on you?"

"Yes, you can! Thank you for calling us." I happily replied.

I know when the prayers of the faithful storm Heaven, things happen, even the atmosphere changes.

I told Mark of the conversation, and he was happy to join with our brothers and sisters all over America and be a part of something much bigger than us. Mark and I sat down with pen and paper to prayerfully ask of our hearts' closest intentions.

1) For our nation—Deliverance and protection.
2) Ben and Amanda's upcoming wedding,
3) Protection—Over us and all we love.
4) All my books to have the favor of God—Open up doors.
5) A home on Nicholas Drive—On time and on budget.

While we waited for the three o'clock hour to chime, we watched stories on the television about the Lord, the Bible and Jerusalem.

When the clock struck 3 p.m., Mark and I went into our prayers. We prayed the Rosary and ended with songs of love for the Lord God Himself. We wondered aloud if we had stirred the atmosphere.

WARRIOR SHIELDS UP!
(Oct. 7th)

Twelve hours later, after the prayers of the faithful, satan went into attack! He started on our weakest link, Annie. For the first time ever, Annie cried out in her sleep, in her bed next to ours.

I jumped up and immediately fell out of the bed! I fell on the right side of my body, my ribs took the brunt of the blow. I couldn't draw in a deep breath! I hurt all the way up to my neck. I called out to Mark, "Warrior shields up! I need your help!"

I didn't know it, but Mark was in a battle too. He woke up hurting in his neck. I told him what had just happened and to put on his healing hands.

I picked up Annie, and the three of us huddled in our bed together. Mark started his prayers over all of us. I felt heat penetrate my injured area from his hand on my back and side. After a few minutes I could take a deep breath again. The pain in my ribs subsided. I could turn my head and my neck, which no longer hurt.

Then, it was my turn to pray over my husband. As I prayed over Mark's neck, I felt heat flow from the top of my head, down into my arms and into the palms of my hands, just as I had been shown in a dream years ago, that healing would flow from the palms of my hands too. I knew Mark's healing had arrived, just like mine. All my pain was gone, and Mark was much better. He continued to recover quickly.

I received a word of knowledge over these incidents. We had been attacked because of the army of believers we had joined with in prayer at three that afternoon — the one million strong.

Well, you know, we are all in an army. The fight for good will not end until Jesus and His army from Heaven end it in triumphant glory!

After all, we are the Potter's clay.
So are you.

WOW!
(Oct. 8th)

It was a day of work for me, and a long one at that. Annie went to work with Mark. I would be there until the store closed.

Halfway through my shift, a woman came in with the hiccups. She had had them for quite a while and couldn't get rid of them. She hiccupped all through the store until she came to my register. My boss was with me in the same area.

As the lady checked out, she spoke to us of her predicament. I stopped, prayed a small prayer, and then waited for her to hiccup again.

"Hiccup, go ahead, hiccup." I touted her.

Nothing.

"I'm waiting." I said again.

Nothing. I knew she was healed.

"My, how unusual." She did not know what to say.

The lady left perplexed in what had just happened. She had no understanding of the gifts of the Holy Spirit.

But I did.

God honored my request for her because of my faith in Him, not hers. When she left, my boss asked me what that was all about. She, too, was puzzled.

I replied that all power was given to all Christians who had the faith to receive it.

Her response to this proclamation of faith?

"Wow!"

UNDER ADVISEMENT
(Oct. 9th)

Sometimes, when I am hearing people speak or arrangements are being made, an angel of the Lord will speak in my right ear, loud and clear, as if standing next to me. That was exactly what happened when our children spoke of our obligations along with their birth- father for their wedding.

"Flowers, invitations and a rehearsal dinner," Ben and Amanda informed us.

As they said "rehearsal dinner," the angel warned me, *"You will pay for it all. Save all your money."*

"Okay."

I was under advisement.

As I caught up my writing, I called Mary, my main editor, publisher, and my very best friend. We realized what possibilities were before us. Could I handle traveling?

I called Deb Grimes to give a report on the other nights' activity and our victory. Somehow, she knew! Deb knew the attack was on us and why — because of the prayers of the faithful.

Mid-afternoon, the double attack came, just like the angel had warned. My ex, the father of my boys, was upset! The seating arrangement he had wanted had been changed. He would have none of it. He withdrew his offer for the nice restaurant for the rehearsal dinner. I quickly canceled the reservation.

Mark and I had ten days to find somewhere for the rehearsal dinner. And who, on such short notice, would cook it?

The word of knowledge from the angel had come in very handy. We still had just enough money put aside to have one of our local grocers put together a meal for 25 people. And Miss Amanda's church opened their doors at no charge as long as we cleaned up afterward.

"No problem."

The Lord had told me from the beginning, we would have to pay for it all.

A NEW CAR
(Oct. 13th)

For as long as I had known Mary Dow Smith, she had needed reliable transportation. I had prayed a heartfelt prayer that God would be as good to her as he had been to me in the way of car blessings. We had gotten my gold car for half the price requested.

So, when Mary came rolling up in a practically new car for half the price they had wanted for it, I knew both our prayers had been answered!

As Mary drove to the Louisville Christian Writers meeting, we both felt that her new Civic would be what we would use to travel in. We would no longer have to worry about Mary travelling from my house to her house. She would be safe.

After the LCW meeting, Mary and I went for a meal with Crystal and David and discussed what to do next for my new book series. The meeting went so well, we felt confirmed in our hearts that we were destined to be a team together.

WEDDING TREE
(Oct. 14th)

When Ben and Amanda asked us to paint them a wedding tree, we had to ask what it was. Mark and I had never heard of it. They sent us several links by e-mail to look at, and I researched it. Mark prayed. Which one Lord?

Instead of having people sign a register book when they came into the wedding reception, Ben and Amanda wanted people to put their thumbprints on a canvas tree. We bought all the fall colors for leaves on the tree.

Mark and I set to work. He wanted me to draw and paint the tree.

"But trees are your specialty, Dear." I responded to his unusual request.

Mark replied back, "I know, but you can do it. I will be working on something special to put at the bottom of the painting."

"Okay." I hesitantly agreed to try.

True to Mark's insight, I drew a beautiful tree and calligraphied their names and wedding date at the bottom of the canvas. The bottom sides of the canvas were left bare. That was where Mark's inspiration came into the picture, literally!

I commented as Mark began to draw, "Honey, it's so pretty, what are you drawing?"

"On the left side, is the lake and forest where they are getting married. On the right side, is our homeland with the two trees we have, holding hands, uh, leaves!"

Underneath the picture of our land, we put our thumbprints together in the shape of a heart.

We took the canvas and paint directly to Ben and Amanda's for their approval. They loved it and took pictures of it right away to send to Amanda's mother immediately to share with her.

On their wedding day, Ben and Amanda would put their thumbprints together beneath the picture of their wedding site.

By 3 p.m., Mark and I went to Momma's for dinner. It was my birthday dinner. With all the wedding plans that had gone on around us, we had to squeeze in my family's birthday party for me. My little brother and his wife came over to Momma's, and we had a nice visit. But the day was still not over! Mark and I had to go way out in the country to pick up all the wedding flower decorations. And they were beautiful! Everything was out on the front porch and ready to be picked up. It was almost midnight when we finally arrived back home. Annie was exhausted from such a long day. So were her parents.

INSPIRATION
(Oct. 16th)

I prayed for God's inspiration to write a letter to the leader of one billion Roman Catholics. I knew the words would have to be special to move hearts. As I sat down to write, the words flowed from my heart onto the paper. I called Mary and read it for her approval. She had two small changes to make—no problem. I would have it typed and ready for her signature.

We also received approval to send a letter and a copy of my books to Ignatius Press to see if there was any interest there as well.

I worked all afternoon and evening on the projects. I daydreamed about what response, if any, we would get from the Vatican.

TWO HEARTS
(Oct. 20th)

Two hearts,
joined as one.
Look and see,
what they have done.

A son and daughter,
our pride and joy.
All we have taught them,
will now be employed.

The groom watched his bride to be
walk down the aisle for all to see.
A day of kindling a lifetime of love
to be blessed from God above.

In a world filled with hate,
darkness and angry fights,
these two have chosen
to be God's holy lights.

As the years go by,
their life will take hold.
And to this union,
they'll add to their fold.

Many years from now,
they'll look back to this day.
At the beginning of their life,
and we will all say...

Yes indeed, they were meant to be,
Husband and Wife.

474

10:20 a.m.

(Oct. 20th)

The big day had arrived. The first of our children was to be wed. Two families were to join.

Mark still had a high temperature, and there was no time to be seen by a physician. I prayed for health and healing to come back to my husband. Annie kept sniffing Mark as if she could sense something was wrong with Daddy.

We were all packed up for the day when we arrived at 9 a.m. to the Forestry. The women of our group got ready in a large ten-person tent. The men were sent to the outside restroom or Mark's truck bed to dress. Why, even Annie had a wedding dress on! She donned a black and gray dress with scads of ruffles. Mark bought her a diamond CZ collar. For a two-and a-half pound puppy, she sparkled!

Guests started to arrive at 10 a.m. Ben and Amanda's nuptials were to begin at 10:20 a.m., on 10/20 in honor of their meeting on October 20th two years before.

People came from all over to attend the feast! The great states of Texas, South Carolina, Kentucky, Tennessee and Indiana were well-represented. Even our local weatherman, Jay Cardosi and his family, who Amanda worked for, were in attendance. It was a joyous occasion!

The colors of the trees in the forestry were splendid. All hues of yellows, reds, browns, orange and umber covered the grounds like a carpet. The lake in the background shone a brilliant blue as the sun's rays danced through the leaves left on the trees.

The wedding and reception were held in a large covered lodge with a stone fireplace at each end with plenty of firewood at the ready to fend off the chill in the air. Multicolored flowers were everywhere! With everyone in place, the Pastor and Ben walked in and stood in front of the arch at the end of the aisle and waited.

Music began, and a host of little girls, hand-picked by Amanda, walked down the aisle and scattered colorful leaves as they walked by the seated guests. Ben broke into a big smile as he saw his bride for the first time. With Amanda's hair in dark cascading curls, flawless make-up, and a dress that draped over one shoulder and across her, Amanda looked like a Greek goddess walking down the aisle with her father.

The pastor greeted the crowd of onlookers. He gave a small sermon before the declaration of the vows. The witnesses were asked to come forward. Amanda's sister, Michelle, and Ben's brother, Andy, walked up to the podium. Witnesses in place, vows were said and rings exchanged.

"You may now kiss your bride." The Pastor's proclamation was made.

The music Ben and Amanda chose to exit on was "Happy Song" from one of their favorite Muppet movies. The two grabbed hands, smiled at each other, and skipped down the aisle. All in attendance laughed and clapped their approval.

The reception did not start for an hour-and-a-half, while family pictures were taken. Amanda's Mom went into action. There were bars set up all along the grounds filled with hot chocolate and hot apple cider. At two different locations were two s'mores bars—

graham cracker, chocolate bars and extra-large marshmallows for those who have never been on a campout—were set up as snack stations.

It was close to Halloween, so Deanna, Amanda's mother, went to each picnic table and put out candy and individual bags of chips and pretzels. There was a party in the air! Six-hundred pictures were taken that day, by the photographer. Friends of Ben and Amanda brought a beautiful Victorian couch to set out amidst the multicolored leaves. The fireplaces with their cheery fires, made wonderful huddling places for families to mingle. Even Annie had a good time all wrapped up in a blanket as light rain brought leaves down around us.

By the formal beginning of the reception, I had a runny nose! I hunted tissues and napkins like they were money! The tree pollen and the rain had won the first round with my sinuses.

Back in the reception area at the bridal table, there was a bride and a groom cake as well as various cupcakes that sat on a stand and waited to be devoured. The bride's cake was covered in roses. Ben's good friend, Rob Walker, had made Ben his special groom cake. It was themed to the Muppet music of the day. The icing was blue and set up as a fight cage. Small figurines were placed on top of the cake. There was Kermit being pinned by Animal, Miss Piggy and Fozzy Bear were on the sides cheering Kermie on. What a sight.

Although the weather was cold and damp, it could not chill our spirits! Deanna had set out a large casual spread of taco meats and cheeses with foods to go along with it. The toast, the cake, and the dancing had all gone nicely. After Amanda and her father danced, Ben picked out a song for us to dance to. The song was about people with caring hearts. Of course, it was.

Different people volunteered to hold Annie. She ate little bits at a time until I could hold her. After everything was all over and I got her to the car, and everything settled down, she finally ate her own special dogfood and water.

I went home to start a dinner for Mark and myself with leftovers from the night before. Mark took a truckload back to the Wilder's and then, he too, headed back to the house. Crystal and David came over for a meal with us and to relax together.

We were all tired and Mark was still sick. Annie laid down beside Mark and went to sleep right after dinner. Quiet conversations about the year ahead lingered for a few hours until we were all falling asleep.

Hugs were finally exchanged as the Murrays left for their temporary home. In six months, our home would become their home.

Six months.
Only six months.

I AM YESHUA!
(Oct. 22nd)

In my telling hours just before I awoke, I heard a voice say out loud,

"I Am Yeshua!"

Immediately, all the pain in my back and neck stopped as if it popped on its own. An out-loud word was followed by an instant healing, and I thanked God! Then I fell back to sleep.

Unfortunately, it didn't take care of our colds. From being out in the rain and the cold for hours at the wedding, Mark and I had caught colds. We took the last of the paperwork to the bank, being assured of a closing date that very week.

I worked, while Mark cleaned house. That evening, we were both wore out and sneezing. It felt like a flu was coming on for both of us.

MAIL
(Oct. 24th)

Many hopes and dreams went out in the mail that day. I sent beautifully crafted letters with a copy of each of my books to Abbey Press, Ignatius Press, National Charismatic Services, and the Vatican to His Holiness, Pope Benedict XVI.

After I mailed everything out, I called Mary to pray with me for good fruit and the favor of God and man!

October flew by with joyful laughter and bliss as happy times, weddings, and births of new babies unfolded before our eyes

As the days of fall gathered speed and October edged to a close, Mark and I both came down with the flu. We needed a timeout. Our long awaited home loan, that we had been promised was just a week away, had been denied. We did not know it at the time, but the paperwork had been sent in with errors.

By the end of the month, Mom Peyron had a light stroke.

November loomed over us like a sour stomach.

DENIED
(Oct. 26th)

The wait from the beginning of the week for our approval was easy. It was such a shoe-in that when the loan processor called and said there was a glitch and to hold on, it took me by surprise. He said he would call me back later.

Not ten seconds after we hung up, Deb Grimes called and said God told her to come and see me. We prayed together and believed all would be well. God, indeed, had a plan and would send the money.

The loan processor called back later that afternoon. We had missed being approved by $50.00 a month. It seemed the cost of living had bumped up over the last six months since we applied.

I hollered into the phone, "Don't you think we can make up $50.00 a month?!"

I was devastated. I knew Mark would be too. Where would we go from there?

When we went to church that evening I told Rabbona Joy. She listened to the Holy Spirit and said, "Don't panic! Don't panic! Don't panic." Then Joy said a few other things that were of interest and unusual — at least for most people. She said getting off on Friday nights wouldn't be a problem for me much longer. She also said we would be spending some time together soon, to go before the Lord for deeper understanding of God's ways.

One of the last things she said to me when she finished reading my first book was that we were twins. We had many of the same gifts — it was hope to go on.

5:10 a.m.
THE BEGINNING OF SORROWS
(Oct. 28th)

Why doesn't anyone ever call up at 5:10 in the morning with good news such as, "I just won the lottery and I want to share it with you!" or "I just got healed of cancer!" or the best of all, "I just got saved in the name of Jesus!"

When I heard the phone ring I knew it was about Mom, Betty Peyron. Mark felt it too. It was Dana. She said Mom was in the hospital and had a mild stroke overnight. They had called us for prayers. We put our phone on speaker as Dana handed Mom the phone. We went to war! The enemy had just made a sneak attack onto our territory, and Mark and I were having none of it! We put on the armor of God, and Mark led the way.

"Lord, we know in Jesus' name, there will be no after-effects of this attack! Mom will walk, and her speech will be just fine."

For two hours, we slept until the alarm went off. Mark put out calls to our sons, and we got ready to go to the hospital. We fed Annie and took her carrier with us to drop her off at Mom's and would pick her back up in a couple of hours.

We got to the hospital after eight in the morning. Much to our surprise, Andy and Samantha had beaten us there! They were already ministering to their Grandma! Just as we had prayed, Betty could walk and talk as good as ever. We all praised the Lord for a quick- answered prayer.

We hadn't been there a few minutes when the rest of the crowd came in—Sandy, Susan, Dana, BJ, Peggy and Mary. There was a roomful of us, and it sounded like a party was going on!

After several hours with Mom, we went and picked up Annie and headed to Ben's for Sunday afternoon football and dinner. I made a veggie dip, chips and dip, and a caramel cake with chocolate cream cheese icing—one of my family's all-time favorites.

During half time, the guys called out for pizza. I wondered where in the world they would put all that food? In honor of fall, Ben put on "Charlie Brown" for all the kids to see; little and big. The big kids were us!

We packed up and left for the hospital right before visiting hours would be over. Mom was still doing well. Betty brought us up to speed on the tests the doctors had done and the ones they wanted to do the next day.

Again, we thanked God for all good outcomes and for her to be able to go home soon.

When we arrived back home, we called Crystal and David to give them an update on Mom.

Sleep was finally achieved by 10:30 p.m. It had been a long, eventful day.

We did not know how many of those long days were still to come.

INVADING ARMY
(Oct. 31st)

A late night turned into an early morning. At 9 a.m., I started a big breakfast for any who were present. Bacon, scrambled eggs, and biscuits and gravy were served piping hot. It was decided, Mark and I would stay with Mom Peyron while she recovered from her mild stroke. Her kitchen had gotten a hard workout that morning. Mom's medications were sorted out, and I checked her heart rate and blood pressure upon waking. Satisfied that all was well, Mark and I sat Mom down after breakfast in her favorite chair, and we did the morning's dishes.

Mark kept his mom entertained until almost noon while I got things ready back in the kitchen for two more meal plans. While mom took a nap, I took off for the grocery to pick up a couple of pie crusts. Mark busied himself in her yard and prepared the bushes at the front of the house for the coming winter. There were two especially large-bushes alongside the house that needed to go, and the flowers needed to be trimmed back.

By dinnertime, the house looked as good on the outside as it smelled with dinner cooking on the inside. Annie went from inside to outside all day long. She wanted to see what Mommy and Daddy were doing as if she was our little supervisor.

From 5 p.m. on, family members dropped by. When they smelled how good the impending supper was, one by one, they decided to stay. When the number of people hit 25, I looked at Mom, and she got her coupons out of the drawer and ordered five large pizzas to go with the large pot pie that would only serve 10!

Every bit of food we put out was eaten. People stayed long into the evening with smiles and laughter that echoed throughout the house. Everyone was happy that Mom was going to be okay.

When everyone left, Mark, our niece Hattie, Mom, Annie and I, stayed up until midnight and talked. Mom remembered days gone by and graced us with story after story of her upbringing and of her and Dad's courtship. When we finally went to bed, we had peace in our hearts.

GOOD NEWS DAY!
(Nov. 1st)

Mark got up early and went off to work. Annie and I stayed with Mom. I drove Mom to her first visit to the cardiologist. They tested her blood, and it was good! No more shots were needed. Mom dropped down to pills only. Our prayers had been answered.

She and I stopped by the grocery to pick up her new medications and a few things needed at the house. Mom happened to mention a type of cookie she liked. We went on a hunt. We looked down one aisle and then another until Mom was worn out!

"Stay here! Sit down! I'll find your cookies." I would not give up!

It took two more tries down more aisles until I found the exact thing she wanted! Once back at the house, I helped Mom inside and Annie outside. I made breakfast for the three of us. I did dishes and packed up while Mom rested in her easy-chair. Annie and I left shortly after lunch. When I arrived back home in Corydon, I called Mark with the good news about his mother. And there was a message on our recorder, while we were gone, about a refund check that was due us. And the last of our good news came later that afternoon. I could pick up the two free tickets to the local theater for their Christmas play. It was about angels, and we won front row seats! It would be on December 2nd.

Shortly before Mark arrived home, we received a call from the new bank we were trying for our home-construction loan. As with all the others, they said it looked hopeful. Once again, we hoped.

WHISKEY
(Nov. 2nd)

It was an early work-day for me. Annie was sent with Mark to work, and I went in to cashier. By early afternoon, I was almost ready to get off when an old haggard-looking man came into our store. He reeked of whiskey. But the Lord showed me his heart. I knew, immediately, to be very kind to him, for who else would?

I gave the elderly gentleman my sweetest smile and showed him great respect. The dear old man gave me his sweetest smile back and said I had impressed him greatly. He called me a princess. For the sake of my kindness, in his eyes, I was a princess. Well, I am the daughter of a King — King of the Universe.

At church that evening, a group of us gathered around Rabbi Joy and prayed for her health. I, myself anointed her with oil, just like in the Bible.

After church, Mark and I dropped the Richmer's off to their car. Suddenly, we smelled good whiskey in our car! It was a strong scent that wafted around us. We felt it was the presence of both our dads.

What it meant, we did not know.

SECOND CONFIRMATION
(Nov. 4th)

At 7 a.m., I awoke with the knowledge of what to write to a new publishing house that Mary and I were inquiring to. The writing took most of the day. At the end, I was finished in time for mass at St. Columba.

Just like the Lord gave me words early that morning, it was the same for Fr. Mike. He started his service like this.

"Whatever your need is, God is here to supply it. After 18 months without a job, I am employed! I am back in the drapery business again!"

The crowd clapped and cheered their approval for the blessing that had come into their pastor's life. As things quieted down, Fr. Mike gave prophesy.

"Someone is being given more gifts as a seer."

I felt Fr. Mike was speaking directly to me. He called out again.

"I have never done this before, but I want everyone here to get their wallets out."

Parishioners looked around at each other but were obedient to his instruction.

Father prayed over his congregation.

"Dear Lord, I ask that you bless our finances to be more than enough to meet every need! Make it more than enough for Your Kingdom's sake. There is no lack in the Kingdom of Heaven. Give us our cattle, Lord! You can believe God for more!"

People wiped tears from their eyes in anticipation of the word of knowledge to come true. Shortly, Fr. Mike gave a personal prophesy over me. He said, "You have a short season where you are now. I see it coming to an end soon."

They were the same words Rabbi Joy had prophesied over me just a few short weeks before. I wondered what was coming down the hatch.

Fr. Mike finished with, "I pray for a floodlight ministry for you and Mark."

Then Father went on with the mass and the readings of the day. He read from Deuteronomy 6:1-9 about Moses and the Ten Commandments. Father spoke on the first commandment—about loving God with all your heart, soul and mind. He said things will go well for you if you do this, and God will multiply you for it.

Father also spoke on Psalm 119:9-16. "Happy are those who seek God with all their hearts and walk in His ways."

"Keep all God's statutes because His judgments are righteous. God will not leave or forsake you. Seek the Lord with all your heart. Things happen in the natural, in the weather or in our nation. Seek the Lord about these things. It is time to return to the altar and our homes."

During high praise, when I took pictures with my camera, there was a purple hue over the area. I felt it was a sign of Jesus among us! Purple is a royal color.

When we got home later that evening, and ready to curl up in our bed, our son Andy called. He was applying for a position with the same hours that Samantha worked. He asked us to pray for God's will.

"Sure thing, Son." Mark answered him.

When Andy got ready to say goodbye, he said to me, "Call us and tell us when you get great news this week."

Andy had felt something great was coming to us. He and Sam wanted to be the first to know. Mark and I looked forward to the week ahead. We speculated on what it could be.

FINAL ANSWER?
(Nov. 7th)

While I was leaving our house that morning, God showed me something — giving out our hearts' desires. For example:

The Lord gives us our hearts' desires the way we will accept them.

My momma was to have a surgery for her heart; a pacemaker. To her, that was healing. My little brother, Ron, was to have surgery for his back. To him, that would be relief. And Pastor Ivie only needed a small amount of chemotherapy this time, not entirely evasive. She knew she was on her way to recovery!

God was giving them answers as far as their faith would take them. I told God at the end of that wonderful revelation that I believed Him for a home on our property, on Nicholas Drive, and for His help with my books to prosper.

Later that afternoon, another bank turned us down. I put up prayers for direction. I watched as everyone else's hearts' desires came true in all the ways they accepted and understood.

Where was ours?

Where was mine?

In obedience, I wrote.

In obedience, I had sold a home, built a home and sold another home. We were ready to sell yet another home. How were we to do this with no place to go? My beloved husband was getting tired of living in everyone else's homes. Mark wanted to settle down for the rest of our lives. Me, too.

But, what if that wasn't what God had planned for us?

Why was it taking so much of our time, energy and money to accomplish our goal of building a home on our land?

Everything fell into place for the Murrays to buy our home on Dutch street.

Where was our help?
I cried out, "Where are you, Lord?"

GLIMMER OF HOPE

(Nov. 8th)

"Daddy's sick, Annie. He can't play with you right now."

The sweet little puppy we called our little girl just looked at me, then back to Daddy with her teddy bear named "Skinny baby" tucked in her mouth. Annie bounced into the kitchen for her breakfast as we got ready for our day.

Mark did indeed feel poorly. Brown, thick mucus escaped his nose and lungs.

"Alright, I'll take off the next three days and go to the doctor! Let me finish up a couple of things, and I will come home early." There was resignation in Mark's voice as he got ready for work.

There was elation in my voice, "Thank you! You know, I shouldn't have to pull teeth from a chicken to get you to cooperate over your health!"

It was a good thing I liked the man!

Lord, help me!

And, He did.

That afternoon, a friend called with phone numbers for two more mortgage companies for us to try. She promised it would all work out fine.

ONWARD CHRISTIAN SOLDIER
(Nov. 9th)

Mark had a rough night. His cough had gotten deeper and I heard a low whistle in his lungs as he exhaled. Annie and I looked at Mark with worried expressions. Our doctor's office was full of patients with the same thing. They recommended the clinic down the street.

Fortunately, our favorite physician's assistant was there to help. She examined Mark thoroughly and said, "Sinusitis and bronchitis." She called in several prescriptions to the pharmacy. The order was written for him to be off for three days. I took care of my husband as I would have any of our children. Breathing treatments were administered, temperature was taken, medications and liquids were handed out at frequent intervals. Whatever Mark could tolerate to eat, I made.

I do not believe I spoiled my husband. No, he probably looked at that in the rearview mirror. Once I had Mark and Annie down for naps, I called the mortgage company that we had been referred to. I left a message, and a short while later, they answered my inquiry. I told her the whole story of our struggle to build on our land. She thought they could help us. She asked me to bring in our packet of information to her office that Sunday and drop it through the mail slot. She would pick it up after church.

"Do you know where the church is?" She asked.

I laughed as I replied, "We just happen to be meeting our son there for the 9 a.m. service." I chuckled; she was going to the 11:00 service, of course.

JUST LIKE MY FATHER
(Nov. 10th)

"Honey, I'm so sorry I have to leave you today! I will check in on you before I go to work."

I had made up Mark's nebulizer medication and put it in the refrigerator. He and Annie looked at me forlornly. Crystal, her family and I were going to Frankfort, Kentucky for a book fair. I would have to be back in town by 3 p.m. to get to work on time. My dear, sick sweetie would have to fend for himself until 9:30 that night! Rats.

I drove and Crystal navigated. Talk was lively while she explained to the rest of us what to expect once we arrived. It was a beautiful late fall day and traffic was easily navigated. When we arrived and went in the building to look around, there was much more than I had expected! If you found a book to take home with you, the author would autograph it and send you to the register with it.

Within minutes, our group split up toward different aisles and sections. I found one of my favorite authors there signing books. Of course, I wanted one of his latest works. Steve recognized me from the LCW meetings and was glad to see me. He writes books about Kentucky's modern day heroes. Steve signed the book and posed for a picture with me. We caught up for the few minutes he had to spare, and all too soon, I walked down the aisle to see who else could be found.

The others of our group found many more books than just one! They walked up with their arms full of books! We took a quick lunch after the fair and headed back to our respective homes a little wiser and a little more broke, than we had left that morning.

Before my friends got out of the car, we all joined hands and thanked God for our safe journey. We looked forward to seeing each other soon.

An hour later, I arrived back in Corydon with less than a half hour before work. I checked in on my ailing husband and made up his next breathing treatment before I flew back out the door.

It had already been a long day, and there was still the other half of it to go. Saturday was the day the supply truck came in, and the afternoon crew members were always the ones to unload it. I must have done okay because we got out 15 minutes early; anything to get me home to my husband! Mark had been alone all day, and I wasn't happy about it.

My arrival would have been met with a cheer if Mark could have gotten out of his chair. Annie was still in good spirits and ran to meet me as I entered the house. She jumped into my arms.

I could hear her in my heart, "Yaayyy. Mommy's home!"

I laughed and hugged her like a baby doll. I always picked her up like you would a baby, up under the arms. I put her over my shoulder as I kissed my husband on his forehead to check for a fever. Then the grilling started.

"Have you eaten today? Did you take all your medication? Have you had any chills? Can I get you another blanket? Ginger ale? Tea?" I sounded like a medical drill sergeant.

Mark smiled good-naturedly as his grilling came to an end. I ran out of questions to ask!

All things accomplished, we curled up in bed together; the two of us. Annie slept in her bassinet, so she would not get Mark's germs. I tucked her in with her teddy bear and kissed her goodnight. She went right off to sleep. Yes, I guess Annie Frances looked spoiled in the rearview mirror too.

I reckon it was my job to love them unconditionally I just like my Father in Heaven does.

MAN OF GOD
PASTOR KEITH TAYLOR
(Nov. 11th)

Some pastors are called, and some just go. For some, it's a family business, and they are very good at it! Others are lousy, and we hear all about it on the 6 o'clock news. And some, a rare few, are men of God.

Mark and I dropped our application papers off that Sunday morning to the private lender. It was just as Ivie had prophesied, no bank would help us. We met Andy and Samantha at the early service on a bright, sunny, and crisp fall morning. After church I sold a book to a lady and gave one to her pastor.

After a wonderful church service—they always seem to have an excellent message—we all headed back to Andy's for breakfast.

Now, let's see, who was there? There was Ben, Andy, Samantha, Lily, Mattie, Mark, Annie and I. Andy made scratch pancakes, bacon, fruit, juice, milk and coffee. What a treat it was! Laughter bounced off the walls until it was time for each of us to head our own way. No one wanted to be the first to go. We hugged with sighs and then hugged some more.

That evening, church started promptly at 6 p.m. Mark and I were excited to meet this visiting pastor once again. We called Pastor Keith Taylor, "Man of God." It had been almost a year since we had last heard him preach. That was the time Mark's high blood pressure was healed. We wanted to give Pastor Keith the good news of what had happened the last time we had seen him. Mark and I wondered how we would be able to catch him for a few minutes and tell him our praise report. We asked God for His help. We needed just a few minutes of Keith's time.

Mark and I arrived 20 minutes early. We followed one car into the parking lot and parked close by them. It looked like the four of us were the only ones there early. As the four of us walked through the church doors, Mark recognized the man in front of us; it was Pastor Keith himself. Our chance to speak to him and give him our praise report happened before we got in the door!

Mark opened the conversation, "Hello! Pastor Keith! I don't know if you remember us, but, earlier this year, we came to hear you preach. You prayed over me for my blood pressure. The next morning, my blood pressure was back to normal! And it has stayed that way." Mark smiled as he ended his testimony.

Pastor Keith was elated!

"Praise the Lord! I love hearing God's good reports." Keith responded.

We went and found seats while others milled in. The service started right on time to a packed house.

As the praise music started, I started to snap pictures and looked for signs of angelic presence. It was during that time that words of knowledge started coming from Pastors Keith and Greg.

Pastor Greg started, "Open doors! Open doors no man can shut nor devil stop! Walk through! No fear or doubt! Don't lose this opportunity or people will die unsaved. Walk through! Now's the time!"

Pastor Keith was introduced and preached a little

as he brought the congregation up to what his ministry had accomplished since his last visit. Then he spoke what the Lord had placed on his heart—a five-fold ministry.

FIVE-FOLD MINISTRY

"Everyone with a ministry, please stand up." Pastor Keith instructed those in the congregation. I felt strongly in my spirit to stand up with the other pastors.

"You see these people—they have targets on their backs. We have to lift them up in prayer so that what they have been called to do will be accomplished. "

The church members prayed health and prosperity over us.

Pastor Keith spoke on Judges 3:31. He spoke on the tribe of Benjamin. Keith said left-handed used to be thought of as not balanced—limited. (I'm left-handed.) Then he prophesied, "God will take you out of your limitations and anoint you! "

He went on speaking to the crowd, "Come against sexual perversions, televisions and computers. Bad passes on bad. Come against it!"

"Never underestimate the power of dreams and influence of the human spirit. The potential for greatness lives within each of us. Guard your seed, and expect a harvest. There will be a harvest! What you sow you reap. The enemy will try to stop you. Take authority over the four corners of your field! The enemy hates teachable sheep, because we then become shepherds. Do what God wants you to do from the ordinary to the extraordinary!"

It felt like he was talking directly to me and my mission field. Miracles! Pastor Keith had a deliverance ministry. He once delivered a witch, who then taught him how to see evil and call it out. Keith spoke on the chapter of Luke 21. He spoke about the signs of the end times. There will be discord in the church.

"Identify any spirits against you. You do not have to be bound by them. Jesus talked more about hell and money than anything else! God is in control with a plan. Move when God tells you to! Be led by the Holy Spirit."

Pastor Keith looked out over the congregation and spoke words of wisdom.

"Faith is daring the soul to go beyond what the eye can see. When God's people move, the enemy is fearful. Get out of your box, and let the Spirit flow!"

After the service, a couple from Louisville approached us. The lady asked me what I did and I told her of my books. She told her husband she knew I ministered when she saw us walk by. They asked to buy a copy of each of my books. I signed and numbered them and thanked her for the monetary blessing.

At the end, there were only six of us left in the building—two pastors, their wives and Mark and myself. It was then that Pastor Keith spoke of the deep things of God. He spoke on how Indiana was integral to the development of Israel. Indiana had ties to the financial start of the country and its first president.

As it got late, I gave him a copy of all my books. He looked at them and said, "You have a miracle ministry. You are doing God's work."

I asked him to pray over a picture of our

homeland on Nicholas Drive. He asked to keep the picture of our land in his Bible. He felt our miracle needed to come quick.

GOD'S RECOVERY
(Nov. 12th)

By mid-November, my mother and little brother were not only at the same hospital, but the same room! As Momma was being released to go home, he went in for back surgery and was assigned her old room.

While Momma's procedure went well with no complications, Ron's was a whole other story. But, what started out as a disaster for him, ended up saving his life. And it went just like this...

I was with my momma at the hospital by 7 a.m. Dorothy Frances needed a pacemaker. Before the nurses took mom to the operating room, she allowed me to pray over her. I anointed her and said a simple prayer for all to go well.

My niece, Kristi, and I kept each other company while we waited for word of her recovery. It did not take long for the nurse to come and take us back to see her. They wheeled Momma into a recovery room. We were there waiting for her. Within two hours of surgery, Mom was up and talking. She was asking for food! Mom was able to eat with just a small amount of help from us.

Four hours after her surgery, Mom had to go to the bathroom. It was all the way across a long hall. I helped Mom with her IV pole, the back of her gown, and walked her to her destination.

By the sixth hour, the staff had moved Mom to her overnight room. It was dinner time and the nurse asked Mom if she felt well enough to eat some dinner.

"Yes!" Momma exclaimed.

When they brought her dinner in, she sat up on the side of the bed without any help and ate every bite of her meal. Momma had not been able to do that for several months!

Eight hours after her surgery, Momma got out of the bed with no help and went to the bathroom. She came back to bed, sat up and turned on the television. Momma then looked at me and said, "You might as well go home. I don't need you tonight."

"Okay, if you are sure." I giggled to myself at how well she had done.

A full recovery in less than eight hours from a pacemaker procedure for her failing heart. Now, that was what I called a "God's Recovery" and an answer to a prayer.

RON'S TURN
(Nov. 13th)

At the same time my mother got out of the hospital, my brother, Ron, was being registered in. The time for his long-awaited back surgery had arrived.

"Would you like for me to come up with you?" I asked him.

"No. I'll be okay, thanks. Devin will be with me," Ron answered.

"Do you want me to come up and pray over you?" I asked again.

"No, just take care of Mom" he answered.

Somehow, I was uncomfortable with his answer.

Ron's stress test went just fine. The orderlies took Ron down for surgery. The anesthesiologist put him to sleep and then turned him over to start the surgery. That was when it all went to poop! Ron's heart rate shot up over 300! His blood pressure went through the roof!

"All men on deck!"

The surgeon stabilized Ron's condition and sent him straight up to the cardiac unit. No one had seen that coming! We almost lost my little brother that day.

"What happened?!" I cried into the phone when Ron's wife, Devin, called me.

"They don't know," Devin replied. She was still in shock over the news herself.

"But they're gonna find out, right?" I wanted answers.

"Yes." She replied. The news had not been good for my little brother. I prayed all day.

My evening was spent with my new daughter-in-law at her sister's Pampered Chef® party. Since it was a small party, Amanda and I agreed to hold a party before Christmas to give her sister more credit dollars. It was the least we could do. We both agreed to go to each other's party. They ended up being scheduled one day apart!

It was already setting up to be a busy month of December.

November 14th

I was working on my second 18-hour day of that week. There were more fires to be put out. The fall had not been a kind season. My little brother was still in the hospital in trouble. Weariness had started to set in for all of us.

Mark took Annie to work with him. I had lots of hospital errands to run.

The morning started with lunch at Vicki Sampson's home. She had been my "go to" person since I was 15-years-old. I was tired, and she knew it.

Vicki set out a lovely meal for me. It was the finest meatloaf, and vegetable soup, I had had in a long time. Rest, for those few short hours, felt like Heaven.

Vicki went with me to see Ron in the hospital. I already knew our way up to his room due to the fact I had just sat there with Momma the day before. For all that Ron had been through, he looked good as we walked in and sat down.

Ron was pleasantly surprised to see Vicki who had tagged along with me. He informed me of all the tests the doctors had ordered.

Vicki chided Ron, "You're too young to be in a hospital bed like this."

We all chuckled and kept the conversation on the light side. Ron had enough of dreary. He was already counting the days until he could go home and recuperate without interference.

I took Vicki back home and headed out to Momma's. She was my next stop on another long day's journey. I spent the late afternoon with her.

"Hi, Momma! How are you feeling? I've been to see your youngest son." I started a whole conversation while I walked in the door.

Momma looked wonderful! She was breathing well on her own and was very curious as to how Ron was doing. Part of our world had righted itself. Momma was going to be well. We were winning one battle at a time.

I was due at Mary Smith's for dinner. We always had a lot of work to do with my books and HCAP. Everyone had told us we needed to make e-books. That was the night's agenda until two the next morning. The mission was not accomplished. It was just another 18-hour day.

November 16th

Several tests later, the doctors found Ron had a 60% blockage, and a stent was ordered immediately. There was no back surgery ordered at that time. But, they saved Ron's life, and we were all very grateful.

AN UNEXPECTED GUEST
(Nov. 19th)

Our dear friend, Deb Grimes, came by to spend the morning with me, and we caught up with each other's lives. While we had lunch together, Fr. Bernie called. He had been praying about taking *Miraculous Interventions II* with him to his Holy Spirit seminars. What good news! He was looking toward the future.

By the time our lunch was finished, I received another call. Deb smiled. My first call was from a priest, and my second call was from a rabbinical minister! Of course.

"Do you have a few minutes?" Rabbona asked me.

Deb and I had just moved into the living room for a comfortable afternoon together.

"For you, sure!" I responded and found paper and a pen. When Rabbona Joy talked, I wrote.

While Joy had been in the shower, singing to the Lord that morning, He mentioned Mark and me for a very long conversation. And when Joy's boss gave her the afternoon off, she knew the Lord wanted her to contact me.

"Get comfortable, "Joy started, "this is going to be a long conversation."

I sighed. What could this visionary have to say about us?

"I saw your property. I saw the hills and the tree line. I saw the messenger angel point to the protector angel. I was reminded how protected the land is by him. There is a purpose for this land. I saw a home with a porch and a big window."

God asked Joy, "*Do you know what you saw?*"

508

"What?" Joy inquired.

*"You **saw through your sister's eyes. She is your close spiritual sister.**"*

"Deb, I saw with your eyes and into your heart." Joy waited a minute and then said, "This all needs to be sacrificed on His altar. You have done everything for your land and your dreams and hope. Lay your vision on the altar of God. He will give it back to you as He sees it. There is a promise and a plan for that land. The promise is out there. You have ran and done all that you can do. God knows your heart and has shared it with me. Sacrifice it on His altar, and He will fulfill in His eyes, the vision and plan. Let the altar totally consume it. What is left is pure, powerful, and will complete the purpose He has. God is going to take your vision for a home there through a spiritual fire."

I was crying pretty hard by then. I did not know how to let go, nor did I really want to.

"Burn up the picture you have of your home in your mind. The modified version will suit the purpose with warmth. You have been willing to walk for the Lord, you have done all, now throw it all down and sacrifice it before God. Cast down your imagination into the fire. Walk with confidence."

As if Joy could read my mind, I could hear her smile as she said, "God understands your desire for shiny or pretty. What is left is His."

Then she made a demand on our time.

"Do this tonight. Mark needs to be in on it. Use your oil and go to the property. Anoint your hands and hearts, eyes and ears too. Then, sacrifice it all back to God. Go all the way back to the age of seven-years-old. Sacrifice all, both of your sorrows and pains, and your sin-nature. Mark knows how far to go back to. God will bring forth victory!"

As I wrote down the instructions, Joy picked up the conversation.

"Do what God tells you. Then your mind set will be a new mind set; a oneness with His. If you are not on the right path, this will not be. Take the spiritual coal and cleanse your lips; it is for a time that is to come, so you can see with clarity. Gather up all your visions, hopes and dreams and hold nothing back. I heard in your heart, you asked the Lord, "Just one day. If I could have it for just one day."

How many times had I said that in my heart without telling a soul but God? Joy had reached right into me and pulled it out.

"God will give you a new vision, better, and Mark will confirm it. Throw, from the first moment you stepped on the land, to now—sacrifice it all. Put on your coat of many colors, Prophet! Your heart is close to mine and His! Now, let Him lead."

Her words settled into my spirit as I readied myself for the task at hand.

"Wait to see what God shows you. Listen to what burps up out of Mark, especially. The burp will be from the Holy Spirit wine. This is what it has all been waiting for."

Joy listened to an unheard voice and said, "You may not be building this month, but your confirmation could come in December. If it's going to happen, it will happen soon."

Then Joy heard something else.

"When you get to the other side of this, God will give you back a promise. A freedom, light heartedness;

all old sorrows and fears will be shed away. It is the knowing. The power to stand in His knowing.

When God does something, it's never about things or land. It's about people. You are one of those people. Mark is one of those people. Mark still sees all this as bigger than him. He doesn't have full peace that God will take care of him in this. Mark is trying to take care of you. It will bubble up in him. He will know. Mark will come through the fire too. What remains is what God okays. God is going to start a fire in Mark. He will have oneness with the Lord like never before."

Joy paused for a moment before she went on, "I want to remind you not to put your confidence in me! Develop your relationship with the Holy Spirit. Remember all the way back to your youth. The Holy Spirit is with us. Invite Him in! He is a gentleman. He wants to be here with us."

Then Joy said something striking to me, "Go back as far as the book of *Alice in Wonderland*. Seven years old! We were the same age when we both started to see and hear. Sacrifice your whole life! This is when God will give back what He sees in you—the promise! God has not forgotten a single tear. He will use them and turn them back into the promise."

I sighed deeply.

"Giving up means you have to let go. Yes it is a sacrifice to put what is so precious out there and lay it on the fire. But sacrifice leads to victory. Present everything you have ever been through as a sacrifice. God will present it to you better than what you had wanted or hoped for. Don't give up! There is victory in sacrifice.

Be ready but not fearful. You are on the threshold,

and the enemy doesn't like it. Come against the enemy, and don't give him any room! God trusts us with what He tells us. Don't tell unless you are told to tell. This is the pearl of great price. If you tell the wrong people, they will turn and rend you with it. When you are responsible with a little, God will show you more and give you more. Trust goes both ways."

Rabbona Joy prayed over us and rebuked the plans of the enemy that would to try to stop us. She asked God to show us what we needed to see for us to have unity.

I told Mark everything over dinner. He agreed to do all that Joy had commanded. Mark drove us to our land and we did as Joy told us. We laid all our lives down; our plans and dreams down. We anointed each other, and fell in love again. As we were leaving I heard in my spirit, *"I am here, go forth."*

What was to come next?
Only God knew.

THANKSGIVING!
(Nov. 22nd)

I was awakened at 5 a.m. to remember the first kitchen we wanted to build, a $40,000.00 kitchen. In our new version, we were trying to build a $1,500.000 kitchen. At 6 a.m., I was up and off to my day job. They were having a special sale, and I wanted to do some serious buying before I had to go to work that afternoon. I spent almost $100.00 at that outing, much to my husband's chagrin.

I arrived back home to a sleeping family and joined them in bed.

A few hours later, Mark got up and started the turkey for the family get-together later that afternoon. It was a 25-pound gobbler. The house smelled of its wonderful perfume while I tried to sleep with hunger pangs on the rise! I worked from 2 p.m. until 6:30 p.m. Mark and Annie went to the Peyron family Thanksgiving.

To my surprise, my dear friends, David and Crystal Murray dropped by to buy a few stocking stuffers and to see me. How nice it was of them! They came all the way from Louisville to Corydon, so I wouldn't be left out on Thanksgiving. What friends! They promised to see me later at the Peyron's too.

When I got off, I raced home and changed clothes. Mark had left me a salad and some turkey. I was sure glad to get it. After all, I was a woman on a mission! After I ate, I went to our local retail store. There were new children coming into our family, and I had presents to get. I stood in lines and inched my way to this and that until I had everything on my list. Mission accomplished.

I arrived at Sandy and Hunter's around 9 p.m. I was ready for my home-cooked meal. Annie jumped up and down to see me.

"Hi, Pretty Girl! Momma loves her baby!" I responded to her warm welcome.

David and Crystal were already there and had given out Christmas treats to the children. They loved it! I had barely gotten down my dinner and dessert when I noticed something amiss.

Our brother-in-law, Tim, had come running upstairs quickly.

Tim looked at me and said, "Do you have any aspirin?"

"No." I replied.

I knew immediately in my spirit that Tim felt he was having a heart attack!

I ran downstairs as Sandy searched her cabinets for an aspirin. I grabbed Andy and Samantha, an advanced care EMT and an Emergency Room technician nurse, respectively, and said, "Get up now! Come with me! It's Tim!"

They were right on my heels.

Tim didn't want to frighten any of the family so we all walked outside together — Andy, Samantha, Tim, Mark and I. Tim told us of the uncomfortable feeling he had been having in his chest for the last several days. He was breaking out in a cold sweat.

I took Tim's pulse while Mark led everyone in prayer around Tim. The longer we prayed the better Tim felt. Andy and Samantha checked him out too. It was our considered opinion, at that time, he was not having an actual heart attack. We all recommended Tim go to the doctor first thing in the morning. Tim agreed to do so. Unknown at the time, Tim would be in for a long haul.

LIGHT UP CORYDON!
(Nov. 24th)

The busy day started with Scripture. I was awakened with the wisdom of Proverbs 15 and 16. I rolled over and opened my Bible. They were good words to start a good day.

I finished the housework for the company that was coming later that day. Mark took Annie to work with him. There was to be a book signing at Arlston's and the reading of "Christmas Chaos!" on the square to open the Christmas season. I was happy to be a part of it.

November had turned very cold overnight. It felt like December! Everyone had to get their winter coats out. The lights around the square were ready to be lit at sunset, 6:30 p.m.

I made it over to Arlston's early. While I set up to start the season, I watched the home-crowd mill through the store. Friends came by to wish me well. Our new friends, Crystal and David, spent a good portion of the day with me. Of course, it was very special to have them there, especially David. David Murray is our resident Santa. With white hair and a long white beard, David was the epitome of St. Nicholas. Several times during the afternoon, he and I would trade off reading "Christmas Chaos!" to the waiting children.

When my time came to go read on the square, family members were in attendance in the audience. It had turned so cold I had a hard time turning the pages! I read several Christmas stories from each book in the *Miraculous Interventions* series, which were well-received. After reading for 15 minutes, the warmth of Arlston's walls was well appreciated.

Mark and Annie came over to visit from next door. Mary arrived near the end. She helped me pack up my car and went to our home for a pizza party! Wherever we have lived, lively has always been a part of the program.

Friends stayed until well after midnight.

Our children, Ben and Amanda, spent the night in our spare bedroom. Andy, Samantha, Lily, Matthew and, of course Nolla, their new puppy, took up our whole living room. What a houseful we had!

I wondered how my husband ever thought we could live in a small house—downsize?! I reminded Mark our family would never be that small again. It would only get bigger!

How blessed were we?
How blessed are you?

BREAKFAST!
(Nov. 25th)

Matthew tried to wake everyone at 6:30 a.m. Andy was so gentle with him.

"Not now, Buddy. The sun's not up yet."

At a more reasonable time, people ambled into the kitchen, and conversations started up.

I said, "We need to go to the grocery."

Andy replied, "Momma, come to the grocery with me; Mark and Samantha can start breakfast."

"Okay, deal."

I didn't realize I had just stepped into a plan. Thomas Andrew and I had barely gotten in the car when he started talking.

"Momma! I have it all figured out."

"Do tell!" I said. Andy's tone and smile were so happy, I was excited and did not even know what about.

"Why, how I want to propose to Sam!"

If Andy was waiting for my approval before going on with his conversation, I sure didn't see it zoom past me! I laughed as he smiled, immersed in his own idea of a Disney wedding.

We arrived at the store with Andy in full conversation. Every once in a while, I would nod, smile and make a quick comment. We wrapped up our shopping when he finally came up for air.

"What do you think?" Andy wanted my opinion.

"Oh, Son! It all sounds wonderful! Sammie and the children will make a wonderful addition to our family."

Finally. I got to give my well received opinion.

"It's a secret, Momma, no telling." Andy smiled.

After breakfast, we all went our separate ways for our errands of the day. Mark and I were due at my mother's to put up her Christmas tree and help decorate.

By the time Mark, Annie and I arrived at Momma's, Annie didn't look very good. Her appetite was off. I wondered what Mark fed her on Thanksgiving. Whatever it was, it was not agreeing with her. A trip to the doctor would be in order for her the next week.

As Momma opened her front door, smells of an early Christmas dinner wafted out to greet us.

"Hi, Momma! Man it smells good in here!" Our noses led us in.

But first, there was work to be done. Momma needed an air-conditioner moved downstairs, a Christmas tree moved upstairs and along with all its trim and lights. Christmas music filtered through the rooms and put us all in a mood to celebrate.

Mark and I looked forward to buying Annie her first Christmas outfit, a coat and boots. Momma looked at Annie so peaked on the couch beside me and said she hoped Annie would be better by Christmas. The look in my mother's eyes told me there may be trouble around the bend.

What did she know that I didn't?

PREPARE YOURSELF
(Nov. 26th)

Early the next morning, I took Annie to the doctor. The diagnosis was not good. She had acute colitis. Where had she gotten that?

I took her to Mark's work to keep her while I worked the afternoon and evening shift.

"Honey, Annie has acute colitis. I need to ask you, what did you feed Annie on Thanksgiving Day while I was at work?"

In all his innocence, Mark responded, "The same things I ate. Turkey."

"How much did you feed her?" I asked.

"Just two meals. One while I was cooking and a plate of it while we ate our Thanksgiving dinner. She ate right next to me. She loved it!" Mark smiled.

Before I could stop it from coming out of my mouth, I spoke in the Spirit.

"Prepare yourself." I knew immediately we would be in a fight for Annie.

Mark's face tightened.

"You mean to tell me I've killed our dog? I've killed Annie?!"

"Prepare yourself." It was all I could think of to say.

When I got home late that evening, Mark was giving Annie medicine and her special food the doctor had ordered.

It wasn't helping her.

Why didn't it help?

We were both off the next day. Little sleep was had that night. It drew me back to the days when the children would get so sick that we had to take them to the hospital. The only difference was she was so tiny! Our tiny baby girl.

Weight and time were not on Annie's side.

DREAMS ON THE TABLE
(Nov. 27th)

Mark and I had an appointment for early that afternoon. One more bank, one more application. We had been referred there from another lender. Our expectations were high once again for a home-construction loan. Where was our promised home?

By the end of our application process, Annie looked bad! We rushed back home to the Corydon Animal Hospital. I ran in with Annie in my arms.

"Help! The medicine and food aren't working! Annie threw up!"

The doctor and nurse looked at each other. A word hung in the air.

"Pancreatitis?"

I knew Pancreatitis could kill a full-grown human. What would it do to a two-pound puppy?

"Save her if you can," we asked with full hearts.

The doctor examined her. "She's very ill and so small. I don't know. We will do everything we can to save her."

They started an IV glucose and piggy-backed pain medication through the line. Special foods were ordered. They fed her every half hour.

"Can we come and see her?"

"Of course, you can."

"How often can we visit?"

"From 8 a.m. to 5 p.m."

"We will see you in the morning."

There is something comforting about having a loved one in the hospital. We expect miracles when they are in other people's care.

The dream I had our first night with Annie now seemed so close to coming true. Mark and I held each other as we slept through the night.

ONE SICK PUPPY
(Nov. 28th & 29th)

Annie had been in the hospital for two days. She was suffering from Pancreatitis with complications. Due to her premature birth and less than two pounds in weight at eight months old, she was in big trouble for a little dog.

Mark and I went to see Annie every morning and evening. Whenever I held her in my arms, she gave me kisses.

The doctor had her hooked up to an IV port with a blanket around her. It had taken us six months to get her up to two-and-a-half pounds. Now she was dwindling down to nothing. There was a problem with her internal organs. It seemed they had not grown at the same rate as her little body.

I worked that morning and early afternoon. As soon as I got off, I went to see her. Annie's doctor looked pensive, "Would you like to take Annie home and take care of her? You'll have to do everything exactly as I tell you." I put on my nursing hat.

He then said, "She is so small. I don't know. I don't know."

The doctor loaded me up with medications, special foods to keep her liver from shutting down, wrapped Annie in a blanket, and sent me home with her.

My husband, Mark, met us at the door with hope in his voice, "Is Annie better?"

"No, Mark. We're in for a fight. Prepare yourself."

We looked at each other soberly. At least we could hold Annie in our arms—surely that would mean something. We prayed into the night. Her poor little body was wracked with diarrhea. We were up all night with her. Mark and I took turns rocking her and taking her outside.

Weakly, Annie said, "Ra," her name for me.

At midnight, Annie had a mild seizure due to low blood sugar. We got up out of bed and fed her special glucose water. Through the rest of the night, Annie seemed to stabilize. We prayed over her at 7 a.m. and took her back to the doctor an hour later for him to check her progress.

The nurse weighed Annie—she had lost two more ounces overnight. We were led to a room and waited for her doctor. He came in and listened to her bowels and chest. Medications were changed and food ramped up. With these changes, she grew a little stronger throughout the day. Her bowel movements were getting back to normal; they looked once again like baby poop.

I called Mark with the good news. Annie and I even took a nap on the couch, curled up in our favorite blanket. While we were resting together, her bowels let loose, everything came out. Annie Frances looked at me with big, sad eyes as if to say, "Mommy, what's wrong with me?"

I thought back to the first day we had her and the dream where she told me she was sick. I felt in my heart, her final day had come. Annie crawled up to my face and kissed me. She was saying, "Goodbye."

Mark called just before his regular time to get off. Our 45-year old brother-in-law, Tim, was taken to the hospital with chest pain. It was not good.

By the time Mark came home, Annie was sleeping a lot. I stopped taking her outside. We put paper all over the kitchen floor as her bowels gave out. I cried, sick with fear and grief. "Please, God! Help us! Help Tim! No deaths, Lord!"

Time was not on our side.

THE LITTLEST ANGEL, Part II
(Nov. 29th & 30th)

By Thursday evening, Mark, Annie and I were exhausted. We had been locked in a battle for her life for 44 hours with no sleep. Mark agreed to hold Annie while sitting up in a chair hoping to make her more comfortable while I tried to get a little rest. I bent down on my knees to kiss them goodnight when I noticed something out of the corner of my eye in the bedroom where Annie's bed was. I saw two light beings with wings walking back and forth in front of her bed. I almost got up, ran in there and asked them who they were and what they wanted, but I knew in my heart they had come to take Annie home.

At midnight, Mark called out to me. Annie was in a full grand mal seizure. He rubbed her throat, and when it was over, we gave her some liquids. We called every veterinarian between Corydon and Louisville. The only hospital open was sixty miles away! I wrapped Annie in her favorite pink blanket, grabbed up her medications and food, and we tore out of town.

No words were spoken. We cried relentlessly. Annie was leaving us and there was no way to stop it. I had seen her angels-in-waiting.

We arrived at the hospital at 1:30 that morning; 47 hours without sleep. The nurse met us at the door. Annie still had the IV port in her right leg. I practically threw Annie at her. I cried out, "Her name is Annie Frances! Her name is Annie Frances!"

The nurse whisked Annie away to see the doctor. A few minutes later, the doctor came out of the emergency room with Annie in her arms. The doctor and nurse were in tears. I clung to Annie's bag of food and medication. As I pushed the bag towards her, the doctor shook her head with two words, "She's enteric."

With deep sorrow, I said, "Put her down."

"It's the kindest thing you can do," the doctor replied.

Mark and I held Annie and kissed her goodbye while the hospital personnel went to ready the shot. Mark openly wept. I left the room, and he held Annie Frances as she took her last breath.

Once it was over, they took our Annie to the back, cleaned her up, took out the port and wrapped her back in her pink blanket. Her burial casket was a sturdy cardboard box.

The drive home was quiet, the fight was over. It was Annie's first night in Paradise.

We put Annie's box in the laundry room and fell into bed at 4 a.m. after almost 50 hours on our feet.

"No more, Lord, no more."

Four hours later, we were awakened by phone calls from family. Tim was scheduled for a triple bypass that afternoon. We were on high alert. After fifty out of fifty-four hours awake, we could barely see.

I couldn't take it anymore. "We have to bury Annie before we leave!"

I cried out to God, "Please send us help." Immediately, I thought of my good friend, Deb Grimes. I called her and told all that had happened. While Mark dug Annie's grave in the flower garden that she loved to play in, Deb came right over. We packed Annie's toys and clothes in with her, and we all wrote goodbye notes on her box.

The three of us walked outside. Deb had gone into

prayer on her way over and asked the Lord what to say. He gave her scripture and a eulogy. She gave a perfect and beautiful eulogy. We said a few, weary words, put Annie's box in the ground, and each put in a handful of dirt.

Then Mark did what we couldn't; he buried our Annie Frances.

"See you in Paradise, Annie."

While Mark and I took showers, Debbie went and bought us lunch. She set out two plates and drinks, and left us $20.00 on the table in case we needed parking lot money. What a dear in our time of sorrow.

ROCKIE ANNIE

Rockie Annie
in Momma's arms.
Keep you safe,
away from harm.

Go to sleep now,
fast asleep now.
Go to sleep now,
sound asleep now.

Close your eyes now,
don't you cry now.
Close your little brown eyes.
Brown eyes, closed so tight.
Brown eyes to kiss goodnight.

Rockie Annie
in Momma's arms.
Keep you safe,
away from harm.

Love, Momma Ra, Daddy Da,
Brothers to lil' sis — Ben and Amanda,
Andy and Samantha, Lily and Matt,
and David

BUSY
(Dec. 1st)

Staying busy was the order of the day. Smiles could not be found in our home. Prayers were still going up for Tim as I cleaned the house and put things back in order. All things of Annie's were given away or tossed. I made a memory book for her and a picture for her death certificate that would go on a wall when we felt a little braver.

As Mark came home from work, I took off to meet with Mary. There was no exchange of our Annie that day. It felt odd; a new normal set in.

My brother, Ron, had just written a book before his hospital stay. It was a book of memories for our five- generation military family. Ron wanted Mary and I to have a look at it.

We picked Ron up to have a dinner meeting about the prospect of publishing his book. He gave us a copy as we settled into our comfy seats at the restaurant. Business was the order of the day.

When I got home, sympathy cards had already started to arrive at our home. Mark was in his chair, crying. I got on my knees, and we held each other — mingling our tears.

Our one and only girl was gone.

FAMILY
(Dec. 2nd)

Good deeds don't wait for your heart to mend to show up at your door. Ron had wood that needed to be hauled away. We showed up early and packed the truck as full as we dared. The old Ford creaked its way home. It was the first time laughter and smiles escaped our lips.

Mark and I unloaded the wood in our backyard. It would have to be split at a later date. After a breakfast of biscuits and gravy, a comfort food at the time, we had free tickets to a Christmas play at a local theater.

Well, I couldn't believe what it was about—a family who lost a loved one at Christmas time and how God sent angels to help them! By the end of the play, I ran out of the building, crying. I did not want to see anyone else that day.

But God had other plans.

The Murray's were coming over for dinner and that was that!

David and Crystal brought desserts, remembrance pins for Annie, bookmarks, prayer cards, and anything else they could think of to get us through our broken hearts. We were not going through it alone if they had anything to do with it. What a team they were!

Before the night was over, real laughter was shared, fellowship was had, and in our hearts, we turned a page.

GOODBYE AND AMEN
(Dec. 3rd)

The words would wait no longer. I had to write a letter telling everyone of Annie's passing. Twenty letters went out to friends and family that loved her. Sympathy cards, meals, gifts and donations were already making their way to us. I mailed the letters on my way to work.

Once again, it was a hard day as I told other employees what happened.

By the end of the night, I was ready for home. When Mark and I talked after I arrived home, he too, had the same experience with the people at work and customers who had known Annie Frances.

Tears were shed all over again.

We slept that night huddled together.

The letter

December 3rd

To: All our dear friends who knew and loved Annie Frances Peyron

We regret with sincere hearts to inform you of the death of our little Annie girl, November 30th at 2:30 a.m.

She became ill shortly after Thanksgiving with Pancreatitis. Annie was hospitalized for two days. The doctor sent her home to be with us for her last 32 hours.

Annie's kidneys soon shut down and she went into complete organ failure. She had a seizure, then a grand mal seizure. At Jefferson Animal Hospital in Louisville, Kentucky, Annie drew her last breath.

We buried Annie in our backyard in the flower garden where the birds perch on a birdhouse to rest. She was buried in her soft pink blankie with all her favorite toys scattered around her. The dress and diamond cz collar she wore to Ben and Amanda's wedding were buried with her.

We wrote goodbye notes on her burial box. Our good friend, Deb Grimes, came over and read Psalm 23 from the Bible and gave a beautiful eulogy.

We will be buying a prayer stone to put as a marker for her in late December. If you would like to be part of that goodbye gathering, let us know. We will not be having our yearly Christmas Party this year or decorations.

We look forward to next year and Christmas of 2013. Please pray for us.

Thank you for understanding,
Love,
Deb and Mark Peyron

TIMOTHY!
(Dec. 4th)

Mark knew in his heart we were to spend the afternoon and evening with Tim at the hospital.

Five days earlier, the day we had buried Annie, and 50 hours without sleep, we showed up at the hospital and prayed over Tim for a miraculous recovery from his triple bypass surgery — and God said yes.

We walked into Tim's room, and he was already hot on it! Tim was busy telling every nurse and doctor he could find that he was going home that day. They laughed at him, and said he could go, if he could find a ride home. No one had been available until we walked through the door. To Timothy, we looked like the cavalry!

The afternoon was spent getting Tim ready with all the doctor's orders, clothes, and medications. At last, around dinnertime, the nurse came with a wheelchair for him. Timothy would have none of that! He was going to walk out of that building! The nurse finally agreed to walk him out to our car.

On the way down the stairs we spoke with her. In short order, we spoke about God and Jesus and asked her if she was saved.

She said, "No."

I asked, "Why?"

She said she felt she wasn't good enough. Well that was all it took! I explained in a few short minutes the real gospel of Jesus Christ. The good news! And right there in the hallway, before we walked out to the parked car, with a prayer, she gave her heart to the Lord, became one of the saved, and we chalked another one up for Christ!

When we walked outside, Tim asked, "Do you think that was the whole reason I was here? To save a soul?"

"Yes. It very well could have been." I answered.

Don't you?

DISAPPOINTING DAY
(Dec. 6th)

Sometimes, no matter where you look, it's not the answer you wanted or needed.

For example, Mark and I had two applications going at once with two banks for a home-construction loan. We were never denied by banks; our credit score and income were too good. But they made it impossible by how much they wanted down.

Both banks wanted $26,000.00 down no matter how much equity we had.

"No, thanks." I went and picked up the papers.

And there were the papers I had received from a big publishing house. They were very interested in my books, but since I was an unknown author at the present time, I needed to send them $16,000.00 to get started.

I appealed and begged for help. Being at the low end of the working, middle class, we were the last to receive help with anything.

I appealed and begged God for help.

Unfortunately, none came.

FIVE GENERATIONS
(Dec. 7th)

My little brother, Ron, has always loved to write poetry and stories. My love of writing started in earnest when Ron came into my room at the age of 15 and said, "Can you help me with a story? I'm stuck."

"Sure!" I replied.

Over the Christmas holiday, Ron and I wrote together "An Old Man's Christmas" (1974). It was love at first type!

Now, at 54-years-old, Ron and I were at it again. All the stories of generations past that our Daddy had told Ron as a child, were being brought to life on paper. I was blessed to have a small part in several of the stories. Five generations of military stories from my brother's memory came forth. Ron asked me to proofread it. I was honored.

I sat for a whole day and read a manuscript that sounded like a cross between Mark Twain and Zane Grey. I laughed and cried, then laughed some more!

The memories of my father on a Saturday afternoon telling us story after story of heroes in our family flooded by me in a wave of grateful tears.

I truly needed that wonderful break from reality.

LOVELY NIGHT
(Dec. 8th)

Mark and I were finally getting back to a new normal. It was time for fun! Louisville Christian Writers held a Christmas Program that night. Mark, Mary and I all attended along with 30 or so other people.

We all donned our nice Christmas clothes and ate a hearty meal together. Games were played and laughter was heard all through the halls! Who knew writers could be so much fun?

Shortly after 8 p.m., Mark and I had to leave to meet Ben, Amanda, Andy, Samantha and the kids at "Light up Charlestown."

"Come on, Momma! You'll be late!" Ben cried into the phone. Children will always be children.

Ben and Amanda brought their new little puppies. It was a cold December night and we were all wrapped up in our furry best, including the puppies!

There were vendors for hot cocoa, candy apples, fudge, and treats. Horse rides and carriage rides could be had for a donation. Christmas carols were sung as we walked around the square toward Ben and Amanda's apartment.

We had to hurry. The fights were coming on, and all the men-folk didn't want to miss them!

Yes, life and laughter had come back to us.

And just in time for Christmas!

ALL OF US
(Dec. 9th)

The more there are of us, the harder it is to get everyone together for our traditional Christmas picture. There were several new additions to our family from the last year.

Ben and Amanda were now married. Andy and Samantha were serious enough for her and her children to be included in our smile fest. Only David, our middle son, had yet to bring someone to the photography table.

Let's see, how many of us did that make? Seven, eight, nine, yes, nine it was!

It took a good two hours, and a hundred and some dollars, to get the results we desired. I wondered if anyone else ran into that brick wall.

The evening was spent at a Christmas concert at Amanda's church. Their best singers had been garnered for the occasion. And their best cooks for the dessert party afterwards.

MOMMA'S
(Dec. 10th)

What a wonderful day! From lunch to dinner, I spent the day with my momma. After a lunch out, Christmas shopping was first on our list of things to do.

Momma and I aaahh'd over different gifts for family members. We walked through all the displays and finery with wide wonder. We finally made it back to her house by mid-afternoon. While Momma cooked us a fine winter meal, I sat in her living room and wrapped all her presents.

After dinner, Momma and I did what we used to do when I was a small child.

We got in the car, and I drove us around the neighborhoods and looked at all the different light displays.

At some houses, we would stop to look at all the different variety of decorations they had. Nativity scenes, blow up Santas, reindeer, snowmen, penguins, Christmas trees, garland, wreaths, snow globes; you name it, we saw it.

The evening ended in hugs and a date for a Christmas celebration.

AN ANGEL OUT OF NOWHERE!
(Dec. 11th)

Wherever Mark and I turned, we were just a few dollars short of being able to build our home. I couldn't understand it. After all the verifications in the spirit, Pastor Ivie was right. The last bank said we were $6,000.00 short. Our new friend at a mortgage company said they could front us the money until we could pay them at the sale of our home in Corydon. I went back to the bank and told them what I thought was good news!

Well, the manager stuttered and stammered and didn't reply.

"What's wrong?" I asked.

"We can't turn you down because your credit score and pay are within bounds. But, it's such a close call, we're not going to take your loan application."

I went to work so sad that afternoon. I had to tell Mark. It was the last straw. I asked the Lord to allow me to give up. A man in line asked about our Annie, and I cried as I told him that story.

The lady in line behind him spoke to me. I thought she was going to comfort me, but she had an entirely different word for me.

She said, "There is a worry on your heart. You have a decision to make."

I told her about our land and the home we had felt compelled to build, and how we were ready to give up. She replied, "Don't give up! Jesus is coming to your rescue!"

"How?" I asked. Jesus would have to come that day!

That night, over dinner I told Mark all that had happened during the day. I told him about the last bank, what the lady said in line; all of it. We looked at each other so weary.

Mark and I decided it was time to put in a call to the private mortgager. We were going to thank her for all she had tried to do, but we were ready to throw in the towel.

We would tell her our grim news that week.

DEPENDING ON THE KINDNESS OF STRANGERS
(Dec. 13th)

Mark and I were out of everything in the kitchen. We had been trying to save every dime possible to get the process started to build a home. I finally broke down and went to the grocery. We were in dire need of something off of every shelf.

"$160.00 please. Thank you!"

It took an hour to put it all away. I made a nice meal for my husband. As Mark and I settled down to eat, the private mortgager returned my call. We informed her of our sad news. Then she told us her family's story and how someone had helped them. That was the catalyst for her starting her own business to help people.

"Don't give up! If you can wait until April, we'll front the whole loan." The young lady waited for our answer.

Mark and I looked at each other. No one had ever offered to help us like that. We were always the ones that helped others out. Could we possibly say yes?

With tentative smiles, and hope in our voice, Mark and I said together, "Yes."

TURN AROUND
(Dec. 13th)

Our whole world turned around in two minutes. The lady in the store had been right! Jesus had indeed sent us a rescuer.

"Oh, my goodness! What do we do now?" We asked.

"I'll contact you this winter, and we will go from there. Update all your bids, and we can start in the spring."

We got off the phone and shouted for joy!

"What a Christmas present!"

We were sure God had remembered us!

The nice dinner I had made tasted 100 times better!

"Who do we call to tell of this miracle?"

After all, we were in the miracle business.

We recognized one when we saw it.

Sleep eluded us. Mark and I curled up long into the night with bedroom talk until we fell asleep between words. We wondered as we dozed off.

"What would Christmas of 2013 look like..."

We could hardly wait to see.

HIC-CUP
(Dec. 15th)

The phone rang at 10 that morning.

"Momma! I am still having an allergic reaction to the dogs even though we sold them and cleaned the house! I am taking antihistamines. What else should I do?" Andy, our youngest son was in a pickle.

"Oh, Andy! Go to the urgent care center! Remember how ill dog dander made you when you were little? Call me when you get back." He promised he would.

Crystal and I spent the day together. We had lunch, shopped, looked at decorations and made dinner together. My husband showed up just in time to eat.

By 9:30 p.m., while we were all talking, Andy called again. He had more problems. He had not gone to the urgent care, and he could hardly breathe! He had no choice but to go to the hospital immediately!

Crystal volunteered to go over and babysit their children for us. She didn't live far from Andy and Sam. We thanked her and prayed for everyone concerned. By 11:00 p.m., I was feeling ill. The battle was now on two fronts. Mark and I went to war and prayed over all our households in Jesus' name.

By 2 a.m., Andy was home from the hospital and was going to be okay, and I was feeling better too.

We all thanked God for His tender mercies.

AN EARLY CHRISTMAS
(Dec. 16th)

My part of the family had an early Christmas with my mother. Mark and I and all our children went over for dinner. We were joined by my brother, Ron and his wife, Devin. I was in charge of desserts. I made a cake and fudge for the children. Mark and I finished wrapping the last of the presents to be taken to Momma's and arrived just in time.

Ben and Amanda greeted us with good news. They were trying to buy a home! They had prayed and God was opening doors for them. We told them our good news about building in April. We all rejoiced over a beautiful Christmas dinner. It was the first time Samantha and her children had joined us. We looked for good in that relationship. Our dear David was there too.

Ben and Amanda had brought their six-week-old puppies with them. The puppies stayed in the backyard during our visit. While Momma and I did the dishes, we talked about their dogs.

Momma commented, "They can't bring those dogs in the house. You know I don't allow dogs in my house."

I chuckled and replied gently, "Momma, you let Annie in your house."

Momma replied without missing a beat, "Annie was not a dog."

End of discussion.

If my mother said Annie was not a dog, I believe her!

And I always knew.

547

THE VATICAN LETTER
(Dec. 17th)

SECRETARIAT OF STATE

FIRST SECTION · GENERAL AFFAIRS

From the Vatican, 17 December 2012

Dear Deborah and Mary,

The Holy Father wishes me to acknowledge your kind letter and gift of copies of your books. He appreciates the sentiments which prompted you to share your writings with him.

His Holiness will remember you and your families in his prayers. Invoking upon you joy and peace in our Lord Jesus Christ, he cordially imparts his Apostolic Blessing.

Yours sincerely,

Peter B. Wells

Monsignor Peter B. Wells
Assessor

Mrs. Deborah Aubrey-Peyron
Mrs. Mary Dow Smith
1544 Dutch Street
Corydon, IN 47112

548

BE NOT AFRAID!
(Dec. 18th)

It was Andy's birthday! I called to wish him a wonderful day and year. That started it all. All throughout the day, he called me with words of knowledge for us.

Andy started with Genesis 15:1. "Be not afraid! I am your shield, your very great reward! Be confident in God, Mom! God knows all for all of us. Pass on this message of confidence. Just because we don't know it all, doesn't mean the outcome won't be a great reward. Have confidence in what God has for you. Don't be afraid either way! Even if you sell that land, God is your shield and reward. He will protect you! Listen to God. Be confident in what God is doing for you. God has no problem having confidence in what He's doing. God will steer you in the right direction. God will work all things for us unto good. Something will happen! Let God make the plans and He will bring it to you."

Samantha added, "Be happy and confident in what God is doing for you. Do not worry! Fear and doubt are from the devil. God's timing is unpredictable!"

"Okay."

CAUTION!
(Dec. 20th)

All the prophets, all the books, all the newscasts had predicted doom and gloom on that day.

It ended up being pretty nondescript.

Until 10:30 that night when Andy called.

"Hi, Momma! We're coming over to spend the night! All four of us! Doesn't that sound like fun?"

"I'll get the bedroom and couches ready! Mark, the children are coming to spend the night." I was smiling.

"Wonderful!" Mark replied.

They arrived 45 minutes later. After greeting everyone, and getting comfortable in our pajamas, we popped in a movie for the children, and the four adults sat down to talk.

Andy began, "I was not afraid of the world blowing up. But, what concerned me was the general public getting out-of-hand tonight. So, I decided to pull my family up and take them to the country."

I replied, "Well, Son, it never hurts to err on the side of caution."

Heads nodded in agreement.

CHRISTMAS BEGINNING TO END
(Dec. 21st)

At 6:30 that morning, I snuck into the kitchen. I was going to make a special breakfast—a Christmas tree out of cinnamon rolls. Not one adult stirred.

But two little elves named Matthew and Lily stuck their heads into the kitchen and asked me, "What's up?"

"Want to help me decorate a Christmas tree?" I asked, stifling a giggle.

Their eyes lit up like candles. And, so did everyone else's when they got up at 8 a.m. to coffee and Christmas Tree Cinnamon rolls!

We received a call that afternoon to make sure we were coming to church that evening. It was a Cowboy Church Christmas Party. We couldn't miss that!

And we didn't. Country Christmas carols, goodies, and cards were exchanged. I got a chance to tell Rabbona Joy that I was off for the next 12 days. She responded with a smile and a nod.

Yes, there would be a meeting soon.

NOT SO HOT
(Dec. 24th)

I called one of my friends to come by for our gift exchange. She was always so practical. They brought us groceries. Pounds and pounds of chicken, juice and chocolate. What a treat!

When she left, I went to the pharmacy and got medication for a cough I had developed.

I packed everything up for a two-day stay at Mom's. We wanted to help fix an early breakfast. Mark and I still had midnight mass to go to. When he came home, he looked at me.

"I know," I said, "not so hot."

He stared at me.

I counter-stared.

"I know! I went and bought medicine! Mom can't make breakfast and dinner on her own. She just had a stroke this past fall. Someone has to step up!"

Mark sighed. He knew he had lost the battle before he had gotten off the first shot.

We unpacked and dressed at Mom's by 10 that evening. It took an hour to get to the church and a half hour waiting time. I cried happy tears as I sat in between my husband and oldest son once again for midnight mass with Amanda's family.

There could be no better start to Christmas for me.

CHRISTMAS WITH THE PEYRONS
(December 25th)

Mark and I got to bed after 2:30 that morning. When the 9:30 wake-up call came, I was sure the alarm time was wrong.

"Nope."

"Rats."

Mark started the coffee, and I started the eggs. Before we knew it, ten people crowded around to help. The dining room table was full to capacity and the living room... oh, the living room! It was overflowing with gifts! Where were we going to put all the people?

The family pictures were taken at 11:30, and the meal was served promptly at noon. We celebrated December birthdays and opened Christmas presents from one another.

The best part was when they gave out the stockings! Mark's sister, Susan, hand sews each stocking. They are all works of art. Every adult in the family buys gifts to put in all the stockings. They are usually filled to the brim with goodies! Money, chocolate, pens, trinkets, notepads, etc...

After all the festivities, the men got together and played cards. The women and the children watched Christmas movies and I took a nap.

A short hour later, I got up and cooked a turkey while Susan baked a ham.

Before we knew it, it was time to eat again!

By late that evening, I was feeling very poorly and took cough medicine for an oncoming illness.

THE DAY AFTER
(Dec. 26th)

While we were eating, weather bulletins started scrolling across the bottom of the television picture. A blizzard was headed our way. It was decided we would head home that night instead of in the morning. We would hunker down in Corydon. Thank God, the blizzard dissipated just 25 miles from us. It was a good thing. I woke up with yellow mucus coming out of my lungs. A trip to the urgent care clinic was in order.

Bronchitis and double ear infections took the place of after Christmas shopping.

"Rats," I said, "Rats."

The nurse practitioner loaded me up with medications and breathing treatments. Mark and I stopped at the store for standard foods for the ill. Mark made us lunch and dinner and took care of me.

"Thanks, Pal."

While I took a nap, Mark balanced our accounts to make sure the New Year would get off to a fine start.

The evening was spent in front of the television, and we watched Christmas movies as we settled in to see the snow.

All in all, it was a quiet day.

OUT OF THE BLUE
(Dec. 28th)

I had a phone call from my sister, Crystal.

"God stopped me while making Kool-Aid for David, who is under the weather. He told me to pray for your strength to be upheld in order to care for sick family members." Crystal was in earnest over the phone.

Something must be amiss. What was it?

"Thanks, but no one is sick but me."

We had dinner that night with the Hornes. There were Christmas gifts to exchange. The children were all old enough to help make the meal. It was wonderful to watch them all with their chores and doing everything their mom and dad told them. They were growing up just fine.

We always have a nice time with Rick, Lisa and their children. It's almost like going back in time, when you step into their home. Obedient, mannerly children; no television in the whole house; just reading and conversations.

Shortly after dinner, it began to snow. It snowed harder and harder. We cut our time short and packed up to come home. We were not in the car five minutes when Mark started to shake.

"What's wrong?" I cried.

"I don't know! I'm so nauseous!" Mark answered.

I felt his head. Mark was on fire!

"What the heck?" I cried.

Six hours after Crystal's call, her prophesy came true. Mark was under a serious attack.

By the time we got home, Mark's temperature was climbing fast! 102.4 degrees. I gave him two ibuprofens and called Crystal for prayer. His temperature was still climbing.

I called Andy and Sam for medical advice.

"Give him 500 mg. of Tylenol, Mom." The nurse and advanced care EMT went into medical mode. Crystal and I prayed and bound satan. We heard in both our spirits, "Virus."

Six times through the night, Mark was up to the bathroom vomiting. By 9:30 that morning, I gave my husband an ultimatum.

"Phenergan suppositories or hospital."

By 11 a.m., Mark was sound asleep in his chair with a blanket over him. It took every 4-6 hours, Ibuprofen, Acetaminophen, and Phenergan to contain it.

All the while, it was snowing outside, stopping at five inches.

It was good I had nowhere else to go.

I took good care of my husband.

ORDAINED BY GOD
(Dec. 20th – 30th)

A minor miracle occurred during the Christmas season of 2012; I was off for 12 days in a row! What a blessing! The Friday before Christmas while at Cowboy Church in Lagrange, Kentucky, I mentioned this to our co-pastor, Rabbi Joy Son. She nodded and smiled. I could already see in her eyes a glint, a spark of interest. We both knew the time had come for our clandestine meeting—a 16 hour space of time away from the cares of the world to glean from one another the deep thoughts of God. Cowboy Church had an agreement with a local hotel for a special rate for their out-of-town guests to stay with them. Joy said she would call me when the time could be arranged.

As Christmas and the days after started flying by, I began to worry about our overnight meeting. The day after Christmas, I came down sick with bronchitis and double ear infections. Two days later, Mark came down sick with the influenza that was wreaking havoc all over America. In all my years, I had never seen my husband so ill. High temperatures and vomiting were joined by aching all over. The dear man was miserable! I surely could not leave him during his illness. I took good care of him, making sure liquids stayed down and no dehydration could set in. Of course, I prayed.

Then I heard from our youngest son, Andy. He was going to need a babysitter for Sam's children New Year's Eve and New Year's Day. Could I manage that as well?

"Sure, Son."

Sigh.

"Well," I thought to myself, "that's the last straw." In all these hours where I was needed by everyone else, there was only one 17-hour time frame in all those days that I could possibly get away.

You got it, and I should have known all along that God was in control of the whole situation. Joy called, and the only 16 hours she had free were the same 17 hours I had. My extra hour? Travel time.

December 30th, I packed a single bag with a robe, house slippers and a gown, clothes for the next day, and a few toiletries. I bought a new pad of paper with 120 sheets—just in case! I had enough money for my half of the room rate and for our dinner out. I wanted to thank Joy for her gift of time with a free meal. It was the least I could do. I made Mark his lunch and dinner, checked his temperature one more time (he was on the mend) and made sure he had my cellphone number close by. I got in the car and started on a journey that I would not come back from the same.

How can I tell you the importance of this?
Why, with a story, of course...

THE WOMAN OF GOD
AND THE APOSTLE
(Dec. 30th)

I arrived at the hotel a few minutes before Rabbona Joy Son. I went in and let the front desk clerk know I was there. When I walked back outside to gather my things, Joy pulled up in her "faithful" van. I smiled and asked if I could help her bring anything in. "Yes!" A light packer she wasn't! It took a couple of trips.

Our room number was 304. We got settled in and went out to dinner – Oriental was agreed on. I drove, and she led the way. I thought dinner conversation would be light, and we would start our real mission when we got back to the hotel. Not necessarily so. I got to know the "woman of God" quickly during our meal. Joy spoke of some of her background and how God had called her at an early age.

She spoke of her mother and father and how very gifted they were in the Spirit. No surprises there; I was getting to know their daughter's gifts rapidly.

Back at the hotel, I got out a pen and paper for our meeting. I wanted to remember everything important she had to say. But the evening didn't start with words, it started with music of a sorts and a candle. Joy put in a CD of a ship on water. You could hear the slapping of the waves against the hull. In my head, it was evening. The candle crackled as we listened to the ship creak as it moved through the water towards the shore. In the distance, a horn from the lighthouse pointed the way home. She asked me if I thought they had been on a journey with great adventures. I smiled as I knew she was setting me up for a look at my own life. And hers. Was I ready to look at that adventure from another set of eyes? She had read my book. I knew revelation was at hand. I prepared to be boarded.

The first thing this woman of God wanted me to know was that I had similar gifts to hers. I could see and hear and smell beyond the veil with words of knowledge and prophesy. Yes, indeed, I was an emissary and an evangelist. But, what I didn't have was discipline. I needed to go deeper into a relationship to hear every day what the Lord God had to say to me. How? This was what the whole night was set up for; the how.

Joy sat quietly as I told story after story that wasn't detailed in my books but felt compelled to tell her then. We sat in our pajamas with a glass of water by our side. When I was drained of all I thought important to tell, then she started...

"Always test the voice you hear."

"Really? Can I do that?" Ignorance abounded out of my mouth before I could stop it.

"Sure, you can!" Joy responded with enthusiasm.

"What about the dumb stuff He shows me? 257 pieces of gum, or the color of a pastor's hair?" I wondered if those things could be important too.

"Relationship building!" Joy Son replied. Everything was becoming clearer at warp speed. "If He can trust you with small things, He can trust you with big things! Test what you hear to know if it's the Holy Spirit by three ways: If it is supported in Scripture, the next if it glorifies God, and the last if it edifies your spirit! This is important for your growth and development!"

Then Joy asked me a second question. "Is God male or female?" Of course, I gave the answer "male" because Jesus himself called God "Father."

Her reply gave me something to think about. Joy said, "God is male, also female. God has the characteristics of both. Strong and brave, yet a loving heart. In the Hebrew, and in Greek the term is masculine and feminine. The Lord God is One. It takes both the male and the female to be whole together — when we love. God calls us to a love relationship. God is whole as both. He has the heart of the mother and the strength of the man."

I again asked how it is that I am able to know things out of thin air sometimes. Joy's answer surprised me. "Deb," she said, "it is like Ezekiel's wheel; you see beyond the veil."

It hit me like a lightning bolt!

"Wow!" "Wow."

I could scarcely take it all in but it was the only thing that made complete sense. I felt unworthy to fill such big shoes. What if this were really true? Had I wasted 54 years with immature understanding? Had I let God down? This line of thought led me to a dream I had the week before and wanted to ask her about.

"Joy, I would like to ask you to interpret a dream I had last week."

"Go ahead."

"I was in Heaven. I could see a great coliseum with white pillars. The people on stage were reenacting the life of Christ. At the end, Jesus Himself appeared. He was beautiful! Once, in a vision I had seen Pastor Fred with a coat of many colors. Jesus had on the Coat of Many Nations. I automatically knew it. There were colors there I had never seen before. I saw Him coming up in the stands to find me. Jesus said, '*You have to be strong now! I have called you out to be strong! Your time is now!*' In the dream I was afraid. Jesus called on me to have His Spirit."

Joy asked, "What season was it?"

I checked my memory and answered, "Summer, I think."

She replied, "Summer represents the end of the Gentile age. It represents the harvest time."

Everything Joy revealed to me took me deeper and deeper into the supernatural world of God; out of time and into His presence. I could barely breathe.

"We are allowed to see when we step through the veil into the Holy of Holies. Our laws and physics don't apply to God. We translate. We step through into eternity."

Joy's words hung in the air. Any words I thought of paled to this. She went on, "Cling to the One who has courage, Jesus. You are called and created for a purpose as a seer and a hearer. I am too. Step into who you are, for the season is right. The deeper you trust, the more you will hear and learn of the secret things of God."

I asked why is it, when I am sick or down for a season, I seem to hear better.

Joy answered, "We are close to the veil when we are ill or quiet; that is when we see beyond. Perspective is everything."

I asked Joy, "Have you known many seers and hearers?"

She replied, "Yes a few. Some less and some more. We glean and share from each other. God brings them.

We don't seek them."

She went on, "What we have to say or think does not matter. It is obedience that matters. It is in those shared moments of obedience with God — with the presence of God and Jesus that matter."

I asked her if she had ever been in the presence of Mary, the mother of Jesus.

"No."

I offered, "I have, once, in a dream. The air went soft, and the smell of a hundred flowers entered the room. I knew it was Mother Mary being introduced by a great saint that had come to tell me they were happy I wrote a book about her Son, Jesus." Again I questioned, "Are people announced into Heaven?"

"Yes and no." Joy answered.

I went on, "I have heard when several people passed over. I heard when a young infant was announced. He was not announced by his first name but by his last name. The youngest male...and with another one, I'm Alive..."

Joy answered me again, "They are announcing a celebration! They are announcing the bride to the wedding."

"What about smells?" I queried. "I have smelled death over people. It smells like a rotten egg. For the flesh without the spirit is but rotten and drops off. I have also smelled the demonic coming out of a poor soul in church. I had been asked to help pray with the women at the end of a mass, and I was given in my spirit what was wrong with her and the cause, which was a demonic spirit. Before I knew what I was doing, I ordered it out of her in Jesus' name, and it came out with a foul smell. And I have smelled when I have been visited, for example, by both of our fathers. I have either smelled or heard them. Our son, Andy smells when good is about to happen to people. It smells sweet to him."

Joy smiled as she replied, "You have experienced all this because you dance in and out of the veil. You can smell the scent of things on the other side, too."

Joy went on, "When He wants you to notice things, He tells you." She smiled. I then told the story of the day that the Lord had told me to notice a certain thing about customers while at work.

Joy responded to this quickly, "Cover yourself! Especially afterwards! So no harassment follows you. Spiritually clean your environment."

"I will! I will." I promised. I had done that on occasion while at work at different times, being told to, immediately in my spirit, not always knowing why. I did not realize how close my enemy was there.

Joy then said, "Deb, you were created to dance in and out of the veil! Be aware and sensitive!" Then she spoke of both of us, "Gifts are placed in us and occasionally an anointing on top of it." I remembered the anointing that fell on me when Pastor Fred prayed over me the first time. He said it was virtue. Power. At the time, I had little understanding of what that meant.

Joy prayed quietly in her heart and then said, "God has said to tell you, '*My Goodness will walk before you*.' Deb, this is the presence of God's goodness. He tells us goodness and mercy follow us all our days. So, what is goodness... it is virtue, truth, forgiveness, and all together they equal power. It will come on you, not as a washing, but as a mantle resting on you. This is beyond just truth or forgiveness. The virtue of God is interchanged with goodness. For example, goodness walked before Abraham and Moses. It is a characteristic of God. You have heard God in different ways throughout your life and at different times. Have a talk with Him! He will encourage you to go on."

Joy then began to tell some of her story, so I could relate to what she had told me. Her first encounter with God's voice was at eight years old. By the age of nine, she was in the presence of the Lord God. Joy could hear the Holy Spirit and converse with Him. She appreciated her angels and prayed for them to have strength for their job. But her real relationship was with the Holy Spirit—the Promised One.

I asked, "Could the voice I hear, and call angels, really be the Holy Spirit?"

Joy replied quickly, "Yes! He wants you to know His voice. You are called to hear. Angels are designed for a purpose. The Holy Spirit is a person of God. He is the Promised One; He sits above the angels for us to have a relationship with."

I commented, "One time, a long time ago, I was shown it this way; God as the proper noun, the Holy Spirit as a verb or action word, and Jesus as the adjective."

Smiling, Joy said, "That would make the veil a prepositional phrase!"

Now, we were both in on it. Silliness abounded as laughter ensnared both of us. Joy went on, "Knowing is a gift of God. It appears with no explanation. Always test and share what you hear. Remember, laughter confuses the enemy; he doesn't know what to do with it. He wants to keep us down."

I told Joy, "Andy is good with laughter! It is one of

his best gifts."

"Jesus came to give a face to God." I nodded in agreement.

"Blessed is He who comes in the name of the Lord!" Joy proclaimed. "He is our specific intercessor. And you are called to be a general." My breath left me. I had been named at birth, Deborah Anne, the Old Testament and the New Testament. Deborah was a judge and a general for the Israelites. St. Anne was Mary's mother. Had my own mother named me rightly from my very beginning? With her words, Joy taught me about myself, "Prior to 2013, it has been important for you to develop and share your story. You are an emissary and an evangelist. But, for such a time that is to come…what you were really created for, God needed to fine-tune and discipline His general — for you to become. Until now, you have been in military school."

"Yes!!" A light had been lit.

"You have encountered gifts and an anointing. You have been brought here to disciple, and others will glean from you and with you."

"Dear Lord, may I be up to the tasks that You have at hand for me."

Joy's father, Jim Chambers had studied with Katherine Kuhlman and had helped start New Covenant Fellowship. Joy studied under great prophets and generals from the time she was a little girl. Her father was the "blind prophet." She asked me about some of the people God had recently placed in my path to help me.

The story became an Ezekiel's Wheel.

*Vicki Sampson had been my best friend for 38 years. Her son, Gary, was my boyfriend all through high school. She asked me to come to a TOPS meeting to speak about nutrition health in the spring of 2011.

*At the same time, Gary looked for a writer's group in Louisville for me. He found a phone number for me to call, which I did. They gave me the date for the next meeting. The president would not be, there but I could still visit. I went, but my work was not well received; they were a secular group. When the president came back from vacation the next week, she called me. It was she that gave me the name and phone number of Louisville Christian Writer's President, Crystal Murray.

* The day I went to speak at TOPS was the first and only class that Fr. Mike and Patti Olsen came to. After class Fr. Mike came up and said, "You're charismatic! The Holy Spirit told me!" He was the pastor of an Anglican Church where they were seeing angelic orbs. Our first night to go to mass there, January 1st, 2012 the Lord told Father Mike to give me miraculous oil for my healing ministry. (My healing ministry?)

*At dinner after the TOPS meeting, Jim and Ann Carter revealed to me Jim had been prayed over by the Hunter's Group — the same group that had prayed over Lee Schwarz, husband to my chemistry professor in nursing school in 1998 — given healing ability — who healed my broken back in December 2004. A second disciple from the group dealing daily in the miraculous! Could this go back any further?

*I called LCW, left my name and phone number with a mention of my books. I received a call back from Crystal two hours later. During that time, she had looked me up, looked up my books, and what they and I were all about. Within ten minutes, we were fast friends; soon to be sisters in Christ Jesus. That was when she said to me, "You deal in miracles. You have anointing in your hands. I am bringing my sister from Arizona here, and she is going to get healed. And by the way, our next meeting is in a couple of weeks. Please attend." As if it was really up to me. By that time, God was showing off!

*Before the meeting with LCW and the official meeting of Crystal and her husband David, we invited Fr. Mike and Patti over for dinner. During the conversation, I asked them how they had come to live in this area after living all over the world. They said in the middle 1990s, they were approached by a Mennonite group they associated with to come and help a lady doctor who was dying of cancer in Louisville. She was my children's pediatrician, and if I hadn't been going through a horrible divorce at the time, I would have been considered for what ended up being their position. They took my place in caring for a dear friend.

*At the end of spring 2012, four days before Crystal, her sister, and David came over for dinner, we had a realtor over to find out how much our house appraised for. He told us, and said we couldn't afford to have him sell it. When he left I asked God what to do now, and He said, *"I have already sold your home."*

"Okay."

Four days later, while the Murrays were having their first dinner with us, Crystal felt called to our home. Even her sister, Candie, told her "this is a perfect home for you." Warp speed.

*Once the relationship with Crystal and David had been established, she wanted Mark and me to come to

"Cowboy Days" in LaGrange, Kentucky, to meet a friend of hers. We had two other things planned for that same day. I made excuses not to go. The day before that meeting at the end of June, 2012, the Murray's came for a visit with Mark. I got off late that evening, and they were still at our home visiting. Crystal looked at me and said, "I want you to meet my friend, Joy. She sees angels and demons. She can see inside people. She talks to God, and He talks back." I got up from my chair, went into the kitchen, pulled out both calendars, struck off both events and penciled in "Cowboy Days with the Murrays."

*The next day, we met Crystal and her family in LaGrange. We were warmly greeted by several in the group, and then taken to meet Parson Zeb and his wife, Joy. Crystal introduced me to Joy. Joy looked up from what she was doing, studied me, looked all around me, then, she smiled at me and said, "Hello."

The Holy Spirit told her that one day soon, we would have time together, and she would answer all the questions I had from all my life — and ready me to be a general in the *Army of God.*

By the time we got to the end of this wheel, my head was reeling! For 27 years, God had been turning events for this very moment. Joy said it was for validation and perspective, so we could know that God sees and orchestrates finite details for such a time as this and is to come. Count on God.

Joy asked me if I knew who Lester Sumrall was. I had heard of him. He had learned from Smith Wigglesworth himself. She had great respect for his faith and gleaned from him. She built her own faith on that foundation. With all the people we had been associated with in our lifetime, she and I felt honored, blessed and unworthy. Who were we? Everything else in this world was small and finite. Our days here are a blessing and a gift – not more than that.

That morning the Holy Spirit had told Joy that I am a seer, a hearer and all I needed was discipline to become a general. I was not prepared yet. It would be a validation for me to know who Joy was.

Joy was and is a people's prophet. She was prophesied over in the 1990s that her mantle was a vest of many colors. What the Lord needs in any given moment, that anointing would fall on her at that time. (I have lived this too.) She wouldn't excel at just one thing; she would flow in and out of the gifts. She was an open and pliable vessel. And, so was I. Joy said, "God waits for us on the other side of those moments; whatever that moment is. When we get on the other side of the moment, God is waiting and proud of us. He waits to thank us."

"Open me up and pour me out!" I cried. This was action-packed.

"Yes, time is short. Perilous times are soon to come," Joy said softly.

Then Joy addressed something near and dear to my heart; our home on Nicholas Drive, yet-to-be - constructed at that time. She said "The house is an illusion for something more that God wants to do in that place. Don't worry, God uses illusions. What looks like an unsafe venture to one person may be security to someone else. God has a plan — hang onto that. It is God's plan and His time. All is perspective. You are not going to be home until you are on the other side of the veil. When you sold or built homes for others, you were building lives. The land is not home. Whatever you build, is not home. Home is on the other side. Every step you have taken for the last twenty years has been investing in that. The land is here for a purpose. It is for a refuge. God calls it a safe place, or a place of safety. Don't mix what you are seeing in the Spirit with what you see in the flesh. What is in the flesh is the illusion for safe refuge. You have two different puzzles you are mixing together."

Joy stopped, so I could take in what she had told me. She listened for a voice that I could not hear. Then she began to speak again, "You are grieving for this! You must be pliable in order to be a general. You set deadlines for God. God sees deadlines differently than we do. You know He works best in the eleventh hour! After all, that's when He gets to show off a miracle. Be mindful of Him and what He is doing. Listen when you need to do something. No longer let this consume you. Separate your puzzle pieces." Joy listened again and said, "The land and the home on Nicholas Drive are resources to provide for you when you need it. The cavern is an important find. The house there will be to meet an ends. It is also to provide a safe place for those who will need it when you and Mark go home." (Rapture) "The eleventh hour is not here yet."

You could have heard a pin drop.

Then we spoke of the *Rapture* to be. I said, "When the Holy Spirit is called up, all who are holy, Spirit-filled, must go up as well. We cannot be split up from our spirits. Is this why there must be a rapture when God's spirit leaves the Earth; all who are attached to it must leave as well?" Wisdom was setting in. Joy nodded, "Yes."

Joy spoke about my husband. "Mark is a treasured gift. God kisses him all the time, but he doesn't recognize it sometimes." She asked me a question, "When disappointments happen, what do you do with them?" Perplexed, I shook my head.

"They can bring you closer to God or you can get bitter about it. God reminds you of the opportunity of choice — to choose between God or bitterness — then it can become a gift. His ways are not our ways." It was hard to hear her at that point, I sobbed as though I was one without comfort.

I asked, "How does this help my husband?"

Joy replied, "Mark is seeing through exhaustion and sickness right now. This is where his perspective is. He cannot base any decision on how he feels right now."

The conversation came back around to us.

"God sees you as more than what you walk in currently. Mark has insecurities. He is a man of velvet and a man of steel. He walks in two worlds. He is sold out to God! But, Mark's insecurity hangs onto what he can see and touch. He needs to let go. When he does, there will be no limit. God sees him as so much more. Mark questions whether he sees or hears even when he does. In his exhaustion, Mark grabs hold of the nearest thing he thinks will help. And all along, God is talking to his heart."

By the late evening, with all my questions asked, my stories told and my tears counted, I had poured out enough to be able to receive what I was really there for; validation on all that I had seen and heard. Joy told of her walk with God, so I would know who it was that was speaking to me and how God had made her to be a pliable vessel with all the gifts poured into her, so she could pour them back out to help others. And what a walk that was!

Like mine, she had started young hearing the Holy Spirit call her name. One night, an angel appeared in her room. The angel told her, "Take my hand." Joy looked down and saw her body. The next thing she knew, she was in a part of Heaven. She felt the warmth of a love so deep surround her and overtake her. As she was standing next to the angel, Joy could hear the voice of God from the Throne Room. He told her He loved her and that she had a purpose. *"Go back. You have a lot to do."*

"I don't want to leave!" the little girl sobbed.

God spoke again, *"I have created you for this. I will always love you and never leave you."*

Joy again took the angel's hand and was led back into her body. Things have never been the same since.

As the years went by, the Holy Spirit accelerated her learning. Visions, seeing and hearing were her gifts. Words of knowledge appeared in her head at God's will.

At the first of every year, Joy would ask for a word for that year. In 2011, the same year I was told to make my manuscript into a book, she too was told to open up and share with people. Just as God had a word for me, *discipline,* God also had a word for her, *stay focused*. Joy saw herself in a vision climbing a high mountain. At the top was God's presence. She was going up for a promotion. The Lord showed her there would be others coming up behind her that she would need to encourage.

I was sure one of those was me. "Why now?"

"Because generals are needed now! Remember, these are perilous times. People have to grow up in the Spirit and step into who they are called to be. All are called. Yet not all will come." God told Joy, ***"When I bring them to you, make disciples of them."***

It was almost midnight. I was weary from our talk together, speaking deep conversations about God. Joy got up off the couch and rummaged through the bag she had brought with her. She took out a plastic container and went into the bathroom. I could hear her running water. Joy came back with a towel over her shoulder and water in the container. She sat me in a chair in front of her. Joy went to her knees, and I sobbed great tears as she washed and anointed my feet. She quoted Holy Scripture, and prayed over me for my journey.

"Now it begins."

I started on this journey 50 years ago as a child, then a student, as an adult, an evangelist, an emissary, a messenger, and an author—and now, a modern day apostle. How can I tell you with mere words the power that was exchanged at that moment in time?

She gave the container to me.

"There is certain responsibility and effort required on our part. We can go to the person of the Holy Spirit and ask for understanding. He will reveal God to you, in you and through you. Say each day, 'Holy Spirit, I invite you into my day.' Establish a relationship with Him. He will show you who you are. Listen when He tells you something or something to do, and respond to it."

In the early hours of the morning, I heard my name called with urgency, "*Debbie*!" On awakening later that same morning, Joy heard with her ears, "*Joy*!" It was the Holy Spirit that had called each of us. He was letting us know He was nearby and in the mix. Over breakfast Joy shared, "When you hear, ask and make sure of what you heard. Start a conversation. Know the voice that calls you to attention. We are called to be seers, hearers, knowers, and have understanding. Cast down all vain imaginations!! Don't let a negative seed-thought grab you and run. As a creative-minded person, you are susceptible. This will be difficult for you, and it will take effort to defeat it. Don't give the dark side any credence. We have a higher accountability. And just because you can, doesn't mean you should."

Joy ended the conversation with this thought, "By the way, where you are working now is only temporary. God showed this to me six or eight weeks back. Don't worry about it."

"Okay."
Okay.

THE LAST MIRACLE OF 2012
(December 31st)

As marvelous as the last 17 hours were, it was time to get back to the every day. I picked up the kids, Lily and Matthew; I shopped for supplies and headed back home to see how Mark was feeling. He said I was a welcome site. His temperature was not!

Mark was still over 100 degrees. What was I to do?

That evening our friends, Jim and Ann Carter, called. We caught each other up to date and before we got off the phone, Jim asked to pray over Mark. I put him on the speaker and said, "Go ahead."

Jim prayed that Mark would be well with no temperature in the morning and that I would not get it. And that is exactly what happened.

REVELATION FOR 2013

(December 31st)

By Pastor Ivie Dennis

To all of my redeemed friends and warriors. We all know that the year 2012 has been full of what seems to be more attacks than victories, but none the less we have stayed the course and kept our aim on our home eternal. As I was praying last night watching the New Year come in God gave me such a strong vision for the year 2013. I hope it will lift you up and encourage you.

This is the year of redemption and restoration for His people. Healing, peace, and joy will come forth. This year is the year of fresh spring rains and new growth. There will be rapid changes for the building of His Kingdom. Many ministry opportunities are coming forth with His blessings. This year is full of favor for the righteous and full of His provision. Get ready children of God. Put your hand to the sickle, it is harvest time. Let us come together in faith and prayer and pray for this prophesy to begin today, January 1st, 2013.

To some this may not mean too much but it spoke volumes to me. Hope you will be inspired if you need some fresh spring rains to rain upon your life.

May God richly bless you all! Please feel free to share if you feel it is worthy of sharing.

Love you all,

Ivie Dennis

JANUARY 1ˢᵀ, 2013
A NEW UNDERSTANDING

Mark and I awoke to a new day. Mark awoke with a smile on his face, no temperature — and energy enough to help with the children. We had Matt and Lily overnight and all day. We played games, colored, watched television, baked a cake together and prayed!

Mark felt so much better, he helped with the laundry and folded the clothes. He played with the children and helped with the dishes. What a great way to start the New Year.

After the children were put to bed and asleep for the night, Mark and I went to our room to go over the notes from my meeting with Rabbona Joy. We got all comfy in bed and I read all 17 pages of notes I had taken. Amazing revelation poured forth. Mark and I went into the New Year wiser than we left the old one.

Whatever happened from there on out, we would never see things the same way again.

EPILOGUE
EVIDENCE OF THINGS UNSEEN

2nd Timothy 1:7 *"For the Spirit God gave us does not make us timid, but gives us power, love and self-discipline."*

An epilogue is usually a summary of the highlights of a book and gives closure to what you have just read. It may also give a perspective of what to take away with you.

As I wondered how to end the year 2012, the year-long events, my little sister, Crystal Murray came up with an idea; count the cost.

"Huh? Clarify please."

"Add up the year. All the churches you attended, where you went, prayers prayed, etc...." Crystal said in her usual, effective manner.

So, I did.

I broke down all the classifications into events, churches, good deeds, attacks on us or close to us, and prayer requests that came across our wires.

I did notice a correlation between the good deeds done in the service of the Lord, family obligations and friendly help, and the attacks that occurred on us physically, spiritually, emotionally and financially. These instances of both good and bad came out even — 110 each category. Every time Mark and I were used in service, there was a counter attack that caused us to be weary in heart, mind, spirit or flesh.

It also came to my attention that the year had moved in seasons. I was not aware of it at first, but as winter turned to spring, I noticed a shift in the spiritual atmosphere around us. Calls out for prayer were replaced by calls for help; landscape, home repair, etc. And we were well paid for all our efforts.

As the middle of the year lined itself up, there came along a prophesy much bigger than what I was used to writing about. This was not just mere miracles, as if they could be "just mere," but a 50-plus-year-in the-making prophesy, brought almost directly to my door step. When I was asked if it was important, my direct response was, "Important enough to be put in a book."

The last months of the year were the hardest to write, "The season of sorrows." Hard times weaved their way through our days and nights. Mark and I clung heavily to God and came out the better for it.

Now, the year in review.

Mark and I attended 12 different church's services anywhere from Friday nights at sundown to Sunday evenings for a total of 50 weekends out of the 52 week year. The churches ran the gauntlet; non-denominational, Christian, Baptist, Catholic, Anglican, Charismatic Catholic, Methodist, and coming in at the end, a Christian Country Cowboy Church.

We attended 19 prayer groups, including ones held in our own home. The most amazing of them all was "Sukkot," held at the sukka of David and Crystal Murray. Their dedication to the high holy days was highly admirable at the very least.

We had 91 prayer requests come to us over the course of the year. Of those, 59 were affirmative answers, 18 answers are still unknown to us, and 14 were nos. One of the "no's" was our deepest desire to have a home on our land. In the end, we had to give up our dreams and hopes, what we wanted and prayed for, become very humble and be homeless for almost a whole year, bow to the will of God and ask for his dream and vision for our lives to take place.

Why?

Only God still knows.

We had 39 instant miracles occur on our watch. They were anything from the alleviation of physical, emotional or spiritual pain to suffering of the individual. The attacks on us or others were stopped in their tracks. It was not due to anything we did, but our obedience of prayer and God's perfect timing that caused the "Yes, now!" to occur. Then, no force in Hell or on Earth could stop the supernatural flow of God from intervening on behalf of man.

"It is finished," the words that fell from Jesus' lips over 2,000 years ago, dropped from the sky, tore through the veil, and saved all who believed.

"It was finished."

Flu's fled, along with headaches, cancers, heart attacks, strokes, allergic reactions, pain and sufferings, injured ribs, chronic hiccups, high temperatures, casting out of demons, even the dying, all ceased in an instant.

What a year!

Eighty-five words of knowledge were given to us, our children or our pastors for us or people we knew and sometimes didn't know. Words of knowledge would even bubble up about complete strangers. Many times I excused myself to people and told them what I was told in the Spirit.

My fear of God outweighed my fear of what the people might think of a stranger who came up to speak to them on delicate matters. Not one person I approached with the Lord's knowledge shunned me or gave me reproach. Many cried, and most thanked me. I am eternally grateful.

Mark and I had 17 visions and prophetic dreams between us. Two were Mark's and 15 were mine. A friend of ours, Kelly, had one vision and one of our pastor's, Joy, had another vision for us. I had 3 visions and 13 dreams of the Lord in my telling hours of sleep. It was definitely not the usual year for us.

There were 58 supernatural events between all the miracles, church services and prayer groups we attended. Some of those were also just for Mark, myself and Annie. We smelled incense, other beyond-the-veil smells, saw and heard angelic presences, Holy Spirit fire, spoke to and heard God speak back! I heard a pastor pass over, felt loved ones who had passed come nearby, and watched prophesies fulfilled.

We had 27 pastor calls or visits from some of our favorite people on the planet.

As much as we grumbled at times, favor was ours. We had almost $3500 worth of meals, gifts, percentages off and money out of the blue come to us that year.

So, out of 50 weeks of the year, we were in church 50 times, 19 times in prayer groups, 27 visits with pastors, had $3,500 total come to our aid throughout the year, 293 prayers or supernatural events occurred, which meant, we were busy about the Lord's work two out of every three days.

Now, what did we get out of this?

When you say yes to the Lord, He may well put you on a fast track of service.

Remember to hold on to your hat.

Dear Reader, what would a year of your life look like if you were to keep track of it? Would it look similar to ours? Would it be a year of service to the Lord or a year of service to yourself?

And, if you look real close, it might just surprise you.

I know for myself and Mark, this was a very eye-opening experience; how much we had been used in the service of God. And it was all because we were obedient to the call and had the faith to believe in the impossible.

I have heard it said, "Extraordinary things happen to extraordinary people."

Go and be extraordinary!

Shalom until the next book.

Deb Peyron

2013
HOMELESS FOR THE HOLIDAYS

You would not know it to look at us by the way we present ourselves, dress or act. We don't fit the bell curve; not any part of it. We are not in the 25% of homeless veterans, we are not addicted to anything, we are not out of a job, or uneducated. Yet, by the circumstances that were in our control and out of our control, we found ourselves homeless, assigned to live with family members. The situation begged a response from God.

We begged a response from God.

My husband and I were square in the middle of the middle class, 55 years old, tithers to several churches we attended, with professions and dreams.

You see, it was a dream that started it all so long ago. In 2013, circumstances fell into perfect line for us to build a long-awaited home on our land and the situation ended up well for everyone but us. But this is the middle of the story. It all started five years before then. After all, it takes time and circumstance to lose everything.

The year 2008 was not a very kind year to almost everybody. The housing market crashed, the stock market crashed, and the job market crashed. The only things that went up were foreclosures, for sale signs and divorces. The trends were on a downward spiral.

Mark and I had just bought a piece of land January 4th, 2008, to follow a dream. I knew I was inspired, and my husband trusted my instincts — until ten days later when my job fell through. So much for my instincts. We had already sold our first "home of our dreams" due to an injury I had sustained and all the medical bills that had come due without any insurance net. The last of our savings was tied up in the new land deal, so we sat.

Over the next three years, we waited and paid down debt, even bought a small house in town until we felt the time was right to move our big project forward. With all our credit cards paid off and the land paid down, our excellent credit and my husband's good work history, we went interest rate hunting. We started with the people who had our land loan. They were so sure we were to be approved, we had the plans drawn up and put our home up for sale. We even found a buyer who was willing to wait until our new home was built to move in.

At the last minute the lending institution wanted $16,000.00 in a savings account in case of overages. We tried to tell them if we had another $16,000.00 we would have paid off more of the land. No dice. We probably had better odds with dice!

The next bank was so sure they could make it all work, if we would just go through a couple of hoops.

First, I needed a job of any kind to show income; I took a job three days later. Then I had to be on the job for six months. We thought at the time, we had waited over four years, what were a couple more months? It was harder to explain to the builder and his whole crew that were being asked to sit and wait.

But, by the fall of 2012, the bank resubmitted our perfect loan application only to be denied at the last minute, due to being $50.00 short income a month, due to the higher cost of living that had occurred in the last six months! That came out short a $1.66 a day. We asked ourselves who they thought they were kidding. Surely it must have been them.

By that time, we had six months before the agreed date of sale of the home we were living in. We had promised. Mark and I were ready to give up on our promised, prayed for, prayed over and anointed homeland when a friend introduced us to a friend who owned a mortgage company. "Great." She heard our story and said they would back us if we could just wait another six months. Our original builder agreed to come back on board. With the sale of the house and our savings, we split all the money we had between the lender and our builder. We moved in with Mom and knew by Christmas of 2013, we would be celebrating. Never count your celebrations until they've hatched.

Ten days after the close of the loan, our builder ended up in the hospital and needed a double bypass. By mid-June, we were up and running again. We still thought we could make our promised December deadline until our builder ended up in the hospital once again. This time, it was just a two week stint with his stomach. July looked good; except for 26 out of 30 days of rain. Bill promised by our anniversary, August 7th, we would have a hole in the ground.

And there would have been one if the mortgage company hadn't called two days before then and told us they rescinded our loan because there was no way we could be done with the project by the end of December. Oh, and they would not carry our land loan, so it would have to be sold.

Happy Anniversary.

We were devastated! They did not offer to give us any of the money back we had given them for closing costs. And all the money we had given to the builder, a good friend, to start the home process was gone. He had been out of work for almost four months, and when we asked him if there was any money left in the account, the look of sorrow on his face told the whole story. How could we be mad that he had fed his family and kept his own lights on with our money? We asked ourselves, "What would Jesus have done?"

On our 14th wedding anniversary, it was official, we were homeless with no savings and nowhere to go. Mom agreed we could continue to stay with her. She had a vested interest in all this; she loved us. So, there we were, occupying one room, sleeping on a 40-year old-mattress, and everything we own locked up for ten months in a storage unit.

We have no bitterness; we were way too tired for that. We have gone on and done good for others as we always have done in our 14 year "good deeds" ministry. We are not mad at God, or the lender, or the builder. And how do you blame a circumstance?

But, just like in a "Miracle on 34th Street," all I wanted was a home for Christmas, Santa. None came our way.

If this story had a moral to it, it would be, if you have a place of your own this holiday season to invite your family or friends to, remember to be thankful. We were thankful for that roof over our heads and the 40-year-old mattress that holiday season. We just walked a little slower, and a smile was a little harder to come by.

*"**Who** shall separate us
from the love of Christ?
Shall tribulation, or distress,
or persecution, or famine,
or nakedness, or peril, or sword?*

*   **Nay,** in all these things
    we are more than conquerors
    through Him that loved us.
    For I am persuaded that
    neither death, or life
    nor angels, nor principalities,
    nor powers, nor things present,
    nor things to come,
    nor height, nor depth,
    nor any other creature,
    shall be able to separate us
    from the love of God,
    which is in
    Christ Jesus Our Lord."*

Romans 8:35, 37-39

We welcome you to share your comments and experiences with us like minded believers. These in this book have been written down in order to encourage the brethren and inspire the secular world.

To contact us, send your e-mail to:
miraculous.interventions@gmail.com

or to the publisher at:

HomeCraftedArtistry@yahoo.com

Or by US Mail to:

Home Crafted Artistry & Printing
1252 Beechwood Avenue
New Albany, IN 47150

Be sure to visit:
www.miraculous-interventions.com

and like us on facebook:
www.facebook.com/MiraculousInterventions
Follow Deborah on twitter:
twitter.com/MiraculousBooks

Made in the USA
Charleston, SC
09 October 2015